D0811728

Eric Clark

Corps Diplomatique

Allen Lane

Copyright © Eric Clark 1973

First published in 1973

Allen Lane
A division of Penguin Books Ltd
21 John Street, London, WC1

ISBN 0 7139 0474 7

Printed in Great Britain by
Western Printing Services Ltd,
Bristol

For Marcelle
For a changeless reason

For Miriam

Contents

Acknowledgements

Those to whom I owe most thanks are those I cannot name: the several hundred diplomats who, over a period of three years, talked to me of their work and their beliefs. So that they could speak frankly, it was agreed that interviews would be anonymous. All those I approached talked readily and – usually – freely. I am grateful to them all, and especially to those who let me join them on their diplomatic rounds or allowed me to stay in their homes so that I could 'taste' the life overseas.

A number of foreign services gave their official co-operation. They attached only one condition: that I should not quote from documents I saw on embassy desks during my visits. Those to whom I am particularly grateful are the British Foreign Office, the American State Department, and the External Affairs Departments of Canada and Ireland. I owe especial thanks to the Foreign Office library and the British Information Services in New York. One or two others, including the French, were not so helpful at an official level. And I am especially grateful to those diplomats from these countries who, notwithstanding this, co-operated on a personal basis.

Several academics gave ready access to their papers and documents, and in particular I owe thanks to Professor Chadwick F. Alger of Northwestern University, Evanston, Illinois, for making available his research on the United Nations, and Professor Donald Klein of the East Asian Institute of Columbia University, New York, for providing research material on Communist China. Others to whom I am grateful are the United Nations, the Commonwealth Secretariat, the Rand Corporation, and the American Foreign Service Association.

D. (who insists on remaining as anonymous as the diplomats interviewed) guided me through material published in the Soviet Union. And Jenny Smith has been a constant help throughout.

'Diplomacy, the patriotic art of lying for one's country'
Ambrose Bierce, *The Devil's Dictionary*

One
The Diplomat Today

'I think the whole concept of diplomacy today . . .
is a little outmoded. I believe much of it goes back
to the early days of the telegraph, when you needed
a despatch to know what was happening in
country A, whereas now you can read it in a good
newspaper.'
Canadian Prime Minister Pierre Trudeau

In an age of fast communications the diplomat, to many, is an
anachronism. Like the sailing barge, he belongs to another age.
Once – separated by time and distance from the policy-makers
at home – his role was a crucial one. What he did and said
mattered.

In the middle of last century Sir Stratford Canning, British
ambassador in Constantinople, made policy and influenced
history. On one occasion he was asked to give an undertaking that
Britain would declare war on Russia and Austria if those two
countries attacked Turkey. He had no authority; to obtain it from
his government would take two months. Yet he gave the guarantee.

Today, wherever he is, the diplomat is a messenger at the
end of a telephone. When matters are important, a statesman,
politician or expert can reach any point in the world within hours.
His despatches no longer contain eagerly awaited news. The recipients will have seen most of it before – on television or on the
news-agency wire machines.

'Diplomacy as once known,' concluded an American commentator recently, 'is at an end.' Yet if the diplomat is dead, the
last person to realise it is the diplomat himself. His profession has
been one of the growth industries of this century. The fifteen
heads of mission who represented their countries in one capital, London, in 1914 had become 114 by 1971. They were

surrounded by other diplomats, from lowly third secretaries to counsellors and ministers: by the late 1960s the number of foreign diplomats and their wives in London entitled to varying degrees of diplomatic privileges and immunity totalled over 3,300, more than double the number in 1945. The privileged few had not disappeared. It had simply become the privileged many.

The first American Secretary of State Thomas Jefferson, had five clerks, two messengers and a part-time translator. As recently as 1936 the entire staff of the State Department could gather on the steps of the old State Building to pose for a photograph. By 1968 there were more than 11,000 American Foreign Service employees, 7,000 of them abroad staffing 261 overseas posts.

In 1914 Britain, as one of the most powerful nations in the world, had 176 staff, including cleaners and doorkeepers, at its Foreign Office at home and only 450 abroad. In 1969, a Britain that had lost much of its international power had 6,400 diplomats, nearly 240 specialist attachés at embassies, and 7,000 locally engaged helpers.

New nations, of which more than sixty came into being between 1945 and 1970, have sent their new diplomats out into the world. Nkrumah celebrated Ghana's independence by opening seventy embassies. In return older nations have posted their diplomats to the new states.

And, even if they are outdated, the flow of information for which they are responsible is vast and real. Every day 2,000 messages pour into the State Department in Washington and another 1,000 flow out. The number of words written and read can total one million daily. The number of documents adds up to nine million a year, and 1,500,000 of these are described as 'current documents' from which information is required every day.

The doctor may have pronounced death, the undertaker may be waiting to bury the body. But the corpse looks remarkably healthy. The diplomat might well describe his obituary notice as premature. Yet the diplomat knows that he continues to exist in a world where his existence is being questioned. Prime Minister Trudeau's utterances were remarkable only in their openness. Diplomats have been called 'glorified journalists', 'cookie pushers', 'a temporarily subsidised aristocracy', and 'redundant and unnecessary'. Their image is not high. They are the men who either do nothing or act stupidly – like the diplomats who, in 1968, argued over the shape of the negotiating table to be used for the Vietnam peace talks.

The questioning of the diplomat's relevance is not confined to one country, and has been reflected in the number of commissions and reviews that have taken place. Nations from Britain to Canada, Norway to Germany, have been examining where the diplomat fits into the modern world. Since the end of World War II there have been eight major studies and scores of minor ones in the United States alone.

Diplomats have been forced to take part in self-examination processes. One, a Canadian, preparing a background paper, said: 'It seems odd trying to examine dispassionately whether I'm necessary or not. But for the first time in my life it has made me query what I am doing.'

The diplomats, in fact, have entered readily into this navel-contemplating process, though it is difficult to decide whether they genuinely seek a role that is relevant (even if this would mean major changes including a vicious slimming process) or whether at heart they are convinced that only minor alterations will ever result.

What most concerns the diplomat is that those criticising him and querying the need for his existence should try to understand what he actually does today.

'Sometimes,' says a Dutch diplomat, 'I get the feeling we are being condemned not on what we are now, but on how people think we are. And their image is of us as people who are responsible for stupid policies, inhabiting a world of diplomacy that has never existed except in fiction, or of how we were forty years ago.'

'We are totally misunderstood,' says an English colleague. 'What's wrong is not what we do – but the image that's held of us by our political master, by the public, and by our colleagues in the civil service at home. I sometimes think that instead of having all these reviews, foreign services would do better to spend the money on hiring public relations firms to show people what they really get up to. Then, people could decide whether they still want to change us.'

Many diplomats will concede that this 'false image' is partly the result of their own passion for secrecy and privacy. One American ambassador, nearing retirement, was self-critical about the way over the years he had dealt with visiting delegations of politicians and others to his embassies: 'I fed them and I wined them and I arranged things for them. But I feel now that I should have forced them to go around the embassy room by room, showing them what every one of my men was doing. If someone was just sitting on his ass, okay. But they'd have seen it was a working place just like any other, and not a round of cocktails.'

The complaint of criticisms over foreign policies is a valid one. The diplomat's job is not to make policy; that belongs to the politician and the statesman. The task of the diplomat is its execution. He transmits details of that policy to foreign governments, he tries to explain it and obtain support, and when told to do so he negotiates agreements that seek to advance and embody it.

The confusion is, however, central to some of the criticism. The great bulk of such criticism, Lord Strang, has claimed, 'turns out, when analysed, to relate to particular foreign policies for which the diplomatist who did not devise them cannot reasonably be blamed'. After President Richard Nixon was reportedly dissatisfied with his ambassador in Japan in 1971 for not being tough enough, a retired American diplomat protested: 'To blame an American ambassador for our present highly complex state of affairs with Japan is a bit like blaming the Western Union messenger for your grandmother's death. He only delivered the message.'

That does, of course, allow the diplomat to enjoy the best of two worlds: if he fails, it is the policy; if he succeeds, the policy may have been good, but success also depended on the way he pressed it.

But, having protested that they are not responsible for policy, diplomats will claim that they are still more than 'mere messengers'. How they present and explain policies formulated by others is important. And as negotiation is perhaps the most important function of the diplomat, the skill and expertise of the man directly involved in the argument, the explanation and the compromise, will be reflected in the agreements reached.

Diplomats claim this is so whether the negotiations involve major or minor decisions – whether to agree a new air route, to fix the terms on which a new entrant will be allowed into the Common Market, or to finalise the detailed points of a Soviet-American agreement on arms' control.

It is the diplomat, they argue, who finds common ground between negotiating parties, assesses how far the other side will go, and then sees that what his political masters want is properly contained within the agreement.

An analogy has been made with the barrister, pleading his client's case to the best of his ability. But the diplomat would claim there is a difference: unlike the barrister he does not set out just to win one case. 'Diplomacy,' says one English diplomat, 'is a continuing process. The skill lies in obtaining what your country wants, whether it is a treaty, an exchange of students, or a trade agreement, while still leaving the other country satisfied. Even when you've got agreement on one thing, you have to remember that tomorrow there will be a different set of negotiations.' Diplomats argue that it is the long-term that matters. Hitler achieved brilliant diplomatic coups but . . . .

They also claim that there is still some latitude in some of their negotiating; there are times when instructions are ambiguous or vague, and decisions have to be made quickly by an ambassador who hopes his government will back him.

But his power in this respect is restricted to relatively minor matters. Today's diplomat might agree to a small change in a resolution at a conference without cabling for fresh instructions; he would not commit his nation to anything even vaguely important or binding without doing so. 'I see myself more as an observer of history than a maker of it,' admits one German ambassador. His mid-nineteenth-century predecessor, living in an age when messages from Rome to London took as long as they did at the time of Julius Caesar, went abroad with wide instructions. And he was often contemptuous of any detailed ones that reached him. 'I never,' said Lord Malmesbury, 'received an instruction that was worth reading.' That kind of power has gone for ever. As skilled and powerful a figure as the late Adlai Stevenson, when at the United Nations, complained to Professor J. K. Galbraith that the State Department 'advises him more or less at what hour to see Gromyko, when to interrupt to go to the men's room and how long to stay there'.

Diplomats also claim that one man can still, on some matters, change the attitude of another. If the other man is in a position to make policy, the diplomat thus still has impact. The secretary general of the first conference to consider the future of man and the world's resources, held in 1972, first had to travel thousands of miles to convince the heads of Third World nations to participate. He succeeded. A former British ambassador to Iran, Sir Denis Wright is widely credited in the diplomatic world with having persuaded the Shah to renounce claims to Bahrain. At a minor level, I watched a European consular diplomat in North Africa persuade a reluctant local official to manipulate the rules to allow one of the diplomat's nationals a work permit.

But such instances seem minor or extremely rare. 'Is the British government going to change its attitude on Gibraltar because our ambassador in London is charming?' says a high-ranking Spanish official. 'Of course, it is not.'

Even if a diplomat concedes that on important matters he has to negotiate within the confines of the most precise instructions, he would still claim that his reporting role has some impact on what those instructions are. A French diplomat argues that if France is about to negotiate with a country in which he is based he can advise his government on the conditions that will influence that country's bargaining position and strength. 'If, for example, the country has internal problems, it is unlikely to take risks in foreign affairs. It is already unpopular at home over one thing; why should it risk being attacked over something else.' It is from this advice that government can decide what specific foreign policies are practical and what are not at any given time.

The diplomat's argument is not that the world has not changed but that his age old qualities of tact, patience, negotiating skills, understanding and precision, are as vital as ever. And that where it has been necessary for him to change his role, he has done so.

The world in which he practises his craft *has* changed and is changing. Modern diplomacy, as an organised craft with its own practitioners and resident missions, began to develop in Italy in the thirteenth and fourteenth centuries, born out of the need for statesmen-diplomats to negotiate constantly changing alliances in the power struggles between individual states. The major step was the opening of the first resident embassy in the mid-fifteenth century. But it is the last century that has produced most of the developments that have a direct bearing on the diplomat's work, worth and role today. Many of these have taken place since the end of World War II.

The most obvious, the development of high-speed international communications, has had an effect beyond that of diminishing the diplomat's power to make decisions on the spot. It has meant that experts from home can rapidly be flown to overseas capitals: Sri Lanka (Ceylon), wanting to discuss a shipping question, sends a specialist in the subject; America, taking part in a whaling conference, heads its delegation with the chairman of the country's Council on Environmental Quality. It has also resulted in an age of statesman to statesman diplomacy. In the days of classic diplomacy, foreign ministers and prime ministers, with rare exceptions, stayed at home. Now it is the Icelandic foreign minister who discusses fishing limits in London, the French defence minister who flies to Washington to talk about general military policy. In just the first twenty-one months of the John F. Kennedy administration, more than fifty heads of government or chiefs of state visited the United States.

This is a development that today's diplomat has to accept, but rarely likes. Policy and its execution become intermingled, and both can suffer, they claim. Diplomats argue that in any event they play a major role in preparing the ground for a statesman's visit. 'He has to be briefed and guided before he arrives,' says a German counsellor. 'Then there are all the arrangements while he is here. And after he has gone – possibly having made some imprecise promise or reached some vague agreement – we have to pick up the pieces and find some way of translating what he thought had been agreed into reality.'

A Canadian ambassador summed up a commonly-held view among diplomats: 'You work on something for months, quietly and patiently. When everything is ready, the minister flies over and signs a piece of paper with a gold pen. Then everyone back home thinks how marvellous he is, and says that we diplomats just aren't needed any more.'

At least as important as the development in rapid communications has been the advent of the power of public opinion. The old diplomat would have been scandalised by the thought that the public should play any part in international affairs. 'Public opinion,' Lord Strang has said, 'did not count for much and the use of secret method in the conduct of foreign relations was recognised and indispensable.'

After World War I the Americans, suddenly dominant, brought a distrust of diplomacy to international affairs. To many people, not just in the United States, secret diplomacy had caused the war; it had to be brought under popular control. President Woodrow Wilson demanded 'open covenants . . . openly arrived at', with emphasis placed on the right of the citizens of a country to know what was being agreed in their name. Later Wilson had to back down from the 'openly arrived at' part of his declaration. In a letter to his secretary of state, Robert Lansing, he explained: 'When I pronounced for open diplomacy I meant not that there should be no private discussion of delicate matters, but that no secret agreement should be entered upon and that all international relations when fixed should be open, above board and explicit.' Despite that, the right of the public to be informed has remained an integral part of most modern diplomacy.

For the policy makers, it means the need to answer to the home electorate, at least on broad issues of policy. For the diplomat it means he has to try to appeal to foreign publics direct. 'The image of ambassadors whispering in royal ears is obsolete,' a report of a Commonwealth seminar on diplomacy has said. 'Thanks to mass media, ambassadors are more often speaking to journalists, farmers, students, industrial workers, etc., than to monarchs and heads of government.'

It has resulted in the development of information work and of cultural activities, of trade fairs and educational exchanges, all functions in which the diplomat is expected to be involved.

In public, at least, today's diplomat must appear to have something resembling a common touch. Yesterday's ambassador would have been shocked if asked to kick off at a football game, open a pub, or entertain a visiting entertainer. Britain's ambassador in Warsaw invited the pop group Marmalade to a steak and chips lunch at the embassy after taking embassy staff to see them perform the previous evening. His colleague in the Hague opened the first English pub there, the Rose and Orange, by ceremonially opening the first bottle of beer.

Late last century one British ambassador in Washington, Lord Lyons, spent five years there without making one speech. Many countries today expect their ambassadors to project themselves – a task that some tackle reluctantly or to the quiet disapproval of colleagues who think they are lowering the tone of the ambassadorial business. The new Spanish ambassador to London in the early 1970s walked out of his residence on his return from presenting credentials at Buckingham Palace to give the coachman and policeman a glass of beer in front of the photographers. He had first cleared such a revolutionary step with the Marshal of the Court. But many of his neighbouring ambassadors in London's Belgrave Square looked on with a quiet disgust. 'Quite frankly', said one, 'I would never do anything like that.'

A number, reluctant and self-conscious about direct publicity, are better at working once-removed, through the press rather than direct with 'the people'. In this the diplomat has had to come to terms with newspapers, in some respects his natural enemy: the press seeks to reveal what he wishes to conceal and, to the diplomat's mind, the newspaperman often projects false and facile pictures of a complex situation.

But several 'handle' the press well, holding regular briefing sessions for correspondents at which they outline and explain their country's policies and actions. Nigeria's high commissioner in London during the Nigerian civil war dealt with correspondents skilfully during days when most newspapers were against his government.

The whole representational side of the work is now more difficult than ever before, say diplomats. 'Once,' says one ambassador, 'all you had to do was walk with kings. Now you have to be acceptable to the president, local importers, television viewers, and the trade unions.' One English ambassador in a small country thought the best piece of image-projecting he had done for his country lay not in impressing local politicians, but in the impact he had had on television with a short, carefully rehearsed, statement given in the local, and highly obscure, dialect. One of his locally-engaged staff, confirmed, 'I almost cried when I saw it.

It did your country so much good. His accent was perfect, and it is not an easy language. It was that he had taken the trouble. . . .'

Another development has been the explosion of new states, each sending and receiving diplomats, all struggling for a voice in international affairs. The diplomat has had to engage in the aid field, negotiating, advising and sometimes also administering.

The growth in the number of countries has also had the effect of spreading the elitism a bit thin. 'Can you take it really seriously any more when we've got an ambassador in *Burundi*,' an American politician exclaims.

The old diplomats were members of a small world, united by class and elitism, dealing with each other like gentlemen. Today's diplomat has had to withstand the impact of the arrival not only of the new states but also of the Soviet diplomat, an animal with his own rules. He is not gentlemanly at all. He fights to win. To him there is only one side to each question; he has a total inflexibility stemming in large part from his need to obey orders to the letter. His manners, too, contrast with the urbanity of the traditionally-acceptable diplomat: where they are smooth-tongued, he is outspokenly tough; where they engage in gentle understatement, making even insults sound pleasant, he argues brutally. The one characteristic he shares with his Western colleagues is that he is no more powerful a figure in real terms in his country's hierarchy than they are, often in fact even less so.

Other major developments have been brought about by the complexity of modern life and, as a result, the vastly increased range of subjects, often technical, that have to be discussed internationally. These range from pollution to monetary policies, from agriculture to labour.

Much of the diplomacy that would once have taken place between just two governments (bilaterally) is now handled in negotiations between several (multilaterally). There has been a vast expansion in international organisations and in conferences: the United States now pays dues to over fifty international organisations and takes part in over 400 major inter-governmental conferences every year.

The effect on the diplomat has been threefold. Firstly, many have had to learn to carry out part of their work in public –

seen, at its peak, at meetings of the United Nations General Assembly where the television cameras are more important than fellow delegates. Secondly, they have had to concern themselves with social and economic subjects that their predecessors, to whom foreign affairs was a graceful political exercise, would never have recognised. And thirdly, they have had to accept that much of today's diplomacy is no longer practised by them but by experts from various fields who meet together to negotiate and take decisions.

The emergence of diplomacy by these non-diplomat experts often means that the diplomat's role is relegated to that of support. With the Organisation for Economic Co-operation and Development, for example, the major task of the British diplomats on the spot is what the British Duncan Committee report on Overseas Representation well-described as 'door opening'. The important work is carried out by experts flown over from London. The job of the seven permanent diplomats there is to alert London if anything important seems likely to happen, to report on routine developments, and to ease experts into the appropriate slots in the complex OECD system when they arrive in Paris.

Some countries now have agencies separate from the diplomatic service to deal with international trade, aid, information work, and cultural diplomacy. Even when most of these tasks are still handled by diplomats (as, for example, in Britain) a large number of home civil service departments have their own representatives at embassies abroad. Today, eighty per cent of the Americans representing their country's government interests overseas are not under the direct supervision of the State Department.

Other countries' embassies have fewer of these 'outsiders'. But the practice is growing. A large Spanish embassy will now have representatives from the ministries of labour, agriculture and information, as well as the defence ministries. Norway had virtually no outsiders until the mid-1960s when the country's application to join the Common Market brought the need for more experts at missions in various fields. Soon, at European embassies, there were men from the ministries of Trade, Finance and Fisheries. Several missions, including Barbados, Ghana, Ceylon and Liberia, have education attachés to look after the student communities of their countries studying abroad. Others, like Ghana and Zambia, have immigration attachés; some, like Cyprus, have attachés for tourism. Kuwait in London has an attaché seconded from the Health Ministry who helps the 80 to 110 Kuwaitis being treated in London hospitals at any time.

Not only do the representatives of other agencies and ministries engage in what could be regarded as wide diplomatic functions, but they also share with the diplomat a representational and image-projecting role. They, just as much as the diplomats, can claim to be seen as prototypes of their country.

The traditional diplomats have to live and work and bargain with all these newcomers. Mostly they do not like it. 'If these people are going to do diplomatic work,' says a Norwegian first secretary, 'they should go through proper training in diplomacy as we have to.'

In arguing that he has adapted as the world has changed, the diplomat points to the range of work now handled at overseas missions: representing and projecting an image of his country; handling negotiations; protecting the interests of his own nationals in the country in which the embassy is based; reporting and interpreting developments; trying to influence public opinion; consular work – from dealing with stranded tourists to witnessing marriages; activities on behalf of all departments of the home government; commercial liaison and trade promotion; and, where applicable, giving or receiving aid and technical assistance.

If a country wishes to emphasise one aspect of the work, the diplomat says that he as a professional is ready to do it: 'All a government has to do is decide what it wants, and we'll do our best to carry it out,' one says.

But central to the question of the diplomat's role in the latter half of the twentieth century is whether he and his traditional embassy structure are right for the job.

If the work involves negotiating trade agreements and promoting exports, why not an official whose speciality that is? If it is aid, why not a professional administrator? If information, why not a publicist?

In large capitals, a number of such specialist functions would have to be undertaken, but why not all of them by experts?

And in smaller countries, where most of the actual work may lie in just aid or trade, why not scrap the whole embassy structure and replace it with one small aid or trade office?

Diplomats claim that, apart from the negotiating skills always needed, the situation is never that clear-cut. A French diplomat argues: 'You cannot divorce aid from the political situation, nor propaganda from what overall you seek to achieve. It is all political. An expert does not realise that. He looks upon his speciality as an end in itself, which it should never be.'

Another says: 'Say this office did nothing but administer aid. Fine. But what do I do if the local government wants to talk to me about things other than that? Do I just tell them to get stuffed? People forget diplomacy is a two-way trade.' After the Duncan Report, several British consulates in America were made trade posts. 'The only trouble,' reports one consular officer, 'is that no one told the people who wanted consular help. They kept coming. And it turned out we were obliged to do certain things for them.'

There can also be conflict of interest between the diplomat and the specialist. At its most cynical extreme, an aid expert may want to build a road because he believes it is needed; the diplomat will debate whether another project might not produce a more striking propagandist success for his own nation. As for flying out experts and politicians when needed, ministers cannot be everywhere, and there is always need for continuous contact and for follow-ups to agreements.

In recent years, however, diplomats have had to endure cuts. In the first nine months after the British Duncan report, eleven overseas posts were closed – though none of them striking (they included Haifa, Oporto, Split and New Orleans). In 1970, Canada decided to reduce its foreign based staff by over fifteen per cent – 'just at a time when it was looking as though we'd soon have an embassy in every capital in the world'. In 1970 alone, the United States, as part of its policy of cutting back on its overseas profile, reduced the foreign personnel of the State Department by nearly 700.

But, on examination, one feels that the diplomatic services of the world, though slightly bruised, remain unblooded. For the moment the growth has been checked, but the suspicion is that the machine will triumph in the end. (A classic example was Ghana's closure of eighteen posts which emerged, on study, to have resulted in no foreign exchange savings because staff had been redeployed to other missions.) In Germany there has been discussion about closing some of the country's smaller embassies. But even if that happened, the number of staff is unlikely to fall because, it is conceded, there are at present too few diplomats for the posts that have to be manned.

The Duncan Report, calling for a British overseas representational machine more appropriate to the country's changed international position, suggested that the present machine could be likened to a Rolls Royce which should be changed for a smaller car of high quality. Despite the changes that have followed the report it seems to an outsider that a compromise of sorts has emerged – the Rolls Royce remains, but its owner has agreed to economise by seeing the chauffeur wears a slightly less costly uniform.

Diplomats are increasingly expensive. Treasury calculations in Britain in the late 1960s estimated that the work of an assistant under secretary in the Home Civil Service cost between £4 and £5 an hour; his equivalent diplomatic colleague, ranking as counsellor, serving abroad might cost £20–£25 an hour.

A basic problem is that it is impossible to calculate the value of a diplomat: if relations with another country are bad, would they have been even worse if the diplomat had not been active? Even if he is involved in a five million dollar export sale, would not it still have taken place without him? If 500 people attend a film show he has organised, will it really help make local people more pro-American or Chinese or French? How can you ever prove it, one way or the other?

Countries have sought new justifications for their diplomacy. 'Keeping the peace' is a resounding phrase; diplomats have argued that now that it is possible for the world to be destroyed, persuasion in international affairs must replace power: military action can no longer be relied upon to settle matters which the diplomats cannot resolve.

The diplomat as peacemaker forms a sharp contrast with the days when diplomats were regarded as war-makers. (A favourite story among diplomats concerns one of their number after World

War I sitting in a railway carriage with three army officers. Finally, goaded by their tales of what they had done in the war, he exclaimed: 'If it hadn't been for people like me you would never have had your war!')

But, with the world apparently settled down to some sort of nuclear stalemate, the current most 'in' justification is that the diplomat is fighting internationally to achieve a whole range of national interests ranging from seeing that his country's farmers do not suffer because of a wheat surplus, to ensuring its holiday-makers can go on charter flights to country X, and helping keep its workers employed and the balance of payments healthy by generating trade abroad.

'The thing today,' says an elderly Italian diplomat, 'is to find a justification. With most people's jobs you can see what they do; there's something tangible at the end of it. With diplomacy, mostly there is not.'

Another, a Canadian, confessing himself slightly cynical after his involvement in an internal review on the role of the diplomat, says: 'I think all countries will establish a justification now diplomatic services are under pressure. But they'll be nice hazy ones. The Americans have already found one – diplomacy exists to protect the life, liberty and happiness of its citizens. Well that's a lovely one – it takes in everything from handing out visas, pushing trade, to defence agreements. We have done nearly as well with our definition that diplomats are charged with pursuing "national aims and interests in the international environment".'

In the British service the emphasis has been placed on helping exports. All diplomats everywhere are expected to regard the trade role as vitally important. One counsellor, with over twenty-five years of service, says he has seen it all before: 'After the war, it was information work that was the great justification. We're still trying to find work for all those people whose informations jobs disappeared when it was decided it wasn't so important after all.' He envisages a surplus of unwanted commercial diplomats in a few years' time when the trade justification is replaced by something else.

The diplomat may have come to some terms with new pressures and developments, but he remains a timeless creature, convinced of both his worth and his capacity for survival.

This, in part, is illustrated by the diplomatic belief that although times change, the qualities needed remain ageless. During lectures at Oxford University, Sir Harold Nicolson listed some of those of the ideal ambassador of the fifteenth and sixteenth century. They included that he should be a good linguist, hospitable, a man of taste, patient, imperturbable, and tolerant of the ignorance and foolishness of his home government. If he still exists, the diplomat of 2500 might well list the same qualities to identify the ideal ambassador of the 1970s. Some older diplomats claim that the best book for any newcomer to the profession to read is still one written by François de Callières – over 250 years ago.

Two qualities are constantly stressed. The first is the need to be skilled in negotiating. The other is sociability.

Because the diplomatic society is a closed one, subject to stringent though often unwritten rules, how the diplomat behaves is regarded as being of prime importance. A diplomat believes he needs to be liked by his colleagues from other nations, not least because over the years he may continue meeting the same men at different times and in different capitals. Diplomats, like elephants, it would seem have long memories for how well or how badly they were once treated.

There is a universal affability and correctness. In meeting groups of diplomats it provides the most immediately striking impression. 'I sometimes like to feel,' one British diplomat says, 'that if I had to tell a friend he'd got B.O. I could do it in a way that would leave him feeling touched and grateful.' You feel he is right. I was out walking with two young German diplomats when it began to rain heavily. They had one umbrella between them. Immediately, they suggested I should take it.

This gentlemanliness is one of the qualities that gives diplomats no matter what their nationality, a sameness and internationalism that is as striking as an airport or a Hilton hotel.

With the pomp and the protocol and the privileges, they also exude an aura of rather faded grander times. In the main, the elitism of class and money had faded in importance (though for some positions a private income is still useful, and in a number of services, like the French, an aristocratic background still helps). Overall, there is this striking uniformity. One writer, Michael H.

Cardozo, has referred to the 'uniform mould from which foreign service officers all over the world seem to have been lifted'.

There are many reasons for this. The first is that the diplomat spends so much time living abroad, and dealing in the main – whatever he may claim – with one special section of society. He loses part of his purely national identity. At the same time, the careful phrase and the fixed smile becomes an intrinsic part of the personality. The diplomat is like an actor who is never sure when he is on or off the stage, in or out of the public gaze.

His work involves calm and caution. He is not keen to commit himself. An Arab ambassador pointed out that, during even routine conversations with officials from another country, he would often pretend to know nothing about a subject even if he was well-briefed on it, simply to give himself more thinking time.

He learns that every argument has a convincing answer. Even his personal convictions recognise there are always conflicting views, and his opinions lack fire. Apart from politicians (for whom he will usually, provided he trusts your discretion, voice disgust and contempt) he seems to have few strong personal views on any important matter.

Even if, deep down, there *are* strongly held views, he is trained to use words with polite understatement. There is a paper currency of conventional phrases that do not quite say what they mean – but are readily understood by other diplomats.

An expert on conference diplomacy, Johan Kaufmann has instanced some examples in his field:

'While I have deep respect for the distinguished delegate of . . . who has stated his views with intelligence and conviction, I must point out that . . .' probably means, 'I do not agree with the delegate of . . .'

'The proposal is very interesting, but we must avoid duplication of activities with certain other organisations,' can be translated as 'The proposal does not belong in this organisation'.

Statements issued after conferences also need to be translated. If the participants reveal they shared 'a full exchange of views', it can be read as meaning they could not agree. 'We have reached substantial agreement' is not as cheering as it sounds; it means that on at least one major issue they could not agree. This cautious language and attitude spills over into ordinary conversation.

Diplomats live and work among other diplomats, and they are bound together in the diplomatic corps (according to one writer, Roberto Regala, the term 'corps diplomatique' originated in Vienna in 1754 and was the name by which a Viennese woman referred to the numerous foreign envoys there). The corps is important to diplomats; one former American ambassador, W. Wendell Blancké has argued that the diplomat has three publics – the country in which he works, his home community, and the corps.

Membership has always been regarded as important. François de Callières in his great work, *De la manière de négocier avec les Souverains*, published in 1716, said: 'Since the whole diplomatic body labours to the same end, namely to discover what is happening, there arises a certain freemasonry of diplomacy, by which one colleague informs another of coming events which a lucky chance has enabled him to discern.'

There can be great closeness when it comes to defending the status of colleagues. Sir William Hayter was British Ambassador in Moscow when Gomulka, then the new Polish Prime Minister, paid a visit. At the Kremlin reception Khrushchev attacked the British and French governments for behaving like bandits over Suez. Hayter told the French ambassador they should walk out. 'Before we left I told Chip Bohlen (the American ambassador) what we were doing, and as Dejean and I stalked out I was touched and grateful to see that Bohlen had rounded up all the other NATO ambassadors (all anti-Suez to a man) like a sheepdog with a flock of sheep, and brought them out behind us.'

Diplomats are happy to be with other diplomats. A young French officer says that when he is with colleagues, whether Japanese, German, or American, 'I know I'll find an ease of manner, an open-mindedness'. An English second secretary says he finds 'a closeness I don't find outside the profession. Like car salesmen together, we have a pattern of thought. And many of our problems are common ones.'

Diplomats from all nations also share the characteristic that they are intuitive animals. They are generalists who fly by the seat of their pants. 'Logic,' said Lord Salisbury to Lord Lyons, 'is of no use in diplomacy.' Describing American diplomats, Henry S. Rowen and Albert P. Williams in a Rand Corporation study said: 'There is probably no group, as a whole, within the United States Government less disposed towards systematic decision-making than the senior members of the corps – officials who either head or dominate our missions abroad. By background, by experience, by selection within the system, they epitomise the intuitive operator.'

One young English diplomat recalled being involved in monitoring a potential crisis over Berlin. He worked on an operations desk with military men. Detailed lists had been drawn up forecasting actions that could be taken by the other country concerned. For each action or combination of actions, there was a pre-planned counter-move. 'I could see the need for that kind of system in the circumstances,' he said, 'but quite honestly I didn't feel at home with it.'

Diplomats have argued whether, despite certain permanent and universal standards, there are discernible national styles.

To an outsider, there are, certainly among Western and European nations: the German diplomat seen in the morning has different characteristics from his French colleague met that evening. Among the Asian and African diplomats, styles are probably more regional than national; it is difficult to find differences between, say, Indian and Pakistan diplomats.

All diplomats, to some degree, are individuals, and descriptions of national characteristics must, necessarily, be sweeping.

The Germans do strike as thorough and punctilious, but though impressive on the outside, nervous and unsure deeper down. (One German counsellor, handing over the most basic facts about his service kept stressing that it should never emerge that they came from a German embassy source.) Younger German diplomats are often giggly and boyish, given to self-deprecating jokes; older ones seem to confirm Sir Harold Nicolson's belief that they feel it more important to inspire fear than beget confidence.

The Italians emerge as being smooth and subtle (perhaps over so) on the surface, but with little underneath. They are great name-droppers, and bad time-keepers.

The Spanish are suave, chivalrous and good mannered; there is an aristocratic feel – one recent ambassador in London was given to riding his white Arab stallion early in the morning across Richmond Park. They are probably the most immediately likeable.

The Portuguese, on the other hand, are dour, not very communicative and – one feels – suffer from a feeling that they are not as rich as their Spanish neighbours.

American diplomats manage to combine a friendly grass-roots quality with the impression that they are in the game to win. The Russians are rather special – and, with their rigidity, probably the most imbued with special characteristics. (The same is not true of all Communist countries; the Yugoslavs, for example, radiate great charm and so – on occasions – do the Poles.)

Latin Americans constitute the most closely-knit of all diplomatic communities abroad. Many of them project a play-boy image. They give splendid, noisy parties, so – even more so – do their young sons.

White Commonwealth countries often like to deprecate themselves as 'raw amateurs', and are probably less subtle and more direct in their approach than the old European powers.

Arabs are passionate and conscious of their reputation for 'Arab hospitality'. Israelis are intense and totally impressive in their single-mindedness. Africans are highly variable, acutely conscious of their 'status'. Asian states, in the main, have a sense of calm and a great welcoming charm; to be greeted by a Sinhalese secretary, in sari, with soft hand outstretched is probably the nicest welcome in visiting any mission.

Despite the closeness between diplomats, in private they can be bitchy about foreign colleagues – perhaps a natural reaction against having to be so charming to them face to face day after day. Their comments too, are imbued with a feeling of superiority of the diplomat's own service. An English diplomat: 'The West Germans start at eight each morning. God knows what they do . . . the Americans all seem the same; they may go into the Foreign Service Institute different but when they come out. . . .'

'In the French service,' one Belgian assures, 'there's a lot of back stabbing. They have people here afraid to go on holiday. You know what one of them once said when he was asked what he did all day? He said, "I get in at eight, work till nine, and spend the rest of the day protecting my position".'

There are two diplomatic services that are regarded as special:

the British and the French. To a very large degree, they have set the pattern for diplomatic services of nations throughout the world.

British diplomacy has a reputation developed during the country's days as a great power. It is still highly regarded; its own diplomats, certainly, almost universally regard it as the best. British diplomats impress as being unbeatable in crisis situations. They rarely take pains to impress; boasting or displaying abilities are, somehow, not good form. Often they act and look like men born to be sleeping behind copies of *The Times* in a London club, but seem well-informed and they are highly respected for their skills by their 'opponents'.

French diplomacy is even more special. It is easily the most disliked and also the most admired. 'It's a diplomat's diplomacy,' says one ambassador. A British diplomat admits grudgingly: 'Even when de Gaulle was postulating the most ridiculous views on defence, the quality of French diplomats was so high that they could put forward good arguments. That's not always the case with other services – including my own.'

French diplomacy has a long and impressive history. Cardinal Richelieu was the first statesman to recognise diplomacy as a continuing process involving permanent negotiations between nations. His other beliefs are largely those practised by diplomatic services and government today: that policies should be based on pragmatic national interest; that allies should be chosen because of their permanence, not because they are liked; and that ambassadors should have a single chief. He saw that foreign affairs in France were handled by one ministry. Richelieu also realised the importance of propaganda and public opinion, writing pamphlets to gain support for his policies from the French people.

Throughout the seventeenth and eighteenth centuries the French set the diplomatic pattern for the world. Its language became *the* diplomatic language, replacing Latin, a position it retained until this century. Its diplomatic machine was larger than any other. For over 150 years, until the Revolution, France remained supreme in international diplomacy.

Today, though no longer supreme, the French are still perhaps the most immediately inspiring, partly because of their manner, partly because of the rude arrogance that seems to be a part of the country's diplomacy. (When, in 1972, New Zealand, as one of the countries protesting about French nuclear tests in the Pacific moved to boycott French ships, the immediate French reaction was a threat of trade sanctions.)

French diplomats are a mixture of great charm and yet self-superiority. They are conscious of their 'eliteness', are very formal, professional and cynical, believers in the right of their own country, in the supremacy of their own culture, and quick to take slight at any imagined offence. They are seen at their best, or worst, in former French colonies – acting like the rulers you feel they believe they ought to be. It is striking that though most non-French diplomats dislike these characteristics, they also admire them.

Two
The New Diplomats: Recruitment and Training

'There are old bureaucrats and there are bold
bureaucrats, but there are no old, bold bureaucrats.'
State Department saying

Those expecting tomorrow's diplomats to be radically different
from those of today seem almost certain to be disillusioned.

'I see them come in like young Turks,' says an American
foreign service personnel officer. 'But within two years they are
becoming diplomatic, cautious and tactful and have realised that
the important thing is not to rock the boat.'

Superficially, there would appear to be several factors that
should prove him wrong – not least among them the fact that
today's newcomers to the diplomatic profession are members of
a radical and questioning generation. Additionally, the recruiting progress in many foreign services has been expanded to try
to get diplomats who will be more widely representative of their
country. And training has been increased, a development that
should ensure that the new diplomats will be less purely intuitive
operators than the old.

Yet still, one feels that the ambassador of the year 2000 will
not be a vastly different creature from the mission head of the
1970s. The newcomers may be, as one foreign service says, 'men
with long hair who even if they haven't been at the barricades
themselves are all for change and progress'. But the pressure of
the diplomatic environment is strong. It is not diplomatic services
that will change, but the young Turks. 'The most important
lesson I've learned is that if you want to get on don't make
mistakes,' says a middle-aged French diplomat. 'It may seem a
negative virtue, but they'll learn it's an essential one.'

This over-emphasis on caution is an important factor, but there
are others. The recruitment process may have been widened – but

the qualities required for a 'good diplomat' have not changed. And neither the selection procedures, nor the training schemes, have been altered as radically as some diplomats would seem to believe.

'Sometimes,' says an elderly English diplomat, 'I think cynically that what we're really doing is trying to find young men as nearly the same as us as possible, and then directing training in such a way that they become indistinguishable'.

All foreign services are today seeking to recruit what one diplomat calls 'an elite – but of talent, not of breeding'. In the main their record has been successful. The academic qualifications of diplomats in most services are high. By the mid-1960s, for example, seventy per cent of Canadian diplomats had two degrees or more.

But foreign services now have to compete harder to obtain the best talent. Bright graduates planning to enter government service are often attracted to more powerful departments like the Treasury. The numbers of applicants fall; in Germany foreign ministry officials concede it has 'lost some of its appeal'; in Spain in 1971 there were less than eighty candidates for admission whereas twelve years previously there were over 400. There are also signs in many countries, say some recruiters, that the standard attracted is beginning to fall.

The annual intake of foreign services is small. Britain needs about twenty-five new diplomats a year, France fewer, Germany seven in a bad year and forty-five in a high one. Many small countries average only about four, and even the United States recruits less than 200. One especial problem for foreign services is that they are buying manpower resources not for next year, but for many years ahead. 'A company can go out and buy fifty engineers if it finds it needs them,' says one officer. 'But if we think we'll need fifty intermediate officers in a few years' time we have to grow them ourselves.'

Some diplomatic services now have to undertake aggressive recruitment campaigns, visiting campuses, publishing glossy literature and sending round ambassadors to talk and answer questions.

Apart from having to compete, there is a second reason for the widening of the net. Many services, in the face of criticisms, are anxious to lose their reputations of being overstaffed with entrants from a few elitist universities. The United States fights its East Coast image, and purposely has no language qualifications so as not to penalise young Americans from areas where language training is not usual. The British strive to lose the Oxbridge reputation, and boast that forty per cent of newcomers now come from universities other than Oxford and Cambridge.

Services rush to stress that they are not exclusive clubs: 'The members of the Foreign Service,' said Dr Paul Frank, State Secretary of the German Federal Foreign Office, 'are by no means concerned with preserving an aura of exclusiveness as is generally imagined.'

But such attempts to widen the backgrounds of entrants are not always totally successful. In Britain Oxbridge *does* still dominate. The Australians from the beginning of their foreign service have consciously striven to avoid an elitist image – but the best educated triumph and, not surprisingly this often means the best schools and the best backgrounds. In France and Germany the diplomatic services are still attractive careers for the upper classes.

Nor are attempts at democratisation always adopted with zest. An Italian Foreign Ministry official, welcoming new third secretaries, began by reminding them that the career was now open to all sections of society. 'You come,' he said, 'from every class in the country. . .' And as an aside he added, 'and you show it'. A titled Spanish diplomat asked me, 'How can you compare a man who had an English nannie and was brought up on Billy Bunter with someone who has studied English for two years?'

It is only comparatively recently that the diplomatic services of the world ceased being prerogatives of the wealthy aristocracy. In the United States, up to World War I, entrants were often forced to prove a private income. An American diplomat posted far afield could find that his travelling expenses (which he had to pay) were more than his first year's salary. Candidates for the foreign service in nineteenth-century Britain had to guarantee a personal income of £400 a year for at least two years. Even though standards of pay and allowances were raised after World War I, the need for private wealth continued in practice. Until 1941 entrants had to pass very severe tests in French and German which meant that normally only those who could support themselves abroad while studying those languages could hope to qualify for the service.

In Spain, diplomats entering the service were not paid until 1923. Even after that, stringent language qualifications, until 1939, meant that parents had to be rich enough to send their sons for expensive tuition. And, even with that qualification removed, another hurdle remained until comparatively recently: recruits, during their two years at diplomatic school, received only £5 a month (it was then raised to £60).

Today salaries are comparable with those in such fields as academic life, though they may not be competitive with those of lawyers, medical specialists or businessmen. In the Canadian service 1968 pay in the lowest grade ranged from $5,400 to $7,860. American foreign service jobs start at about $12,000. In the British service, an ambassador at a major embassy was receiving £14,000 a year in 1972. But, taken by themselves, salaries are misleading. For the diplomat overseas there are a host of allowances which ensure his standard of life is high.

Because the pay is coupled with the comparative security of life in the public service, it provides one incentive to seek a diplomatic career. This is especially so during periods of high unemployment. 'You have the uncertainty of where you will be going next and what you'll be doing there,' says one middle-grade English diplomat. 'But you do have the overall security of knowing you will be all right unless you do something really stupid.'

But, by itself, it seems not to be a major reason (though it may be a strong one for not resigning later). Talking to young diplomats, a wide range of reasons for joining foreign services emerge. Three recur. The first stems from a desire to be involved in the government machine. A sense of public service and adventure, thought the British Plowden Committee Report on Representational Services Overseas, should be the 'real incentive to join'. Americans frequently give their reason as the wish to take part in making foreign policy. A young Russian explained that his incentive was a desire to serve his country and the cause of international peace.

Nevertheless, some recruiters report a lesser degree of dedication and motivation than ten years ago, with more taking on diplomacy just as they would any other job. An elderly German diplomat claims that entrants who think they will make an impact on policy 'very, very quickly get disillusioned'. McGeorge Bundy, American Presidential Special assistant for National Security from 1961–66, told Harvard students in a speech: 'It would be hard to demonstrate the best way to affect foreign affairs is to enter the foreign service.'

A second is the desire to work and live abroad, which many young German diplomats give as their major reason. On this, there seems to be less disillusionment as the diplomats progress in their careers. 'This,' says one, 'is the thing that keeps me in the service. Whenever I get a bit low, I think about the alternative – being chained to an office desk at home.'

The third involves all the prestige and status inducements in being a member of what is still regarded as rather a special profession. This is a real inducement in many countries, including France. It is not quite as special as it was before World War II, when it was very much a business run by gentlemen for gentlemen. In the 1930s, a current British Foreign Office joke was that work did not begin until 11 a.m. in order to allow the messenger crossing the Channel time to reach London. A story, still told with relish, is of the new entrant who was told his working hours were 11 a.m. until 12.30 and then 3.30 to 4 p.m. He commented, 'But that doesn't seem much.' His incredulous superior retorted: 'It may not seem long laddie, but you'll find it certainly cuts into your day.'

But there is still a mystique. Some new recruits dream of being called Your Excellency one day. 'When I entered,' says a young English diplomat, 'the only thing I'd read was Sir Harold Nicolson. I suppose I did think it was going to be nice being secretary to our ambassador in Paris. . .' And there is an incentive, too, in the relatively small number of entrants allowed into foreign services a year: by succeeding in joining, the new entrants confirm a superiority. 'There may be more diplomats than ever before today,' says an American deputy chief of mission, 'but there are still a damn sight fewer of us than there are businessmen.'

For every foreign service there are precise and basic qualifications, such as age limits, fitness, and minimum academic qualifications (in most, a university degree, although America is a notable exception). Germany sets out to attract men with law degrees and, as an inducement, makes the initial probation period shorter for them than for non-lawyer entrants (eighteen months as against two and a half years).

But equally important in all countries are the intangible qualities. Many are those needed for any civil servant, but there is stress on ones that make a diplomat a good representative of his country abroad. The list is seemingly endless: moral integrity, political sense, ability to communicate, flexibility, loyalty, accuracy, courage. . .

Central to the qualities sought is the belief that diplomats are what has been called in Britain 'professional generalists' and in the United States men with a command of the 'core' diplomatic skills. These 'core' skills are considered essential whatever the work a diplomat does, whether he is working in a political field, economics, or trade. Some services, including the German, have examined whether there should not be more concentration on specialist diplomats, but have decided against such a change.

What it means in some services is that the diplomat is expected to be what one calls 'the multi-headed genius beast – the man who can handle political and economic analysis, turn his hand to information or aid work, and yet still knows how to get someone out of jail or send a body home.'

Basically, there are two methods of selection and training adopted by foreign services. The first relies on gauging potential and then letting the new diplomat learn while working. This could be called the British system. The other, involving a long period of formal training, could be called the French. Methods adopted by other countries are all, to some degree, variants on these two systems.

The system adopted by the British diplomatic service is designed to cream off a group of applicants already known to have high intelligence and extended education. 'It assumes,' said a British Government Committee that examined it, 'that candidates will quickly need to display the qualities for which they have been chosen.'

There are three stages of the selection process. The first part is a written examination, lasting a day and a half. It includes a test in summarising – typically, a complex 1,400 word piece to be reduced to no more than 350 words – and a general paper to test constructive thinking and the ability to set out ideas lucidly and cogently. In recent years changes have been made to redress the advantage said to have been given to arts graduates in the past. The essay section has now been discarded, and there is a diagrammatic test – 'for candidates with a background in science and mathematics who may be more accustomed to working with symbols than with words'. (All services contain a large majority of diplomats with backgrounds either in the arts or in law.) Each year, between four and five hundred applicants take this part of the test, and about half get through to the next stage. This lasts two days, and the potential-diplomats are interviewed and tested by a panel of three, consisting of a senior or retired civil servant, a psychologist and a middle-ranking civil servant. What should emerge, it is claimed, is a rounded picture of the candidate's personality and ability.

Those who survive this process, go before a final selection board where seven people, from inside and outside the public service, conduct a thirty minute interview. It is claimed to be the most intensive selection test in the country.

In America the procedure follows basically the same pattern. Since 1970 Foreign Service candidates are no longer expected to be as 'generalist' (they opt to specialise in political, administration, consular or economic work) but stress is still placed on the 'core' skills and recruiting a 'good diplomatic'.

Again, there is emphasis on the oral examination, and on the successful candidate learning on the job. The written examination, which is meant only to measure aptitude in order to allow a broad base of candidates to pass to the next stage, is not very difficult. Although the oral examination specially covers the field in which the applicant wishes to specialise, he is judged also as a potential Foreign Service officer. 'In this way, it's different from hiring the way a firm does,' says an officer involved in the selection process. 'Say a man wants to be an administrator. First we'd press him on why he wants to do this in the Foreign Service when he could earn three-and-a-half times as much in Standard Oil. Then we'd throw at him something like, "What's the purpose of NATO?".'

There will be questions to test his political awareness and arguing skill. 'Imagine yourself working in Beirut,' one is told.

'You meet someone who's the son of a Palestine refugee. He asks you "What the hell is the U.S. trying to achieve in the Middle East?" What would you say?'

Compared with the oral questioning in Britain, the American sessions are brief, only sixty to ninety minutes long. Many selectors believe it is too short a time in which to gain a fair impression. They become guarded when asked how they rate the President or what they think about a specific U.S. policy. It does not matter what they say, only that they should argue it well. But they have no way of knowing that it will not be held against them if their views are opposed to those of the Administration.

Criticisms can be made of this sort of selection procedure which is also followed by a number of other countries. All try to sift out men who can go to the top – notwithstanding the fact that most are never expected to rise that far. Sir Douglas Busk, who has sat on British recruitment boards, likens it to trying to ascertain whether every corporal has a marshal's baton in his pack 'disregarding the fact that no army is staffed with just marshals and that you need colonels and captains'.

Another is the difficulty of assessing whether young men really have all the intangible qualities being sought. In Britain itself time is spent over this, but it has grown more difficult a task since compulsory military national service in the country was ended. Now candidates come straight from university, and admits a Foreign Office man, 'It's a lot harder to assess a man at the age of twenty-one than at the age of twenty-three or twenty-four'.

A third concerns the qualities that will impress a panel of selectors. A number of countries now claim they are determined to broaden the base of candidates. But the qualities of personal ease and character formed at the elitist schools and universities are exactly the ones that will count most. Some older diplomats believe that the fault lies not in this, but in trying to attract more representative candidates in the first place. 'What we should want is the best,' one Briton says. 'And if the best people happen to come from certain backgrounds and schools, fine. You don't get the French giving in to this nonsense.' Nor, in fact, do many others, including Arab and Asian States.

There are three arguments for this system as compared with the French: diplomacy is a profession best learned on the job;

after leaving university, candidates are impatient to get down to practical work; and a procedure that involves lengthy formal training deters many good applicants, reducing the overall quality of the intake.

A newcomer to the British diplomatic service is, on his first day, placed in a department of the Foreign Office. During the first week he acclimatises and learns the most basic routines: the layout of the building, where papers are filed, and some of the strange customs of the Office such as not knocking at doors or calling anyone 'Sir' except the secretary of state (or, when he is posted, his ambassador).

He then takes a two week course. This consists mainly of short lectures, on the organisation of the Foreign Office, the work of various departments, and on welfare in the service. He receives a security briefing and (seemingly the only concession to technology) is given a short lecture on 'The use of dictating machines'.

After this it is back to his department where he remains for twelve months. 'We just chuck them in and let them get on with it,' says one department head. Departments in foreign ministries are geographical, covering areas of the world, or functional, handling such matters as trade policy or research. In a geographical department, the newcomer will be given his own little bit of the world to handle. Telegrams and despatches from embassies there will come to him first.

The system assumes that, from the start, he knows about the country or subject with which he deals, an inducement meant to make sure that he soon does. One British diplomat abroad recalled that as a new entrant he was involved with aid, a subject in which his superior was not very interested. The result, he reported, was that much of the British aid policy was formulated by him, a third secretary fresh from university.

During the first year, the new diplomat's only formal training is in improving his knowledge of a foreign language. (After that, about half of the newcomers go on to study a 'hard language' such as Arabic, Japanese or Russian. Perhaps oddly, British diplomats are good at these more difficult languages, but less good on more common ones.)

In the American service, initial training takes place at the Foreign Service Institute but is also short – six weeks – and is aimed at giving the recruits a broad picture of the service. But there are special features. The first is in the degree of participation invited. One course leader told his new entrants: 'You are welcome to help work out a curriculum. You don't have to have anything on commerce, but I'm bound to tell you that you'll find it helpful later. . .' 'This approach,' reported the Deputy Director of the Institute, 'went a little further than the usual degree of participation – but it's an example of the kind of thing we are trying to do.'

Lectures lead into discussion sessions on controversial issues. At one a speaker warned American diplomats not to expect to be liked abroad. There were reasons why they would not be: America was powerful and powerful countries had always been hated. America was imitated by others, and this caused resentment. And some countries hated the United States because it treated the masses as people.

The recommended reading list of books for the trainees provides a moment of pleasure. A pro-C.I.A. book by a former director, Allen Dulles, comes next to *The Invisible Government* – an anti-C.I.A. bestseller that gave the American establishment high blood-pressure when it was published.

The recruits are also invited to participate in the choice of their first overseas posting which they take up about six months after appointment. During the first weeks a list of posts available is displayed in the Institute building and recruits are asked to mark their first, second and third preferences. 'I think this is a more open approach especially when young people all over the world are clamouring for more responsibility,' says one officer. 'Mostly they spread themselves around very well, but if six want to go to the same place, we have to decide.'

Before being sent abroad, however, the new American diplomat spends five months learning a language. The choice available, ranging alphabetically from Amharic to Vietnamese, covers six pages of the Institute's schedule of courses. Foreign services lay great stress on language training, and usually there are rewards (in the form of allowances) or punishments (in not being promoted) linked with the training in them.

In the American service the number unable to speak a foreign language fell from over fifty per cent to less than a third between

1958 and 1962. By 1970, it was said that most spoke at least two. Now a diplomat has to speak one before being allowed overseas.

One problem is that recruits learn a language, and are then posted to a country where they cannot use it. 'We teach him German and then he ends up in Australia,' says an Institute official. 'Then of course Congress starts asking questions. . . .' This is a problem that continues throughout a diplomat's career, and is common to all services. A well-known joke in the Swedish diplomatic service is, 'If you *don't* want to be sent to Moscow, learn Russian.'

Diplomats of all nations are constantly being moved around; consequently, a diplomat who has learned, say, Chinese may find himself spending part of his working life in Europe or America. A far-sighted young diplomat can, however, exercise some influence on his career and on the countries in which he will serve by his choice of languages. 'There's a boy we taught Portuguese,' says an American officer. 'Now he's doing French. He wants to go to Africa, and with those two languages he could cover the whole continent.'

The training-by-doing starts at the officer's first post. One American ambassador said that he instructed juniors to write memos on anything they think might be of interest to the embassy: 'I have instructed their superiors to take what is said seriously, and, whenever possible, to leave the junior officer with his pride of authorship.' Another pointed out that he sometimes directed young officers to give their views on actions under consideration: 'Surprisingly enough, their recommendations are frequently sound enough and original enough to cause us to review our staff findings and even to alter our plans.' And a third put them to work quickly as possible: 'It isn't a matter of "sink or swim". If the water is too deep for them, a senior officer is there to give them a hand. . . . Instead of merely *getting ready* to work they are actually *working* – pulling their own weight so to speak.'

It conveys the impression that it is a real man's life in the diplomatic service. But it is not quite that rosy.

In 1967 the State Department courageously published a study by Professor Chris Argyris called 'Some Causes of Organisational Ineffectiveness within the Department of State.' During his research, Argyris was given this account:

I was given a job to type 3,000 file cards after I had been told in my orientation how much the Foreign Service valued initiative. I was furious. Why not use a girl for this? I asked and was told that secretaries were scarce. I thought, if they'd get rid of some of the excess officers they might afford secretaries.

Anyway, I started typing. But I decided to research the job on my own. I found out:

1. Another Foreign Service officer had done the same thing one year ago.
2. The process was so slow that by the time I finished the last one, the first one would be obsolete.

I came up with a simple solution and took it to my boss. He told me that was a great idea but it wouldn't work. When I asked him why, he gave me a vague reason. I felt that either he didn't want to bother with developing the idea, or that he didn't want to admit to a superior that a junior man thought this out. He told me to go back to my typing.

I continued my typing so that no one would consider me as a troublemaker. But I wrote up the plan as a beneficial suggestion. Nothing happened. I decided finally that there was nothing that I could do. So I started asking around. First thing I found out was how many people had experienced the same kind of thing. 'Join the club.' I was taught to complain about my job to certain people but not to be too obvious about it. Finally, I got out. One good thing I learned was how to beat the system.

There is another inbuilt disadvantage to the system of learning by doing. The success or failure depends largely on the amount and the quality of the guidance exercised by superior officers. 'We have some great people in this service,' says one senior English diplomat, 'but we also have some duffers. Heaven help the youngsters supposed to accept guidance from them.' Another says: 'So many elder diplomats are ultra-cautious, that the one lesson the newcomers learn is: If in doubt, do nothing.'

Even if seniors are good at their own jobs, they may be busy, or poor at communicating advice. As in many professions, experienced seniors often find it quicker to do a job themselves than to explain to juniors how it should be tackled.

The alternative to this method of training is the French system which involves a relatively long period of formal training.

In France itself university graduates under the age of twenty-five are selected to study at the Ecole Nationale d'Administration which produces senior civil servants and diplomats. Each year there are about 1,000 applications for the 100 places. Once admitted, they become salaried civil servants under service discipline, but they do not know until the end of their training which French ministry will finally employ them.

The first twelve months are usually spent in prefecture, with the student attached to the prefect's office as an assistant. Some of his time is spent in sub-prefectures and in the local offices of ministries. He will be given a report to do, and copies are sent to the E.N.A. with the prefect's comments.

He then spends eighteen months at the E.N.A., where most of the teaching takes place in discussion groups. A study group has to produce a report on a current issue. All students take the same subjects, and these include economics, social questions, international relations, judicial and administrative matters, accountancy, business management, organisation and methods, and languages.

At the end of the course an order of merit, based on performance throughout, is published together with a list of vacancies. The man with the highest marks gets first choice at the ministry of his choice, and so on down the list. The first choice is normally the powerful Inspection Générale des Finances which usually has seven to eight vacancies. The French diplomatic service takes about a dozen students a year from this source. (A smaller number of entrants consists of graduates who can offer two difficult languages.) Although the E.N.A. is the longest established example of the system, other countries have adopted variants of it.

German newcomers to the foreign service spend eight months at the diplomatic training school in Bonn after passing stiff entrance exams in English and French, history, politics and basic economics. After a probationary period, part of which will be spent abroad, there is a second examination. But few fail this one: 'The state have spent so much on you by this time that you would have to be really bad,' concedes one young attaché.

In the Norwegian service, there is a one year fulltime course covering such subjects as history, law and diplomatic practice. While at diplomatic school, students have to bring themselves up to the same level as their companions. A recruit with a degree in

history, for example, would need to spend most of his year studying law, and the lawyer his time studying history.

Several advantages can be claimed for the French system. The
training is both wide and thorough. If all civil servants are
taught in the same academy, at the end, home civil servants have
some knowledge and understanding of foreign affairs, and diplomats similar insight into the workings and problems of home
departments. The new diplomat arrives at his first post with a
grounding in his subject. And because the training system is so
competitive successful candidates will have really worked. Critics,
however, claim that the competition is unhealthy. This is particularly so in the Spanish service. In recent years entrance
examination standards to get into diplomatic school have been
drastically lowered. Each year about fifty get through to spend
two years formal training. But this does not mean they have been
admitted to the Foreign Service. At the end of the period there is
a stiff examination. Between ten and twenty people pass (depending on the number of diplomatic jobs available that year). Those
who fail can either go through the whole course again, risking
another two years of their lives, or try to get a job outside. The
French system is a tough race in which the elite come out first.
One consequence for countries that practise this approach is that
their new diplomats are older when they begin work than their
colleagues in the British or American Services. In Britain, a
young diplomat can be a third secretary at twenty-three; his
French, Spanish or Italian counterpart may be nearing thirty.

Its opponents claim that the training comes at the wrong stage
in a diplomat's career; that far more important is training that
continues right through a career. At present, the most basic training programme consists of the introductory tuition, languages,
and specialised (though short) instruction during the diplomat's
career to equip him to handle specific functions or understand
particular countries or areas.

The great need, in addition, claim many diplomats is much
more mid-career and early senior-level training. The American
Foreign Service Institute now aims at four essential levels after
the introductory orientation. The first is for diplomats getting
ready for the middle of the careers, and includes intensive courses
in speciality. The second, at mid-career, is aimed at ensuring

the officer does not become *too* specialised, and includes seminars which in one particular week included ones on science technology and foreign affairs, and on the international implications of the New Left.

The third stage, at which officers are poised for the top rank, can include sabbaticals and advanced research. And the fourth, for seniors, consists of the Senior Seminar on Foreign Policy, a ten month programme of studies to expose future mission chiefs and other top officers to 'the latest developments worldwide in science, arts, communications, space, atomic energy, industry, commerce, agriculture, labour, education, transportation, the communist threat and counterinsurgency, the poverty programme, the Peace Corps, race relations, city-state federal relationships, automation, computers, and systems and functional analysis.'

Other countries have their own schemes, though none as ambitious. On paper, the presence of such training is a valid and sensible alternative to long formal tuition at the start of a diplomat's career. But there is a large gap between the desire and the actuality of current schemes. In the United States there have been recommendations that diplomats should spend ten per cent of their careers in non-language professional training, but in 1968 the percentage of the service totally engaged in such training was only 2.6 per cent.

One major problem is that the service providing such training needs a manpower surplus. In Britain the Plowden Committee report in 1964 recommended this should be ten per cent, but five years later the Duncan Committee found that the highest authorised had been seven and a half per cent, and margins were less at two key levels – six per cent at counsellor rank and nil at first secretary.

Other services have had the same problem. Many have found it difficult to implement any systematic programme of such training at all. Germany has suffered especially. With virtually no manpower surplus, the problem has been less fitting in training but avoiding months' long vacancies at posts. In the early 1970s a German diplomat going to a new country could expect a fourteen-day briefing; someone taking up a scientific job could anticipate a swift tour of a few German factories. The need for a manpower surplus has, however, been accepted, and the target is one of just under eight per cent by 1978.

It *may* be that, given time, training schemes will have some real impact, and that diplomats will gradually change. But it seems at least highly debatable. Even in the unlikely event of the amount of training reaching the levels that have been envisaged as ideal, the impact of the diplomat's working environment will still be critical.

The impact of the system in all services is deadening. Professor Argyris looked at what he calls the 'living system' of the State Department and the American Foreign Service. His findings specifically concerned the United States but they would seem to coincide with personal experiences of the other services. 'The system,' he concluded, 'contained norms that inhibit open confrontation of difficult issues and penalise people who take risks.' He illustrated his points with interviews with officers:

'Open hostility is not very good form. Negative comments are always made subtly. Until I came here I never placed my ideas in such cautious language.'

'Senior people are rarely open. So you have to discount what they say.'

'If someone is incompetent, he is not fired. He is given an assistant who will do most of the work.'

'Some superiors – I'd say the majority that I know about send everything upstairs. Even the most trivial things. Superiors send them upstairs for approval for fear of sticking their necks out.'

'. . . On balance, there is strong pressure to keep your mouth shut because you may be labelled as an unrealistic thinker.'

A young British diplomat claims that one early lesson he learned was to say what he thought others wanted to hear. 'This I very rapidly realised was essential if you weren't to be regarded as some kind of bolshevik. So you learn not by doing or thinking, but by copying, attitudes as well as methods.'

Sometimes one meets a newcomer and knows instinctively that unless he does change, his future in his diplomatic service will hardly be spectacular. A young Italian, abrasive and self-confident, was – perhaps unknown to him – attracting adverse comments from his older colleagues. At some point, one suspected he would realise it and conform or else . . . .

It is likely he will, for one is struck by how cautious and conformist diplomats do quickly become. And then they begin to justify it. A youngish member of the British service says: 'I believe there is good reason for our over caution. If you say or do something that you shouldn't, it can cancel out a year of doing and saying the right things. In diplomacy there is little room for error. If you are a home civil servant and plan a school for the wrong place, you can always put it right. But as a diplomat, if you let out information that upsets another country. . . .'

Each year a few 'late entrants' are admitted into foreign services after deciding to change their careers. They often find it harder to conform. But this does not have much impact on the services concerned. They are rarely ever admitted to full membership of the club and their status has been likened to that of immigrants.

An 'outsider', now working in a foreign ministry in a specialist role, claims that he was soon 'stunned' by the rapid effect of the system on new diplomats. 'They seem to get frustrated and disillusioned when they find out the smallness of the work involved. At first they kick, but they soon find it doesn't get them anywhere. It is frowned upon and even the most modern-minded intermediate or senior officer will say "They'll get over it." And they do. I watch them taking on the colourisation of the department. They start to water down and to compromise. Their caution spills over into every sphere. It does mean, of course, that it's a very polite place.'

Another official, a Scandinavian, in a similar outsider position, says: 'I know we used to say "Left wing at twenty-one, liberal at thirty, and conservative at forty", but this happens so much quicker. They realise that the rewards for simply playing along and waiting their turn in line are very real.'

This appears to be supported by the fact that although young diplomats are initially highly vocal in their condemnation of what they find, the number who leave is small. In some services it is as low as three per cent; even in the United States the number who leave within the first five years is only twelve per cent (compared with about fifty per cent in business firms).

Later on in their careers the caution is reinforced by the fear of not being able to find work if they resign. 'As a diplomat,' concedes one, 'you're not really fitted for much else.' American recruiters say that they accept this point, and hope that it will be remedied by recruiting for the four specialities. This they hope will reduce the percentage of entrants with arts degrees. One says: 'Say we can now attract a boy with a business master's degree. Well, he can give us the farewell any time, and I like that. Now what happens with an officer who has got a faded bit of parchment saying he's got Spanish literature? If he doesn't like something, he can knuckle down or quit. If he quits, he's qualified for nothing, so he knuckles down.'

The pressure of the system is strengthened by the fact that despite the attempts at broadening the range of recruits, diplomats from all countries do still come from a vaguely similar mould, and most enter the service straight after schooling. One English first secretary says: 'I feel that the office should make more effort to rub our noses in the reality of life. Most of us have no firsthand experience of the kind of life ordinary people in Britain live. I think really I should have been shipped off to somewhere like Bradford before starting in a department and made to see what it was all about – what makes up the country I'm supposed to be representing and what ordinary people's problems are.'

This applies at home but even more so when the diplomat is sent overseas. The young diplomat's working and social hours are spent with other diplomats or with the members of one section of local society. A diplomat can live in a foreign country and hardly ever try to come to grips with its everyday living conditions.

Ambassadors are the most cut off, of course, but it happens right down to the lowest level. A secretary at a British embassy in a Middle Eastern country admitted that she had never been on a local bus and wanted a description of what it was like. She had waited at a stop once, she said, but had grown nervous at the last moment. Despite her youth, there was a striking similarity between her words and those of another woman attaché nearing retirement who said she had been personally grateful for the war 'because I did see another class of person for the first time'.

Many elderly diplomats agree that changes are likely to be few. If anything, some feel, the new diplomats will become even more conformist than their predecessors. 'Of course my generation conformed to the right sort of thing,' one says. 'But, my God, we threw up some eccentrics as well. I can't see *this* lot doing that. . . .'

Three

The Diplomat at Home:
Foreign Ministries

'There are three species of creatures who, when they
seem coming are going; when they seem going, they
come: diplomats, women and crabs.'
John Hay, U.S. Statesman and author

Although a diplomat can expect to spend two-thirds of his working life abroad, from the moment he enters his profession his life
will be dominated by the organisation at home.

His first experiences of his new career will be gained inside the
foreign ministry where he will work until he receives his first overseas assignment. Thereafter, a third of his career may be spent
within its environs during home-postings.

When he is abroad at an embassy, the ministry is his 'head
office'. It will send him orders, decide what happens to his reports,
and his colleagues there will be the link with the policy-makers
that he hopes to influence. It will decide where he is posted, when
he is promoted, and in some services it will send forth the teams
of inspectors who will examine his embassy and him personally.

The home organisation and the foreign missions are the two
elements that together form a country's diplomatic machine. They
are interdependent; without one the other could not exist. Head
office has been likened to the central and nervous system; missions
feed it with information and act as a channel of communication
between it and foreign governments.

The diplomat serving abroad today may be working at home
next year. Officers rotate through home and overseas postings,
and in the United States service, for example, a third of the
country's diplomats are in America at any given moment.

Despite that, distinctive head office and branch mentalities
develop. Depending on whether the diplomat is working at home
or abroad *they* may be head-office or embassies. And it is *they*

who are usually hide-bound with bureaucracy and are out of touch with reality.

To a diplomat at head office '*here* is where it really happens'. And, at least in terms of the massive inflow of material, complicated organisation and hierarchies, and enormous concentrations of effort, he is right. Whether the end product justifies it all is a different matter.

Although the home organisation, and how well or badly it operates, is crucial, it has escaped the scrutiny of most diplomatic reviews, with the possible exception of the German Reform Commission that made it clear that the most urgent immediate task was a reorganisation of the central office. The steps being taken – notably regrouping working units into sections to deal with areas of the world rather than specialised subjects – were hardly radical. At least there, however, there was acceptance that something needed to be done.

The British Duncan Committee report, the most quoted and most closely studied examination of overseas representation, hardly looked at the head office situation. If missions are in danger of being over-investigated, as some diplomats claim, home organisations certainly are not. They are certainly ripe for scrutiny. Douglas Hurd, a former British diplomat, has described the organisation of the British Foreign Office with its 'so many Under-Secretaries . . . so many Parliamentary Under-Secretaries and Ministers of State, each needing his own little organisation, each sucking in copies of every document, each marking out frontiers of power, a crowd of admirals making navigation baffling for the ordinary seaman.'

The home organisation collates and analyses reports from abroad, and sends out instructions and guidance. Its officials advise their minister on policy, liaise with other government departments who have an interest in what happens abroad, and they conduct business with the diplomats of foreign nations based in their country.

The buildings in which all this happens range from squalid to luxurious, from architectural monuments to air-conditioned modern blocks, from the elegance and formality of the Quai d'Orsay to the pinnacled skyscraper oppressiveness of the Soviet Foreign Ministry. The atmosphere can be of faded grandeur, as with the

British Foreign Office, a mid-Victorian building in Whitehall, loved by preservationists and hated by those who occupy it. Ministers work under vast oil paintings in rooms that are deep-carpeted; officials often operate in incredibly squalid conditions. The waiting-room for one department head consist of three cheap steel-frame chairs in a main corridor, the floor covered with brown linoleum. Lord George-Brown, former Minister, found: 'People literally still work in corridors and what were once upon a time intended to be cupboards. Quite senior officials interview foreign diplomats in the most incredible little cubby-holes.'

Or it can be functional like the $50 million, eight-storey high, mini-city State Department in Washington, a warren of corridors, row after row of rooms, and exhortations (on the wall) for walkers to keep to the right, especially on corners, to avoid person-to-person collisions.

All, to some degree, are oppressive; the State Department, perhaps because of its size, the most so. People seem a little superfluous; they vanish into the vastness. It is not only that Mr X can't reach Mr Y; not even X's secretary can reach Y's secretary. One feels that someone could vanish for weeks and never be noticed. And, alternatively, that an outsider with access could move into an empty room and, provided he shuffled the right papers, would never be exposed as not belonging. Kafka, one feels, would be at home.

President John Kennedy, according to former aide Arthur Schlesinger Jr, complained that he and his assistant for national security affairs, McGeorge Bundy, could 'get more done in one day at the White House than they do in six months at the State Department'.

Foreign diplomats are awed by the number of people, 'State *is* too big,' concedes an American ambassador. 'But if you ask me what can be done about it, I'll tell you the answer: nothing.' A colleague suggests there is only one answer: to adopt a suggestion first aimed at the Pentagon. This would involve sealing off all the offices except those on the first two floors one Monday morning. As staff arrived, they would be directed to those offices. Once they were all occupied, the State Department would be considered fully staffed and everyone else dismissed. 'I'd say State was easily the worst,' he says, 'but from my experience I doubt if there's a foreign ministry anywhere in the world that couldn't benefit from trying this scheme.'

If State does seem the worst, this is partly because it is such an open organisation. It is easy for an outsider to wander, watching the organisation in action. Other foreign ministries are much less open, and are often, because of the ever-increasing staff, spread out over up to twenty separate buildings, often far apart from one another. But all, from the French to the Ghanaian, seem to be equally effective at playing the bureaucrat game, at creating paper work and, if they are not underworked, at proving the truth of Parkinson's law that work expands as the work force expands. The French, in particular, are experts at conducting weeks-long series of formal correspondence when a telephone call would do. Paper swamps and dominates foreign ministries. An official may write to a colleague whose office is two doors away. A British Foreign Office Department head stressed that he was trying to curtail this practice – but conceded he would write to people next door 'if I was telling them not to split infinitives'.

The bureaucracy can be deadening. During the Arab–Israeli Six Day War the Canadian ambassador in Cairo, afraid the embassy would be set on fire, wanted to buy $200 worth of fire extinguishers. At that time an ambassador was not authorised to spend over $25 without clearance, so he requested it. He was then asked for a reason. He replied, citing the war. The department then sent another cable. It wanted more details about quantities and costs and, in particular, advice on whether there was not a cheaper way of providing protection. The ambassador gave in at this point, bought $25 worth of buckets, and filled them with sand and water.

The number of staff at head office needs to be related to the number abroad. A proportion of two abroad to one at home has been claimed as ideal. Sometimes when there are not enough diplomats to staff the home organisation, the home civil service can be used to build up the ratio. Diplomats claim this presents especial problems: officers at home cannot properly appreciate the difficulties of those abroad, and if there are too few home posts, officers may spend so long overseas that they lose all perspective of their own nations. The problem is most acute for countries with small diplomatic services. Luxembourg, for example, has less than forty diplomats, about two-thirds of them overseas. There are ten ambassadors abroad, but it is hard to bring them home for a posting: there is only one job of ambassador level in the home organisation, that of secretary general of the department. Sweden, with about 300 diplomats, faces the problem at all levels of the service. The majority of officers are always abroad; even getting a home posting is difficult. In consequence, they can be hopelessly out of touch with what is happening at home. Diplomats get paid home leave every two years – and *have* to take it in Sweden, one way of ensuring they still know what the country looks like. And diplomats have to be recalled from time to time for short courses to brush-up on home politics.

Without a sufficient number of home postings, the head office-branch mentality will be especially strong. Even with a good rotational system, it is real. 'You don't have to be back overseas long before you start thinking of those bastards back there,' says an Australian diplomat. From head office, though, the view is different: 'What's important at the post is just a drop in the bucket here,' says one home-based diplomat.

Once reports reaching foreign ministries were few. When Thomas Jefferson was the U.S. Secretary of State he pointed out that it was over two years since he had heard from his ambassador in Madrid. If another year went by with no news, he planned to write to him.

But today the amount is vast. It comes in by telegraph and by courier. Foreign ministries have their own radio services linking them with missions, and says one head office diplomat 'It's going full blast twenty-four hours a day seven days a week'. Couriers roam the world; the American service has ninety who in an average year travel nearly ten million miles between them, their pouches bulging with reports and documents.

The State Department not only sucks in thousands of messages a week but even more startling, an incoming one may be copied a hundred times and the copies sent whizzing around Washington. Even a middling-size service may process about 10,000 incoming and outgoing telegrams a month. Telegraph messages alone at the British Foreign Office increase by an average seven per cent a year: 'It's a growth we think will continue,' says a diplomat there. 'I just don't know where saturation point comes.'

A few years ago German diplomats conceded that the material that reached the foreign ministry in Bonn 'was too much and too late'. Today it may be on time; it is still too much.

An ambassador at a major German embassy confesses: 'When I consider the size of our Foreign Office and of the desk that deals with this country and the size of this embassy, I am afraid we are giving them too much. It is so easy to send a long report, very difficult to *précis* a difficult political programme into a short telegraph. And these days it is so easy to send a telegram. In the past they had to be ciphered by hand before being sent which was a big inducement to keep them short or few. Now there is no technical reason for not sending them because you cipher automatically by machine.'

As it is, diplomats overseas often feel that their reports are simply filed or are moved around from person to person, and then are lost or pigeonholed at some stage in the process. A European head office diplomat confirms: 'The real problem today is just keeping it moving.' Another, an American, believes: 'The intelligence that flows into foreign ministries is often excellent. But the trouble is knowing what to do with it.'

Walter Hines Page, the American ambassador to Britain during World War I, became so angry at the little attention paid to his telegrams that he threatened to send a message saying that an earthquake had swallowed up the Thames, that a suffragette had kissed the King, and that the statue of Cromwell had made an assault against the House of Lords just to see if anyone in Washington would take any notice. Even today it is an experiment that would be worth making.

Although head offices complain about the deluge of paper, they appear to see their main task as absorbing rather than cutting down the quantity. Occasionally, they will complain to a mission that too much is being sent by expensive telegram instead of by the courier service. But the ambassador will not be given a list of reports emanating from his mission that were regarded as unnecessary. As it is, the only way an ambassador can ensure a measurable head office reaction is to send a view at variance with the ministry's collective thought, or report that locally a minister's policy is going down badly.

J. K. Galbraith, from his embassy in New Delhi, sent the State Department his views on China and the United Nations. It brought, he recorded in his diary, 'one of the rudest and certainly the promptest response in the history of the Department: "To the extent that your position has any merit it has been fully considered and rejected".'

The bulk of material that pours into foreign ministries goes first to officers whose daily dealings are with the country concerned. The structure of ministries is elaborate. Basically, they are divided up into departments covering functions such as economics or politico-military matters and departments dealing with geographical areas. (In addition there are all those handling administrative matters.)

The hierarchy is structured like a pyramid with the minister and his senior advisers at the top. Below them are several layers of officialdom, with diplomats dealing with individual countries at the bottom of the pyramid. In the American service the officers handling specific countries are known as country directors and are answerable to a deputy assistant secretary, who in turn is under an assistant secretary who is responsible for an area of the world such as Europe.

Similar systems are operated in other ministries, although titles given to the officers will vary, and the elaborateness will depend on the size of the organisation. In the British Foreign Office what the United States calls bureaux are known as departments. Under the head of department and his assistant come diplomats who, depending on their rank, may deal with major countries or groups, or with less vital ones.

Most of the material that enters foreign ministries is routed to departments and individual officers there. Because of rankings in the service, correspondence on the same subject may be carried on simultaneously at different levels:

For each rank abroad there is an equivalent level in the hierarchy at home. In the British service, for example, the permanent under secretary in London equates with the ambassador at a major post, the deputy under secretaries with less grand ambassadors, assistant under secretaries with ambassadors at minor posts, and heads of department with counsellors. The ranks of first, second and third secretaries are the same at home and overseas. In practice a first secretary at home might deal direct with an ambassador at some small post – never with as high a figure as the ambassador to Washington. In the American service, an ambassador might insist on dealing with someone higher up the ladder than the country director.

The bulk of incoming material is for information only, and needs no action other than being read and filed. A great deal of the rest can be handled at the bottom level.

According to the British Foreign Office, a day in the life of a third secretary dealing with Norway, Sweden, Denmark, Finland and Iceland, could go like this:

Morning: Drawing up a list of the pros and cons of a proposed visit by a Scandinavian minister to London at the request of his department head. This involves gathering reactions from other departments.

Collecting information for a reply to a question in Parliament, drafting the reply, and clearing it with the assistant head of department.

Sitting on a Cabinet Office working party to put his department's view on a fisheries question.

Afternoon: Dealing with a note from the Swedish embassy asking if a Swedish training ship can visit Liverpool. He calls the defence ministry, confirms there are no obvious problems, and drafts a formal letter (to be signed by his department head) conveying the inquiry to the Ministry of Defence.

Chatting with the third secretary of the British embassy in Helsinki who is on leave in London.

Studying the programme of a visit of Swedish economic journalists who will be visiting London as guests of the Foreign Office.

Dealing with a telegram from the ambassador in Denmark about the import of Danish goods. He sends a copy to the trade ministry for its views and discusses it with the Foreign Office's own economic relations department. When the trade ministry replies, he will draft a reply.

Considering a request from a philatelic organisation in Helsinki asking to borrow stamps from the Queen's collection for an exhibition. He decides that there is no political objection, and suggests that the request be sent to the Keeper of the Privy Purse at the Palace.

The problems with which this third secretary has dealt are comparatively minor ones. But, on those calling for action, it should be noted, he was primarily reacting to events, and he involved others in the decision-taking process – his superiors, other departments and other ministries of government.

These two elements – reaction rather than initiative, and group decision making – are common and basic to all foreign ministries at all levels.

Two factors make decision taking even more complex in foreign ministries than in other agencies of government. All ministries have systems whereby recommendations travel through the hierarchy, being subject to change and compromise on the way. But in the case of foreign ministries this is complicated by the excess caution of the officials involved, and also by the number of outside agencies interested in foreign affairs who have to be consulted.

Recommendations for action normally start with the area expert or the desk officer. A British department head explains how it works: 'You start with a problem that requires a decision. An officer will draft a recommendation with the pros and cons. I'll consider it and it may be changed. Before it leaves this department it will be cleared with everyone who needs to see it in the office. If, for example, it involves the Portuguese in Guinea, it would be dealt with by the West African department. But it would also be shown to the United Nations political department and the departments covering Southern Europe and Central and South Africa.'

Changes may be made; if the other departments simply concur, this fact will be minuted at the bottom. This then moves on to the next stage in the hierarchy. 'Practically always what goes forward,' says a department head, ' is a consensus review. In the last report the initiating department could say, "We believe this, but they believe that." But there's always an attempt to sort it out. It's a question of give and take. One department gives a little of something it would like in return for a concession from the other department.'

The paper which reaches the minister at the top of the pyramid is, in Britain, known as the submission. Lord Chalfont, a former junior minister at the British Foreign Office, has described it in

an article in the *New Statesman*, as always being 'lucidly presented, persuasively argued, and formidably monolithic. Dissent
and reservation is carefully ironed out at the official level; what is
presented to the minister is the considered, agreed Foreign Office
view. If he is disobliging enough to reject it the process has to
begin again; and in case ministers should disrupt the machine by
trying to initiate policies themselves, they are kept busy with an
endless stream of telegrams, despatches, cabinet papers, parliamentary questions and miscellaneous correspondence.' Chalfont
has pleaded that submissions should submit various courses of
action in the form of options with the arguments for and against
each 'so that the minister has a real choice to make, not simply
the illusory one of accepting the advice of officials or persuading
them to change it'.

The Trudeau Government in Canada enforced what Chalfont
wants: 'The attitude to us now,' reported one Canadian diplomat, 'is that the minister and the cabinet don't want a consensus
of opinions. They want options; they want papers to stimulate
discussions.'

One of his colleagues is sceptical about this system: 'Of course,
it's right politicians should make the decisions. But if you don't
give them a consensus, how wisely do they decide? What happens
is that they decide not on the arguments with which they are
presented but on their political beliefs, where they come from,
and what they've read in the newspapers.'

There is also such an amount of cross-checking with other
ministries to make some express wonderment that any decisions
are made at all. An American under secretary of state for political
affairs, U. Alexis Johnson, has said: 'I cannot think of a single
problem that crosses my desk during the course of the day that
doesn't involve at least two or three, and often fifteen or twenty,
different government agencies, and their interests are often conflicting. This is where the State Department comes into it.'

Some foreign ministries are more powerful than others in the
home governmental structure, and can adopt near-bullying tac-
tics. The British Foreign Office has a tendency when calling other
ministries to say, 'We propose to do this . . .' leaving the other to
produce a convincing reason why they should not. In the United
States and a number of other countries the other ministry would

wait for the diplomats to convince them. In Australia, the likely reaction from the civil servant in the other department would be, 'Now hold on . . .' heralding a fierce battle.

The need for continuous cross-consultation is often the reason why diplomats at embassies cannot obtain fast decisions. And diplomats abroad are not expected to make direct contact with other agencies; even the most routine of inquiries made direct to another ministry at home may be frowned upon.

One consequence of a complex, wide embracing decision-taking process, is that all officials become caught up in it. Where they should be planning, they are reacting, keeping up with the daily and weekly pressure of events. 'The people who should be making policy,' says a German head office diplomat, 'spend all day keeping their desks clear.' Sir David Kelly, in *The Ruling Few*, has referred to the struggle to keep pace with papers which 'leaves senior officers literally no time for reflection. In such circumstances planning can well become a gigantic bluff.' Another diplomat, Sir J. Headlam-Morley has claimed: 'The most important decisions are often made, not as a part of a concerted or far-sighted policy, but under the urgent pressure of some immediate crisis.' One feels that foreign ministries are quite good, given time, at dealing with problems once they arise; nowhere near as good in anticipating and helping prevent them.

There are planning departments, and Sweden is a country which has a Report Secretariat which brings together reports on one subject from all over the world and produces detailed papers. But nowhere does their influence on the system seem strong. And, as it is, the section of any foreign ministry that most impresses is one at the State Department that was formed to fulfil a crisis function.

The focal point is a closely guarded suite of rooms on the seventh floor, known officially as the Operations Centre but popularly as the Crisis Centre. The Centre, which is linked to the Situation Room in the basement of the White House, to the Pentagon's own crisis center, and to the C.I.A., dates back to 1961 and the Bay of Pigs. Before then, officials admit that co-ordination of information and intelligence was bad, not only between State and Defense and C.I.A. and the White House but within the department itself.

Inside the first door leading to the centre, a guard sits on duty twenty-four hours a day. He opens a second door after checking identity, telephoning ahead and issuing a badge.

Into the Center streams the most important diplomatic and intelligence material. In one of the rooms are banks of telex machines, including F.B.I.S., the C.I.A. service which monitors foreign radio and television. In the corner is the 'hot line' to Moscow – a telex machine, kept operating twenty-four hours so that it is *known* that it works. Operators in Moscow and Washington tap out poems and short stories. Those in Washington say that from the content they can tell who is working the machine at the other end. Green telephones with black handsets are 'scrambled'; white phones link with the White House; blue ones with the C.I.A.

The Center has three main functions. Its primary one lies in watching developments so that the Secretary or officials can be alerted to a situation day or night.

About twenty-five foreign service officers take it in turns to man the room, working in shifts of 8 a.m.–4 p.m., 4 p.m.–midnight and midnight–8 a.m. The duty team consists of a senior watch officer who is a middle-grade diplomat with a background of various parts of the world, together with a junior and an editor.

Messages entering State carry four gradings: Routine, Priority, Immediate and Flash. Immediate and Flash are ones the sender believes need immediate attention day or night. The computer scans the messages, carrying Immediate and Flash directly through to the Operations Center. In any given twenty-four hours, there are normally about 300 such telegrams.

The senior watch officer can call whoever he thinks necessary: 'He can get the Secretary out of bed if he likes; he's authorised to,' says an official, 'but not unnaturally it's something he exercises rather sparingly. . . .' It is said that at night the watch officer is the best informed man in the United States as to what is happening throughout the world. And, points out one Crisis Center official: 'Secretary Rusk used to say in here – "While Washington is asleep, two-thirds of the world is awake, and I'm sure one-third is making trouble for us." '

Most of the information that reaches the room is diplomatic. The second largest category of material is military information.

A team of six officers from the Pentagon have a room in the Center, and provide liaison with the Pentagon's own crisis room (where there are five officers from State).

This is the Center's first function. Its second one is to provide twice daily Top Secret digests for the President, the Secretaries of States and Defense, and the C.I.A. Each summary contains a briefing on the most significant reports of the previous twelve hours.

The reports are prepared at 5 a.m. and 5 p.m. each day; the editor's job is to decide which of the 150 or so messages of the previous twelve hours should be included, and then to edit them. Usually he decides that between eight and fifteen are significant enough to be included. Each is summarised in no more than eight lines. The report goes into a folder marked TOP SECRET, with copies of the full telegrams attached. The morning folder is white with a red border, the afternoon one buff coloured. For years invariably one of the messages has concerned Vietnam.

The Center's third function is in establishing emergency task forces when a crisis situation appears imminent. Often this is heralded by a FLASH message: the computer is programmed to send through such telegrams immediately, downgrading all other material in the pipeline.

In a crisis, the senior watch officer calls the country director or assistant secretary for the area and warns: The situation in X is getting out of hand. Officials from State Defense and the C.I.A. move into the Center and stay until the crisis is over. Vietnam, which was a continuous problem – never *per se* constituted a crisis; the Lebanon situation in 1969 did. Foreign diplomats whose countries are involved may also be invited to sit in. There are beds and showers so that officials can stay in the Center. 'But not many, because we don't want to have empty space around,' says one official. 'If you have any empty space in this building, people want it.'

The Center is on alert whenever U.S. astronauts go into space, from before blast off, and then for the last hours of the journey. This is in case landing takes place in foreign territory, an accident which could lead to international problems.

The atmosphere within the Center is businesslike and non-bureaucratic. 'We try to keep it as spare and spartan as possible,' says one officer. 'It's stimulating because it's the most anti-bureaucratic office in State. We resist filing cabinets; we don't want them. We don't want to build up a bureaucracy. We don't want too many routine procedures.'

The Center may alert the Secretary of State to crisis situations, but what of other occasions – the majority? The relationship between the policy maker at the head of a foreign ministry and his civil servants is a crucial one. With material filtering up the hierarchy, the key officials will be the ones at the top in regular contact with him.

The most important of these is the official who is chief and spokesman of the service. In Britain this is the permanent under secretary, in the United States the under secretary, in Russia the first vice-minister, and in a number of countries including France, Belgium and Italy, the general secretary of the ministry. In many respects, this official is the link-man between the civil servants and the minister, needing to retain the confidence of the first, and to exert influence on the second.

In a service where this position is occupied by a permanent head, his power is especially strong: as ministers come and go, he remains, and his contact with the diplomatic machine, at home and abroad, is superior and his knowledge of how to use it better.

High career civil servants in many countries share an attribute which gives them strength. As the British commentator Paul Johnson has pointed out they 'seek power and influence for its own sake; they are not distracted by the desire to produce or the longing for money.' Nor are they the political eunuchs some would claim: their views are no less strong because of their own facelessness, nor because of their conservative nature, nor because of the need at times to put into practice policies which they do not favour.

Their strength will depend on the strength or weakness of the minister. Arthur Henderson, a former British Foreign Secretary, said of the British Foreign Office: 'The first forty-eight hours decide whether a new minister is going to run his office or whether his office is going to run him.' Another British Foreign Secretary made an early attempt to exert his domination. Ernest Bevin found a pile of documents on his desk before leaving for a weekend. A note with them said, 'The Secretary of State may care to peruse these at his leisure before Monday'. Bevin left the documents undisturbed, but added his own note: 'A kindly thought, but erroneous'.

Lord George-Brown, another Foreign Secretary, complained after leaving office that it was officials who decided the 'areas I should be briefed about'.

French and German civil servants have a reputation for intriguing. In Germany leaks have been common – notable among them that of the proposed treaty between Germany and the Soviet Union to the press in 1970. With many civil servants distrusting Chancellor Willy Brandt's Ostpolitik campaign, some suspicion of sabotage has fallen on them. But to an outsider what is most notable is not that there have been leaks, nor that there is distrust, but that German diplomats have been so well able to adjust from a policy of anti-Communism to one of achieving better relations with the Soviet Union and bloc countries.

It is because of distrust of permanent civil servants that new foreign ministers in some countries surround themselves with their own advisers to lessen the impact of the permanent civil servants. In France ministers at the head of departments have a personal cabinet of advisers selected by them. In the United States the Secretary of State places a number of his own men in key positions. Even though Disraeli, over a hundred years ago, advocated such a system, Britain has never adopted it. And it does create problems. The newcomers create a new series of empires between the Minister or Secretary of State and the permanent civil servants. This, in itself, generates more work and means an even bigger bureaucracy.

In any system, however, the minister is far from powerless: those surrounding him are seeking advancement and have to strive to win his favour. They also need him to fight for policies. 'What I want from a minister more than anything else,' says one high ranking official, 'is that he should carry weight in the political machine.' Lord George-Brown, as British Foreign Secretary, was not liked by diplomats. But he had one quality they admired: 'He did carry weight in the cabinet . . . and he was prepared to fight for the policies he believed in,' Sir Patrick Reilly, the former British ambassador in Paris said.

For diplomats, the political weight and fighting power of a minister has become more important as the position itself has decreased in power. All governments are now more concerned with domestic matters than international ones. In cabinet, foreign ministers have to compete for resources with colleagues who can demonstrate that if the money is given to *their* departments the results will be seen to be real, and may be politically advantageous – more schools or houses or not raising taxes. The trouble for foreign ministries is that all their department is selling is words.

The power in important matters of foreign policy has now shifted to the offices of prime ministers or presidents as faster communication has resulted in direct contacts between leaders of state.

In the United States, where the Secretary of State is an appointed official and not an elected one, policy-making rests with the president, and most presidents have guarded it jealously. Few have delegated their powers to a secretary of state. The sole exception in recent years was John Foster Dulles whom Eisenhower allowed to be his own master. Franklin D. Roosevelt did not always take his secretary of state into his confidence on major policy matters; Lyndon B. Johnson was virtually his own country director in the case of Vietnam – wandering over to look at the tape machines regularly and then calling the State Department.

Although the situation is not new, many diplomats feel that foreign affairs will continue to concentrate more and more in the White House. It was Dr Henry Kissinger, President Nixon's adviser on national security affairs, who flew to Peking to negotiate the president's visit to China in 1972, and who played the key role in so many other foreign policy initiatives including Vietnam. The question now is whether presidents even listen to the State Department and, through it, its diplomats.

The situation has been paralleled in other countries. On election to power, Canada's Trudeau rapidly took over foreign policy. Major initiatives came from his office, among them the decision to cut back on NATO commitments, to establish rapport with Red China, and to call for major rethinking on Canada's role in the world. Trudeau even set up his own corps of foreign experts, led by two former diplomats. One of those flew to Lagos to negotiate with the Nigerians when Canada wanted to discuss relief flights to Biafra – thus, taking the matter completely out of the hands of the Department of External Affairs.

In Germany the Ostpolitik has been conducted mainly by the Chancellor's office, and the Foreign Minister was not told of some of the correspondence involved. Chancellor Brandt sent one letter to Gomulka, the Polish Communist Party leader, which German Foreign Minister Walter Scheel knew nothing about. One cartoon joke at the time had Willy Brandt asking, 'Is it important or can we send Scheel?'

The one major distrust that diplomats have of elected Ministers is that they are first and foremost politicians, and as such often initiate policies the main purpose of which is to improve their public relations. (The diplomatic initiatives towards the rebel Rhodesian regime by the British Government in 1971 were largely motivated by the desires to achieve a resounding success for the government and to satisfy the party's right wing.) Towards their own minister, officials have loyalty because of his position. Towards other politicians there is often little but contempt.

Sir Alexander Cadogan, a former Permanent Under Secretary at the British Foreign Office, wrote in his diaries of MPs: 'Silly bladders! Self-advertising, irresponsible nincompoops. How I hate Members of Parliament! They embody everything that my training has taught me to eschew — ambition, prejudice, dishonesty, self-seeking light-hearted irresponsibility, black-hearted mendacity.' However extreme Cadogan's views, echoes of the sentiment can be found in many diplomatic hearts. Politicians are regarded as being uninformed on foreign affairs, and what is more they don't want to know about them: they are more interested in domestic matters that will win them votes. Following foreign affairs is a minority interest in most parliaments.

In most services, the foreign minister does act as a buffer between officials and antagonistic politicians in Parliament. The American service, on the other hand, has to face politicians direct. Ambassadors have to have their nominations confirmed by the Senate. Normally consent is given, although its attitude on some occasions has been such that the President has withdrawn his nomination. In the winter of 1971 the Senate refused to confirm the nomination of Howard P. Mace as American ambassador to Sierra Leone — after, it is believed, several colleagues testified against his appointment in private. Mace had been director of personnel for four years, a job having great influence on the lives and futures of diplomats. In it, he made many enemies.

Hearings, conducted by the Foreign Relations Committee, have proved embarrassing for some nominees: a man destined to become ambassador in Sri Lanka a few years ago could not tell the Committee the name of the country's prime minister. President Eisenhower's nomination of Mrs Clare Boothe Luce as ambassador to Brazil was confirmed by the Senate, but her comment later that one particular senator with whom she had clashed must have been kicked on the head by a horse aroused so much criticism that she found it advisable to resign.

Individual queries or complaints from politicians in all democracies are taken seriously by head office diplomats. In the State Department mail from congressmen is placed in special folders marked 'Urgent. A Congressional – for immediate action. A reply or written acknowledgement must be made within three working days.' The folder is conspicuous so that it does not get lost among the other mounds of paper. In Britain, too, the quickest a foreign ministry official is called upon to work is when he is providing information for a minister to answer a parliamentary question. Officials hear about questions at 11 a.m. and have to have answers ready by 2.30 p.m. the same day.

Although in most countries politicians stay outside the actual conduct of diplomacy, confining themselves to matters of policy, in the United States their involvement grinds small. Committees of Congress frequently call on individuals for information they need to fulfil their function as legislators. When Congress is in session, senior officials from the State Department spend much time appearing before them. In one year, 1962, eighty-seven senior officers testified a total of 224 times, and this was in addition to twenty-five formal appearances by the Secretary of State. The Department has its own Congressional Relations division whose job is to 'sell' policies to Congress.

Diplomats have mixed feelings. Some believe it gives the foreign service a chance to put its side. Others resent it, believing it hampers action and, by bringing into the open frank detail, can embarrass the United States in its relations with foreign powers.

One diplomat critic especially commended the following inter-

change between politicians and a State Department official at
the subcommittee of appropriations in 1969. The acting assistant
secretary for Educational and Cultural Affairs, Jacob Canter, was
being examined about educational and cultural exchanges by the
chairman John J. Rooney and Mr Frank T. Bow. 'It's a great
example of how ludicrous it becomes when the politicians really
get going,' said the diplomat.

MR ROONEY   Although I was a charter member of Local 802
of the American Federation of Musicians, I must confess, I never
heard of the Junior Wells Rhythm and Blues Band. Can you tell
us anything about them?

MR CANTER   I recall that the visit of Junior Wells and his
Rhythm and Blues Band was reported in most favourable terms
by our embassies.

MR ROONEY   Can you give us some real information, not
what these people at the Embassy say?

MR CANTER   They went to thirteen countries in Africa.

MR ROONEY   I didn't ask you that. What do you know about
Junior Wells? Did you ever hear of him before?

MR CANTER   No, sir.

MR ROONEY   You're as bad off as I am. I am just trying
culturally to find out who the gentleman is. I want to know
whether I should pay special attention to the fact that he is in
Washington and whether I should go to hear him.

MR CANTER   Mr Chairman, I am not a follower of rhythm
and blues, either.

MR ROONEY   But I am. I'm an old Dixieland man.

MR CANTER   I understand that Mr Wells is a competent
person with a very competent group and he went to these countries in Africa. The group was composed of a bass guitar, a guitar,
a saxophone, drums and a singer. He is director of the group. He
also sings. It was brought to my attention that he did have a
particularly successful tour, and I can only cite, I am afraid, the
reports of our embassies.

MR ROONEY   Their reports have never influenced this committee one way or another because we have seen them so wrong
in so many instances.

MR BOW   Was it not Dizzy Gillespie who rode a horse and
pretended he was a gaucho?

MR ROONEY   Is he in this programme?

MR CANTER   No sir.

MR ROONEY   I thought there was some publicity a while back that he was going to be sent. I wondered if everybody had forgotten what happened on his last trip to South America.

MR CANTER   He is not in our programme, Mr Chairman.

MR ROONEY   He is a good musician.

Perhaps surprisingly, in view of the bureaucracy and the decrease in power, there have been few attempts to cut foreign ministries down to size. Any such efforts have been directed at overseas missions.

One American planner thinks rather than being cut, home organisations will take on a new importance in future years. 'Today you have someone here who calls up our embassy in Xland and tells them to go around to the Foreign Office. Given, say, twenty-five to thirty years, communications should be such that embassy channels can be virtually cut out. You could have someone here with a videophone on his desk make a direct call to his counterpart abroad without going through the embassy at all.

'And look at embassies in the sense of being their own memory banks for information we may want. Each one has its own memory now: hundreds of filing cabinets. The availability of large computers is going to make all that outdated. There will be one central memory for the whole of a country's diplomacy. A bank to which all embassies, and all officers here, have access in seconds.'

One feels if that day ever comes embassies *might* get slimmer; head offices will get fatter.

Four

The Diplomat Abroad:
The Embassy and Reporting

'Knowing who the Prime Minister goes to bed with
may win you a treaty – or sell you a power station.'

British diplomat

Diplomats prefer being abroad, not simply because of the allowances and the style of life, but because they are freer there. The
decision-making apparatus may be far away, often leading to frustrations – but so too are the tiresome politicians and the need to
continuously consult other departments and other ministries.

During his working life, a diplomat on average will work
in six or seven different embassies. These can vary enormously
– from a two diplomat mission in an office block (like the Irish
embassy in Ottawa) to a miniature replica of the home government (like the British embassy in Washington with its 700 staff
and its operation costs of £2.5 million a year).

Often they are enormous and impressive – sweeping stair-
cases, red carpet, chandeliers and gold decorated ceilings. But
occasionally they are far from grand. One Caribbean mission
in London is a few small offices, stained carpets, old-fashioned
kitchen-type chairs and bare walls.

When they are stripped of their image and their immunity
embassies are offices populated by civil servants who happen to
work abroad. But they are more than that: they are little bits of
the home country overseas. If you want afternoon tea, British
embassies are superb, as are American missions for coffee and ice-
water. They always manage to convey an impression of having
provided a haven of elegance and culture in the midst of the
uncivilised. In a Kuwaiti embassy, there is an aura of discreet
but enormous wealth. Next to the open safe in an Australian
diplomat's office stands a case of Fosters lager. A Russian embassy,

characteristically, is a largely unknown place; visitors see nothing except the hallway and one room.

A few things are common to all: the deference accorded to the ambassador; the inevitable portrait of the country's leader (and Lenin too in a Soviet mission); the racks of home-produced newspapers and magazines from *Country Life* (Britain) to *The Buddhist* (Sri Lanka); and the desks piled high with folders and documents.

Embassies are always found in capitals – essential for their dealings with the local foreign ministry and other government departments, but a fact that means they are often cut off from regular contact with people representative of the country, industry and sometimes the main communications media which may have its headquarters elsewhere. These limitations are particularly acute in 'false capitals' like Bonn, Ottawa, Canberra and even Rome.

Although there is a vast difference in size, all embassies are animals of the same species. The small embassy in some remote non-place, staffed by an ambassador and one other, is simply a scaled-down replica of the enormous one.

Home organisations send them all roughly the same circulars, treat them administratively similarly, and all are expected to fulfil broadly the same functions, and follow the identical rules of procedure.

Diplomats at all missions, whatever the size and whatever the place, are expected to gather information, pass on messages, negotiate, try to build up friendly relations, get involved in helping trade to some degree, give out publicity material, and on demand help their own nationals who happen to live in a country or are visiting it.

The great difference is that at a small embassy one man will be expected to do all of them; at a large one, work will be compartmentalised (rather as at home) and specialisation may grind small. 'It's not unusual,' says an English diplomat at a small mission, 'to find myself writing a report in the morning, lobbying a local journalist at lunchtime, calling on the foreign ministry in the afternoon, and giving a gramophone recital in the evening.' His colleague at a larger embassy, on the other hand, may be operating in so limited an area that the only way he knows what is going on more generally in his post is through meetings.

With the vast divergence in size, it might look as though embassies perfectly represent the varying workloads in different parts of the world. After all, it makes sense that the British embassy in Washington should be bigger than the mission to the Vatican, or the American in Paris larger than the one in Ireland. But it is doubtful if this is ever so. Embassies that are large get larger – not just because Parkinson's law applies abroad as well as at home, but because so many ministries other than foreign offices now want their men overseas too. 'The view is often that if you need to do something in Washington, you need a man at a mission,' says one American ambassador. 'The next stage is that you need two men. Bureaucracy exists to justify itself. And home departments can always find justification for these men.' 'They clutter up the premises,' Ellis Briggs a former American ambassador has said. But others claim that the proliferation of representatives of home agencies overseas is inevitable and necessary: a former head of the U.S. Mission in Tokyo, recalled that he had twenty-three Government agencies represented there, justified because 'it is the fact that there is almost no agency of the United States Government that is not interested and directly concerned in some way in what is going on in Japan.' (Japan, in turn, sends to Washington officers specialising in: commerce, labour, economic planning, agriculture, transport, post and telecommunications, construction, finance, science, information, administration and defence.)

Sometimes too the size of a mission represents past historical importance of links between two countries as well as some reality. The massive Australian High Commission in London is a classic example.

The biggest missions, not surprisingly, are usually the American and Russian. Normally British embassies have larger staffs than the French and German, particularly at the lower level.

At the other extreme, some embassies are so small that, given the workload, it is hard to see what they can do that could not be better handled by other means. The problem with small ones is that they are expected to cover so much. In consequence, everything has to be treated superficially. 'My reports home,' admits an Irish diplomat at a tiny mission, 'can hardly ever be anything more than a rewrite of the local papers. There just isn't time for anything else.' A Latin American ambassador at one, asked to justify his mission's existence, replied in one word: 'Prestige'.

The apparent size of a mission is sometimes misleading. One South American embassy, for example, which appears to contain half a dozen diplomats in fact does hardly any work. Three of the 'diplomats' are simply ordinary nationals of the country concerned, temporarily living abroad and–with the connivance of their nation – using this ploy to obtain diplomatic facilities and privileges.

The organisation of an embassy will depend on its size. All are headed by an ambassador (the exception to this is when two countries consider their relationship not friendly enough to give their chief representatives in each other's capitals that title and call them *chargés d'affaires*, but they do the same work). Ranking below that are ministers (found at the larger embassies), counsellors and then first, second and third secretaries.

A very small mission may have just an ambassador and a first secretary, but a medium or large one will have diplomats of all ranks, and will have a formal organisational structure. In the American service there is a Deputy Chief of Mission who almost always takes temporary charge when the ambassador is away.

A typical medium-size British embassy has diplomats divided up into sections dealing with political work (the Chancery), consular, information, commercial, and administration. A similar size American embassy might have political, economic, consular and administrative sections. At British embassies and those of countries that follow the British pattern, the head of Chancery is not only the ambassador's adviser on political matters, but is also generally responsible for 'seeing the whole embassy works as a team'; and the Chancery itself handles not only political work, but also all matters not dealt with by the other sections or by the attached specialists.

Embassies are usually in the 'best part' of any capital. In London, for example, they predominate in rich areas such as Mayfair, Belgravia, Kensington and Knightsbridge. Communist missions are not an exception: in the early 1970s the East Germans paid over £250,000 for a house in exclusive Belgrave Square to house its trade delegation (the nearest it was allowed to an embassy by a country that had not recognised its existence diplomatically).

Wherever the embassy building, ambassadors usually like to keep the consular department away from the main part of the building. 'We usually get relegated to the furthest wing,' says one consular officer. 'You see, we get *ordinary* people coming to see us and wandering about the place. And it does lower the tone.' A similar situation applies when there is an immigration department. 'Broadly speaking,' says one Canadian officer involved in that work, 'ambassadors prefer us to be some way away from the rest of the operations. Then they don't have to see our visitors – parents with kids with snotty noses, or people breathing out garlic fumes.'

Apart from secretaries and clerks, visitors will see few women at any embassy. Women are a minority group in the diplomatic services of all countries. America did not employ its first woman diplomat until 1922, and the British service was completely closed to them until World War II. Today, officially, they are 'encouraged', but in the late 1960s there were no ranking women diplomats in the French service, and only one in thirteen German diplomats was a woman. America was worse (one woman in every sixteen diplomats) and Britain much worse (one in seventy). In Spain they were allowed entry until 1936, then excluded, and have recently been declared 'acceptable' again – though there were only two in 1972. In Norway there has been great political pressure for full equality for women in diplomacy – but strong opposition from within the service. Some countries have had woman ambassadors, among them the United States, Cuba, Canada, Germany, Russia, Morocco, Guatemala and Sweden. But a high-ranking woman diplomat is very rare.

Despite the official encouragement, male diplomats argue that women are not ideally suited to diplomacy. 'In some countries,' says an ambassador (male), 'women are regarded as inferior. So you have to be careful where you send them. They'd be useless in most of the Middle East, for example.' Others argue, nowhere near as convincingly, that even in countries where there is no prejudice, a woman diplomat's worth is curtailed. 'A male diplomat can easily invite another man for dinner or drinks to talk something over. But a man, especially if he's married, might well hesitate to accept a woman diplomat's invitation.'

And several claim that some postings are 'too tough' for

women, and complain that, as it is, female diplomats often get the pleasant assignments while men get the postings to primitive or unhealthy countries.

There is, also, the problem of marriage. The British service expects women entrants to be single or widowed, and warns 'Women members of the Diplomatic Service may be called upon to resign on marriage'. In the United States most women leave on getting married. The problem, it is explained, is what happens to the husband when the diplomatic wife is moved to another country: does he follow behind? A few women diplomats have married and continued working, but their married lives have been somewhat unusual. An American woman ambassador Carol C. Laise married another U.S. ambassador, Ellsworth Bunker, in 1967, and the two carried on working, at their separate posts in Nepal and Vietnam. In 1970 a woman third secretary at the Thai Embassy in London was married to a diplomat serving at the Thai Embassy in Bonn.

Apart from the diplomats and the officers of other agencies, mission staffs are swelled by locally-employed workers whose jobs range from driving and carrying messages to being involved in the political, economic or labour work. The numbers involved are large. American overseas agencies, including the foreign service, are backed up by over 25,000 local staff, Germany employs over 1,700 (roughly one for every two diplomats), and Britain has more local employees than diplomats.

Many carry out responsible work; commercial matters, on a day to day basis, at some smaller posts are handled by a local national. They have the advantage of language, and a good knowledge of local people, customs and practices. 'They're a key part, and no embassy could function without them,' one German diplomat says. But they are also often undervalued and even regarded as inferior. The British Plowden Committee on Representational Services Overseas, after noting their worth, commented: 'Yet we had an uneasy feeling – we do not wish to exaggerate this – that some posts have not altogether succeeded in ridding themselves of traces of the once prevalent idea that locally engaged staff are in some undefined way inferior to home-based staff.'

Dependence on them has increased as diplomatic services have been forced to economise. Local staff are much cheaper. Even at the lowest levels, one administration officer estimates a local employee costs much less than half someone posted from home who receives allowances and free housing. The higher the level, the greater the saving. 'I sometimes feel,' one British first secretary confesses, 'that foreign services are able to function courtesy of financially-depressed local labour.'

The height that they can reach is low compared with the diplomats around them. An elderly local employee may find himself still doing the work, and carrying the responsibility, of a diplomat twenty-five years younger. It is hardly a way of attracting the best people. There is the security problem too. Locals are not employed in positions where security is involved. They may have to work on a different floor from the diplomats who handle sensitive or secret material.

The operating staff at large missions need a host of support facilities: cars and drivers, files and clerks, secretaries and guards, cipher clerks and radio operators. There may even be a large maintenance section to back up the embassy, with a warehouse of furniture and material for exhibitions. The Canadian Public Works Department has forty staff based in Britain. Self-administration will be a major function, involving renting housing accommodation for staff, supervising the accounts, and managing the daily housekeeping. Diplomats are usually poor administrators. And although they will concede that more expertise and training are needed, administration is a slightly dirty world. The administrator is a little like the man who comes to fix the plumbing (a state of mind reflected in the French service where administration is a task for juniors). As it is, one of the most cutting remarks any diplomat can make about another embassy is: '*They* spend most of their time administering themselves.' Some services have teams of inspectors from head office, who can spend up to eighty 'inspector weeks' in the largest missions examining efficiency, but doubts can be cast on their effectiveness, not least because they are members of the service they are examining. In some others, such as the Australian, the work of the inspectors, in any event, is largely restricted to examining the terms and conditions under which the diplomats live and work.

Ambassadors are far too high up the ladder to get involved with the daily nitty-gritty of making sure the place functions, but those with large staffs of diplomats and experts now have to fulfil a managing role. 'I see myself as captain of the team,' says one British ambassador at a major embassy. But it is not much good being captain unless you control the players. And, often, in practice, ambassadors admit they do not: 'With people from nearly twenty different departments at this mission', says one American ambassador, 'it's all a bit of a mess.' Larger missions may have a series of committees meeting regularly to compare notes and to try to get cohesion. Many ambassadors hold formal meetings, sometimes daily, with key staff gathered together.

Ideally, as co-ordinator and controller of a mission, an ambassador should play a key part in defining priorities to be pursued in any given country. 'Embassies no longer should have *a* role,' one German says. 'What they should have is certain functions depending upon the particular country they are in.'

To some extent this happens. The Canadian mission in Washington, for example, spends about forty per cent of its time developing trade and trading opportunities; the Mongolians in London concentrate on cultural work, keeping in touch with universities and the British Council; African missions in Bonn lobby for aid.

Embassies representing other countries in other capitals can produce similar breakdowns. And sometimes the emphasis is forced on the mission by events: one in Dublin during the Ulster troubles, for example, could hardly fail to concentrate on attempting to forecast Eire's reactions. But it remains that much of the time the emphasis is determined not by a carefully considered list of needs and priorities but by what the ambassador likes doing.

Whatever the emphasis at a mission, the two key elements of diplomatic work overseas are collecting information, some of which will be sent home, and negotiating in its widest sense. The latter may involve simply the exchange of messages with local officials or actual detailed bargaining.

The information gathering function is an important one, raising questions concerning both the worth of the material and how well it is utilised. A diplomat today will claim that he has downgraded this part of his job. It is easy to see why he does so; it is a function that is easily criticised; after all there are newspapers and radio and wire machines, also pouring back information. But the

amount of diplomatic material he sends home continues to increase dramatically. And whatever he claims, the reporting role
is vital to the diplomat because it helps determine the view held
of him at home and also constitutes his bid at exerting some
influence.

Every diplomat pays lip service to the need for discrimination
in what he reports home. An Indian diplomat says: 'The amount
we send back is relatively small, but we are expected to know
much more. Then if something blows up, we have the information here.' One Canadian first secretary dealing with economic
matters says he had a personal criterion: 'I ask myself if I don't
do this, will it matter? I could do a long report on inflation at
the moment. But does anyone at home *need* to know? There
should be a great difference between reporting and reporting
just to keep people rather generally informed. One should report
on things we can do something about; not things we cannot.'

A German first secretary agrees that an embassy should concentrate on matters where action at home is likely. The problem,
he explains, is that diplomats sometimes have to guess at the
priorities; head office will usually complain if they do not get
reports on a subject that interests, but will rarely mention it if
incoming material is simply filed. The natural tendency, therefore, is for a diplomat to play safe and send everything they
might want.

As a result diplomatic pouches still bulge with reports that seem
to have little purpose beyond creating employment for those
who write them and those who read them. 'When the decision
is left to individual officers in the field,' says an American diplomat at head office, 'you tend to get what interests him – not
necessarily stuff that's of any interest here.'

Often too the diplomat is never sure of what his head office
does want. Sometimes the closeness of diplomats at the same
level from different embassies can be helpful here: some countries'
interests are very close. A Dutch diplomat confesses that if he is
not certain, he will see if a Belgian colleague has been given instructions – 'if he has you're probably safe to follow the same line'.

A lone Western European diplomat in Canada confessed he
had been sending reports on the Quebec situation because it fascinated him. 'But sometimes I ask what practical value it has to

anyone back home. I suppose if Joe Smith from Quebec visits them, they'll know who he is. . . . This isn't the only example. When I came I was asked to do a report on Canadian foreign aid. I did it, and I've been sending further reports on the subject every two months. Whether anyone still wants it I don't know. . . . No one has said.'

One of the rare diplomats who has been told his reports are too long swears that the requests from his ministry to make them shorter came in a letter which was six pages long.

Not knowing what is wanted, says another, means 'you keep yourself busy – but it doesn't mean you are *doing* anything'. One German believes that the more remote from head office the post, the more likely to be the over-reporting. 'You feel so cut off. You are a voice in the wilderness who wants to be heard, so you keep sending reports.' Another recalls a former colleague who used to save up all his messages until his ambassador was away, and then enjoy an orgy of communication. Often the diplomat is brought down to earth when he is posted back home, and finds a third secretary has simply been filing his priceless reports.

Frustration and a 'branch office' mentality is created as strong as the 'head office' one at home. There are constant written briefings, guidance papers and copies of speeches sent from home; at a large embassy these can total between fifty and a hundred pages of text every day. But what is needed say many, is more frequent visits between head offices and missions. 'We ought to send someone out every six to twelve months,' says one diplomat at home. 'It needn't be for more than a day. Any individual talking to someone can get things across far better than you can in any number of telegrams.' Henry M. Jackson, in *The Secretary of State and the Ambassador*, recommended that ambassadors should visit Washington two or three times a year – an impossible suggestion even for the wealthy United States and even more so for other countries. As it is, diplomats often feel left out in the cold. Canada, preparing a series of policy studies, asked few abroad to contribute (when individuals were consulted it was because of their personal status and not because they happened to be centred in an area being discussed). One commented: 'You then tend to think of yourself as just someone implementing policies that you've had no hand in – just doing the dirty work.'

The methods of collecting information have changed little in the past two centuries. Diplomats talk with ministers and officials, collect gossip at parties and dinners, and chat with journalists, politicians and local figures.

In some democratic countries, the diplomat's reporting role consists not so much in seeking information – but in selecting it from the mass of detail that is made public. 'Here,' one Asian in London says, 'I've not only got newspaper reports, and official documents, but debates in Parliament and the mass of detail fed to me by the Foreign Ministry. I don't claim to know any secrets, but I've got more information to go on than anyone at home could ever want to know.'

Newspaper reports often play a large part; it is significant that during a newspaper strike in New York, a number of foreign offices found a drop in the information reported back from their Washington embassies. Reading the local newspapers is a major first task for embassies each day. One ambassador admitted that without them there would be great difficulties over reporting. The press told his embassy what was happening within the country, and could be used as a starting base. 'Without this we would have to find out all the information ourselves – and we would need an enormous staff and still never know whether or not we were missing something.'

But policy makers back home also see the newspaper reports. More than fifty years ago, Lloyd George's private secretary wrote: 'The truth is that one derives far more news from the press than from any other source, and every day in the club (The Travellers) one sees long rows of foreign office officials, including Balfour, going eagerly to the notice board to find out what is really happening.'

A German ambassador conceded that the reports sent home by German newspaper correspondents resident in his capital had a more immediate impact than his despatches. 'You can be sure that with any important matter, whether political or economic, the Chancellor and the Parliamentarians will first turn to the press. Later a restricted circle of people will see my telegram.' He, like a number of ambassadors, tries to keep in close touch with newspaper correspondents of his own nationality, seeking to exert some influence over the way they see events.

The diplomat claims that his despatches do matter in that it is his *assessment* of the information that is important. 'What can *I* add?' says the same German ambassador. 'First I can look at something the press reports and say whether it *knows* it or *assumes* it. I can add the government's official reaction, together with those of the opposition, civil servants and others like trade unions. If the newspaper has a bias on a subject, I can remove that. And I can say what my colleagues think and know: I can ask the French ambassador for his views and find out his information on the subject.'

What is important, claim diplomats, is not what emerges publicly, but what it really means. A diplomat, by cultivating the people in power can gauge this. And then he can comment with authority.

The degree of interpretation a diplomat includes in his reports increases the longer his service in a post. Middle-ranking officers are expected to start functioning almost immediately on arrival. 'When I came to London,' says one Commonwealth diplomat, 'I had never worked on European affairs before. When it all falls on you suddenly it's very formidable. One may not understand fully what one is saying in the beginning, but a large part of the work is reporting what other people are saying. After a while you begin to understand the implications. At the beginning you are careful to keep out personal assessment; as time goes on you put in more. When I refer to telegrams I sent soon after arrival, I like what I write a lot better now. I put meat around the bone.'

Despite this, it remains that the *New York Times* and the London *Economist* are probably as good an intelligence source, if not better, than most diplomatic despatches.

And allowed to see, or hear, some of the information diplomats have collected during a day or evening, and on which comment is based, one is often struck by the minutiae of it all: excitement over a casual word by a Church leader, or flurry over a hint by a high official. In one country, permitted to compare diplomatic and clandestine intelligence material on a specific but confused, even taking place in the Caribbean I was struck months later by how much more accurate the intelligence source had proved to be. This might, of course, be an isolated case. Without seeing *all* reports, it is impossible to know.

Journalists in all countries are regarded as good sources of information if they can be persuaded to talk. Today's diplomatic platitude is of a two-way exchange of information, but in practice diplomats often want more than they give. Apart from his natural caution, the diplomat is hampered in the exchange by the convention that he does not reveal new, major information. All important statements have to come from head office or from the foreign minister or premier. It means there is usually very little he can do except to try to explain the background to an event or situation. Even in this he draws a sharp distinction in whom he talks to between the journalists on the spot whom he knows, and the ones who fly in for a crisis. 'The dangerous ones are those who fly in to cover one story,' says an English counsellor. 'They swarm around the bars and don't know the facts and get the perspective wrong. They refer to facts or events as startling when in the context of the country, they are not.' At least one diplomatic service has put its relationship with journalists on a paying basis. The Japanese pay journalists to supply reports. One writer who gets the equivalent of $2,500 dollars a year from a Japanese embassy for supplying a 2,000 word weekly breakdown on the political scene (his speciality) justifies it by saying that 'I only give them stuff they could have read in the papers anyway'. Only the embassy knows how many other journalists supply information in this way; at least one other writer visits this embassy once a month to answer questions posed by a 'panel' of diplomats.

Information is also drawn in from other diplomats. The degree of contact depends mainly on the place; in, say, a totalitarian country where there is a scarcity of information, diplomats will be highly dependent on shared gossip and tit-bits of information. Between friendly embassies there will be mutual help anyway. In Lomé the American mission feeds the British a lot of information; in Lagos the British, who are better placed to get it at source, help the Americans. A diplomat from a neutral or universally loved country is often considered worth cultivating. The German diplomat, for example, does not have the same sort of rapport with say American and British colleagues that a Canadian diplomat has. Therefore, it may be worthwhile for the German to try to extract information about the Americans from the Canadian at second-hand.

One criticism aimed at all diplomats is that most of their information comes from establishment sources. In democracies, they are free to contact opposition parties. But in totalitarian states – precisely those places where violent change is likely – they are out of touch with opponents of the ruling regime. Ambassadors dismiss this criticism on the ground that they are accredited to the ruling faction in any country. In an extreme case, where the opposition is 'illegal' or consists of rebels, contact would simply mean the ambassador's expulsion. Despite that, the practical criticism remains: diplomatic reports from such places will often be one-sided and, therefore, inaccurate and unbalanced.

One comes across rare instances of reporting that do seem to justify a diplomatic apparatus. An example is the role of the British embassy in Dublin over the Northern Ireland situation. Today political reporting involves supplying background information on key Irish figures (where they were born may be a major factor in dealing with them), detail on clandestine groups and their power at given times, and general background, including the way the south sees and reports what is happening in Ulster. What impact, or worth, the information eventually has on the policy-makers must always be debatable, but the embassy is supplying a reporting and interpretive function not in this case supplied by the press. British newspapers, radio and television give spasmodic attention to Eire, and what there is is often of doubtful worth.

But such examples are hard to find – and, even here, it could be argued that the work could be handled by a simpler piece of apparatus than the traditional embassy. It is also worth remembering that only a small percentage of information reaching governments now comes from diplomatic sources. They also have intelligence reports, direct access to newspapers and journals of all varieties, the interpretation of monitored radio and television programmes, and academic analysis.

It is debatable how much effective prediction results from diplomatic reports. No one, for example, predicted the Hungarian Revolution. The overthrow of Prince Sihanouk, the Cambodian head of state in 1970, was greeted by at least the British Foreign Office with incredulity; they had believed his position was very strong.

And, even if predictions are accurate, how much notice of them is taken by policy-makers? Three British diplomats, with special knowledge of Pakistan began warning of a possible conflict, three years before the war with India over Bangladesh began. Their warnings were ignored by two successive governments, and, according to the London *Times*, on one occasion one of the diplomats threw up his hands in despair and said, 'Interest in Britain does not extend east of London docks'.

In the United States, perhaps the major fascination of the so-called Anderson papers – records of top level meetings that fell into the hands of columnist Jack Anderson in 1972 – was the revelation of President Nixon's remoteness from the decision-making process, and the importance of his personal biases. They gave the impression that, as far as his foreign policy decisions were concerned, the State Department and the diplomats need not exist.

Diplomats at embassies have mixed feelings about politicians, just as do their counterparts at home. They need them to translate (they hope) their deliberations into actual policy. They also have to suffer them, particularly when they pay visits. Politicians have to be well treated, but they are also regarded as not very well-informed nuisances who need to be cossetted while they go about seeking publicity. 'Let a politician say cocktails to me,' says one American diplomat getting down to the emotional side of it, 'and I'll say junkets to you.'

Certainly the ones met on their tours abroad were hardly loveable. One British, not very senior, spent part of an evening threatening what he was going to do to a consul who had not been waiting at the airport with a car to greet him: 'And the luggage got lost; I tell you, he's just not with it.'

'What do politicians mean to me?' says an Irish diplomat. 'M.P.s back home complaining that they visited an embassy, and that we didn't offer them Irish whiskey.' An Australian ambassador says: 'They object when they can't get the latest sporting results. And then get down the booze.'

Diplomats of all nations resent having to accord them especial and deferential treatment. One young German diplomat was complaining about his ruined Sunday; a politician had arrived by plane, and the diplomat had been deputed to meet him at the airport. 'There ought to be a law about them travelling on

Sunday, or they ought to be told to make their own way about like everyone else. All I had to do was say "I hope you had a good flight," and drive him to his hotel. Surely he could have taken a cab like anyone else. . . .'

A Canadian diplomat, serving in an Arab country recalls a politician who visited Israel and Arab states. 'Back home he gave a speech full of praise about Israel. He said nothing about the Arabs. Surely he could have said one bloody word. And you get ones back home going to Jewish and pro-Zionist functions. You never hear of them going to Arab ones. Those things make a difference to us here.'

Others complain that it is impossible to control what visiting politicians do or say. Sometimes they make public statements that are at variance with their country's official policy. Then the diplomat has to explain that the speaker was just an individual giving his own personal views.

There are some who claim that, despite the problems, good must result from politicians' visits – because they will absorb some knowledge and also develop a better understanding of diplomatic work. That may be so; it is still difficult to find any politician who, quizzed long enough, will not confess to seeing diplomats as striped-trousered, cocktail pushers, or any diplomat who does not regard politicians as necessary crosses to be borne.

In both his information-gathering and negotiating roles the diplomat's main focus of contact will be with the local foreign ministry. Though his welcome will be largely determined by what is thought of his country, diplomats claim that personal relationships do count.

Negotiations can take place on several levels, depending on the importance of the subject matter. Much of it consists of simply routine contact fairly well down the line, and may involve simply calling to notify officials of a minor decision in the diplomat's own nation that might marginally affect the host country.

Such contact starts with instructions from head office. A diplomat's first task on arriving at his embassy in the morning is to read all the telegrams that have come in. Most are just for information. If they do call for action it is not a rushed process. The diplomat first gets out the files and reads the background. Most of them mean going round to the ministry, either with or without a written note. As at home, the note is discussed with, and cleared by, someone higher up the hierarchy.

In most countries contact between diplomats and officials is a mixture of formal and informal communications, written and verbal. In some, however, where relations are not friendly, it may be confined to written notes. 'And often,' says a diplomat, 'you don't even get an acknowledgement. It may be silly, but it's the only channel you've got. . . .'

But even in non-extreme situations like this communication between diplomats and a ministry is a cumbersome process. One young Luxembourg diplomat complains about the 'quite unnecessary formalities', and explains: 'If my ambassador feels that it's something that can be dealt with at my level, I approach someone at the same level in the ministry. But, say, the ambassador wants to be taken as seriously as a foreign minister over something important. He has to write a highly formal note. When it is delivered, it goes round half a dozen departments and everyone writes notes on it.'

The formality and protocol of such correspondence is extreme. In the handbook *Diplomatic Ceremonial and Protocol*, by John R. Wood and Jean Serres, twenty-five pages are devoted to such matters as how to start various forms of notes, end them, when to sign or simply initial and whether to give the recipient's address. Anyone wishing to wrestle with the intricacies is referred to manuals like this, or Sir Ernest Satow's classic *A Guide to Diplomatic Practice*.

But in general, official communication between a mission and a Foreign Ministry takes one or another of three principal forms The first is the *Note* – the most official and formal way of corresponding, addressed to the foreign minister, signed by the ambassador. It can be in the first person or the third person. The second is the *Note Verbale* – almost always in the third person, and not signed. The third is the *Aide-Mémoire* which, again has no signature. Unlike the *Note* it has no courtesy beginning or ending, and is used mainly to list facts or record statements already made orally.

There are three kinds of note that are rarely used. The *Collective Note* is when several governments send a single note to one foreign government. The *Identic Note* is when several send separate, but almost identical, notes to one nation. *Parallel Notes* are almost the same – the difference is that the words in the notes are not the same but the basic point is. All convey an impression of ganging up which, depending on which of the three forms is used, varies in its degree of offensiveness. Routine notes may be delivered by embassy messengers, more important ones by an official, and the most important by the ambassador to the foreign minister.

There are often reports of notes 'being rejected'. Usually this is not true; what had happened is that the government is only rejecting what is contained in the note. True rejection, in diplomatic terms, means physical refusal to take delivery of a note. It is rare. One instance was in 1943 when Stalin sent a telegram to Winston Churchill protesting that a British Arctic convoy had not properly protected certain shipments. Churchill summoned the Soviet ambassador. He then handed the telegram back to him. The ambassador protested that he had been instructed to deliver it. Churchill replied: 'I am not prepared to receive it.'

The diplomatic formalities are observed even when a country is castigating another in its notes. Guyana, in 1969, protesting that Venezuela organised, equipped and supported an insurrection within its country, had a Note of Protest delivered to the Venezuelan Ministry of Foreign Relations and to Venezuela's embassy in Guyana.

The note condemned the 'hypocrisy of the Government of Venezuela', and contained words like 'invidious' and 'disgust'. It accused the Venezuelan Government of trying to 'advance its spurious territorial claims under cover of subversion or terrorism'.

The condemnation and protest, however, was sandwiched between these two paragraphs – the opening ran: 'The Ministry of External Affairs presents its compliments to the Embassy of the Republic of Venezuela and has the honour to request that the Embassy bring to the closer attention of the Government of the Republic of Venezuela certain incidents of a nature deeply disturbing to the Government of Guyana which have recently occurred in the Rupununi District of Guyana.' The note closed: 'The Ministry of External Affairs takes this opportunity to renew to the Embassy of the Republic of Venezuela the assurances of its highest consideration.'

Five
The Nomadic Diplomat

'Am I going to London or Ghana?
Am I going to Ouagadougou?
Am I going to Spain
Where it rains on the plain?
Will my language be Czech or Urdu?'

Part of a poem circulating in an American
consulate in Turkey

Moving, settling for a few years, absorbing a new culture and
environment, making new friends, and then moving on again is
the constant reality of being a diplomat. By the time he retires
he may have lived in up to ten or even more countries. One Finnish ambassador came to London having already served in Paris,
Stockholm, Washington, Belgrade, Vienna and the Holy See; an
Indian colleague has lived in British East Africa, Central Africa,
New York, Sikkim, Indonesia, Norway and Egypt.

With the growth of new nations and of foreign services, a
diplomat's temporary home today may be in any one of over
a hundred countries, conditions ranging from the heat and the
flies of Africa to the civilised surroundings of the great European
capitals. Geographically, there may be little pattern in his assignments. A Canadian officer, in fourteen years, has already served
in Uraguay, Lebanon, Haiti, and Britain; a British diplomat, in
only ten, has been in Baghdad, Lomé and Luxembourg.

The country of a diplomat's next posting is vital not only to
his career but also to his personal life: Will his wife like it? What
of the educational facilities for his children? Can he save money
there? 'You find that as time nears,' says one American diplomat,
'wondering *where* makes it hard to concentrate on anything
else.'

A diplomat normally stays in one post for between two and
five years, depending on whether it is classed as a pleasant or an
unpleasant one. The 'good' are primarily in Western Europe and

North America. The 'bad' are those with an unhealthy climate, extreme isolation and rudimentary facilities, and include most African and Asian ones and those behind the Iron Curtain.

Members of large foreign services can expect a mixture of both types of posting. Countries generally practise a policy of giving a diplomat who has had a tough assignment a pleasant one to follow – an unhealthy tropical state, plagued with amoebic dysentery, will be followed by a city like Paris.

Although North America falls within the pleasant postings, it proves more difficult in many diplomatic services to persuade men to serve there willingly. 'They hate New York because of its general unpleasantness, and Washington because of its crime,' says one European assignments officer. In the last three years of the 1960s foreign missions in Washington suffered forty-four robberies, twelve cases of breaking and entering, two bomb attacks, thirty-nine threats of violence and sixteen acts of vandalism.

In countries where diplomats face disease, bad sanitation, poor medical facilities, bad climate and the absence of amenities, they fare badly compared with colleagues in sophisticated capitals. But diplomats everywhere are insulated from everyday worries; it is only the degree to which this is possible that alters. At a hardship post, the diplomat will still be cossetted and protected from the problems of local life.

They will also receive hardship allowances – a salary increment that in some services can range up to twenty-five per cent. As there is often not much on which to spend the money, a diplomat can leave such a post with an impressive savings account. For diplomats in such posts there will also be extra leave: a Canadian serving in Djakarta periodically gets his air fare paid to Hong Kong, an American in Moscow his fare to Frankfurt.

Some services, including the German, often choose a bachelor instead of a family man for such a post – a fact of life that pleases married men but annoys their unmarried colleagues. A few, including the Spanish, frequently send newcomers to such places, a policy that often has sad long-term results. The new diplomat, at what is often a two-man post, may find himself in charge of a mission when his ambassador goes on leave. Suddenly he personally has ready access to the foreign minister. His next posting is almost invariably to a large embassy, where his status falls immediately and his work becomes menial. One diplomat recalled that it was mostly involved with the boredom of ciphering telegrams by hand. He rapidly became frustrated.

The diplomatic community at an isolated post will be a tight one. All the resident diplomats may gather together regularly to watch American films supplied by the United States army. In Saudi Arabia where cinemas are banned, diplomats watch film shows in turn in each other's embassies – a particularly prized privilege granted only after the diplomats promised to allow no outsiders entry.

Some diplomats like such postings. Whatever the diplomat's rank, he will feel important. It really is a question of being a big fish in a small pond. An ambassador, very low in the hierarchy of his own service, can be in daily touch with the nation's prime minister. He is especially powerful if his country gives aid to the host nation.

'My ambassador,' says a British diplomat in an African state, 'is still an old timer in the sense that he is never going to have any politicians cabling him instructions. To people here he still represents the Queen. They don't see him as a man on the end of a telephone, the way governments see ambassadors in the West.' Even though protocol plays a part, there will be more informality. A diplomat posted to Europe from Africa says: 'After six months here I still find it strange. I can't turn up at an ambassador's house in jeans as I did there or find the foreign minister in a bar downtown.' This diplomat is anxious to return to Africa: 'I always felt being greeted in a village by the chief with a bottle of Black Label whisky – a flag waving on the Landrover – was trail-blazing in a way.'

There may be activities far divorced from the diplomatic whirl of the civilised capitals. An American sent to the Yemen in the early sixties for two years travelled to areas never previously visited by Americans to gather information on the economy. 'Travel was usually by jeep along desert and mountain trails frequently washed out; average speed was around twelve miles an hour. In one area with no roads I walked for two days over mountain terrain up to 10,000 feet, with mules carrying supplies. Some places were too steep even for loaded mules, and tribesmen carried the supplies while the mules were led unburdened. From time to time I stayed in the 'assembly' rooms of local sheikhs.'

But it would be wrong to overstress the hardships or the horrors of the diplomatic life; most postings are still in civilised capitals. Missions there, in any event, are bigger (and – some cynics claim – it is hardly coincidence that the nicest posts often have the largest staffs). And even though a diplomat in Iran, for example, may make the occasional mule journey, his life still revolves around the Shah's court.

It would be equally untrue to claim, as some do, that today's important postings are necessarily to places that are remote. There, it is argued, the ambassador remains important because he still has to make rapid decisions. By that criterion a far-flung South American republic is now more important than Paris. It is not true. The mission there *is* allowed to get on with its work, undisturbed by over-detailed instructions or directives from politicians, but simply because the home country has decided that what happens does not matter too much. They are used, sometimes, as pre-retirement presents. In the ones on or near the sea it is best, explains one elderly Austrian diplomat, if the ambassador can sail.

The most important posts today vary according to the diplomat's nation. London, Washington, Paris and Moscow are key ones for most. Bonn is a very important one for African nations because of aid and scholarships. Madrid is a major capital for Latin American countries and Delhi for Asian nations.

Just how important though must always depend on the sending nation, its size and seriousness. Many small nations in Washington, for example, appear to have little to do but compete for the reputation of being the most avid socialisers (the list changes each year, but in the late 1960s Algiers was highly regarded in this respect although, in the 1970s, Morocco and Kuwait appeared to be overtaking it).

Apart from finding himself in a 'hardship' post, a diplomat today is also more likely to find himself in a country whose regime is repugnant to his fellow citizens. Missions are established in foreign countries (with that government's permission) not on the basis of love and trust, but because it is believed they are needed. The one factor not involved is any *moral* judgement on that state.

Louis J. Halle in *Diplomacy in a Changing World* has compared having diplomatic relations with another government to buying groceries: the customer 'does not ask whether his grocer has ever committed adultery before he buys his groceries because it would seem irrelevant to him'.

A paper prepared by the American State Department for internal guidance – 'GIST: Recognition U.S. Policy' – reminds diplomats, often called on to justify the morality of posts, that 'The decision to accept a new regime as the government of a state is based on what best serves our national interest . . . recognition of a foreign government does not imply approval of the government's domestic policies or the means by which it came to power.'

The diplomat himself may abhor the politics of the country in which he works. But he is expected to rise above it – just as diplomats have always been expected to argue for policies in which they do not personally believe. One service at least, however, will not make its officers serve in South Africa if they have strong personal convictions.

Not only is there now a readiness to open embassies, but increasingly in recent years there has been a reluctance to close them even when relations are reduced to threats (a contrast with the past when major rifts often led to nations withdrawing their missions). Diplomats may have to serve in countries openly hostile, as in Peking during the Cultural Revolution when the British mission was attacked by mobs, or in Djakarta in the 1960s when the British embassy was systematically destroyed. Diplomats agree that, hardship or not, it is right relations should continue: 'It's when things are bad that we are most needed,' says one Briton who was in China during the worst period. 'Our job is to try to ensure they don't get even worse, and if possible to improve them.'

In filling vacancies at posts foreign services try to fit requirements to the qualifications of diplomats available. The fact that diplomats are regarded as generalists, and, therefore, a man in a political job can be posted to a consular or economic one, helps the assignments officer. Personal circumstances and wishes are taken into some consideration; in the German service, for example, this can be done in about thirty per cent of the vacancies. In the rest, needs have to triumph. None of this means, however, that diplomats are simply like pins on a map-board, passively going where foreign ministries want to send them. If they do not like an assignment, they will lobby to change it even though, theoretically, they are supposed to be prepared to go anywhere.

John E. Harr, in a Carnegie Endowment study *The Development of Careers in the Foreign Service*, pointed out that the American diplomats prepared to take virtually any assignment without flinching or much foot-dragging are 'in the minority'. He concluded that the ideal of a world-wide commitment was misleading if it conjured up an image of selfless men who silently go their appointed ways. 'The correct image is one of a group of men who are highly vocal about their assignments, but who are generally willing to deliver when the chips are down.'

He instanced one 'classic case of artful dodging' – a diplomat perfect for a posting in a newly independent African country, but not keen to leave his comfortable European post. 'When word of the pending assignment got around, a steady stream of visitors returning from Europe to the Department (of State) carried back the news that the officer, for a great variety of reasons, was not suited to the African assignment, was uninterested in it, and was needed where he was.' He won his battle. And Harr reports that the assignments panel involved were, despite themselves, 'full of admiration for the officer's rearguard action'.

Lobbying to obtain, or to avoid assignments has a place in all foreign services. Partly, successful lobbying is possible because diplomatic services usually assign themselves: 'Today you're in the field, tomorrow you may be in career management and assignments, and next year you may be on a promotion panel,' says an American. 'So there is built in empathy to the problems of everyone in the system. Tomorrow it may be you.' There is sympathy from fellow diplomats too: not only is it accepted that assignment is so important to a diplomat, but also the process by which it is carried out is a much criticised one in most services. In America diplomats refer to it as 'the flesh market' or the 'auction block'. Anyone who succeeds in beating such a system is to be congratulated.

It is not always successful, although those who fail in their attempts seem to accept it as the luck of the game. One English first secretary recalled how, as a head office diplomat concerned with Berlin, he had tried – unsuccessfully – to use the Cuban missile crisis as an excuse for not being posted to Guatemala.

And there are unofficial rules that the lobbyist disregards at his peril. The most important one in all services is that a diplomat can only take the issue right up to the point of near-refusal once in his life. 'You just cannot say "no" more than once,' says a Swedish counsellor. 'If you do, it has bad effects on your whole career.'

Once he is in his new post, there is a limit to the time the diplomat will be kept there irrespective of the conditions. This is because it is accepted that a diplomat's worth in a country increases for a number of years – and then declines, sometimes sharply. One reason is that the diplomat gets too out of touch with his own country. There is also a tendency after a time for the diplomat to become too emotionally involved with the country in which he works. 'You may start loving the place and wanting to be liked by local officials so much that you lose objectivity,' says one German. Diplomats frequently begin over-estimating the importance of the country in which they are based: 'Suddenly,' says one, 'you're believing it's the centre of the world.' The worst cases may, as they say in the British Foreign Office, 'go native'. The American service now insists that its diplomats spend at least three years out of every fifteen in Washington. 'This goes back,' explains one, 'to when some diplomats were recalled from London to talk to senators. Some had been in Britain for twenty years. And, suddenly, there they were back in the States, rolled umbrellas and British accents. A senator took a look at one, and said, "*That* represents me!"' Contrariwise, the diplomat's dispassion may become hatred. One diplomat who spent five years in an Arab country confessed that he grew to loathe the Arab world so much that after the first three years he took no interest in anything he did.

Foreign services try to cushion their diplomats and their families from the routine problems of living abroad with a system of allowances and by supplying, or paying for, housing. In the British service, for example, diplomats receive a local cost of living allowance, a supplement to cover their representational role, an entertainments allowance and an amount based on salary simply for being overseas. Additionally there will be allowances for children's schooling, and free housing. The quality of housing is one of the factors that often sets the diplomat apart from residents of the country in which he lives. Ironically, the poorer the country, the better the diplomat's house may be. The people there are often either very poor or very rich and the choice of housing lies between a mud hut or a palace. Even the most junior staff are never put in mud huts.

In countries where the disparity is not so great, diplomats still live in the nicest, most desirable sections of town. They may occupy accommodation that has been leased by the embassy, or they may find homes themselves and claim the rent. In many capitals there will be a mixture of both sorts of accommodation. British diplomats prefer the post-hired ones – because the houses are then decorated and furnished by the British Department of the Environment, generally up to a much higher standard than a private landlord would supply.

Though these post-hirings generally work out cheaper for the foreign services concerned, there is a limit to their number in any capital: 'You can't have too many in one place because you'd find yourself with a house for a couple empty and a diplomat and six children wanting accommodation. What you do try to have is a mix of sizes, so that you can be fairly flexible.' There are parts of the world, too, where landlords do not like letting to embassies as distinct from individuals. America is notorious for this. 'A landlord knows that if he leases to you then he would have to lease to the diplomatic mission of a black country,' explains a diplomat there. 'If he's renting to an individual he can always say he doesn't like the man, and that his colour doesn't come into it.'

Some countries, including Sweden and Germany, pay for the diplomat's furniture to be moved wherever he goes; others, like the British, make the diplomat take furnished accommodation. In the Swedish service, extensive repairs and renovations will be undertaken at the service's expense. In one I visited the whole building had just been fitted with new plumbing – even though the diplomat only had it on a short lease.

There is a temptation for new diplomats to seek something even grander – and to pay the difference themselves. If he does that, however, he will find considerable pressure put on him by his embassy chief: 'He may feel affluent and think he can easily manage £10 a week more – but he can't and we do our best to stop him,' one high-ranking English diplomat says. Older diplomats, though, are left alone: 'You can't tell a counsellor he doesn't know what he's doing with his own money.'

Landlords and estate agents like diplomats: they seek expensive homes, with entertaining facilities, and are not – as one London estate agent puts it – 'affected by the normal economic problems'. In the late 1960s a married British counsellor in Paris was receiving a rent allowance of £250 a month.

A Swedish counsellor, with three children, in London in the early 1970s was getting his rent and all household bills paid – a total of nearly £100 a week.

Different parts of the world present different housing problems. If a diplomatic service wants more accommodation in Africa, it often has to build it. In South America, there is a constant battle with landlords – described by one diplomat as 'rapacious and inconsiderate'. European landlords are judged good, but Belgium and Swiss law is heavily balanced in the landlord's favour. In Saudi Arabia, though prices are high, diplomats are lucky. Property speculators built more accommodation than the market will take; a diplomat can be offered fifty to sixty houses.

Officials dealing with housing for diplomats note a global tendency for standards to creep up. One believes this is due to rising expectations generally – 'and the fact that when someone moves into an above-average home, by the time he leaves it's become average to him.'

They get angry over some of the criticisms however. 'We get asked why we put single girls in two bedroom flats in Damascus, wasting money? The answer's simple – they don't have any one bedroom flats there.' Rent allowances do get cut. British diplomatic inspectors reduced rent allowances in two European posts in 1969 because diplomats were living in accommodation better than they needed.

Even if they are in the best areas, rented homes provide some contact between diplomats and the cities in which they live. This is not so in the case of another form of accommodation – compounds which bring together the embassy, the ambassador's residence and housing in one area. The American ones have been called 'golden ghettos'.

In Bonn, the U.S. compound consists of rows of neat apartments together with public and social buildings; in Rangoon, there are stately houses around a lake; in Saudi Arabia modern bungalows are set in spacious grounds and there is a golf-course and four tennis courts. The British compounds are found especially in the older established missions in Africa and Asia. One in Addis Ababa covers eighty acres and includes a village for servants. In Teheran there are two, one in the city, and another – originally intended for summer use – in the foothills. The compound in Tokyo is now valued at over £12 million – but cannot be sold. It is owned by the British on a perpetual lease granted by the Emperor in 1869. As it is technically unsaleable, its market value to the British is nil.

The advantage is that they help management. The disadvantage is that they cut off contact. This was accepted in the United States in the late 1950s when a commission recommended that senior diplomats with representational responsibilities should move out into town. The suggestion was shelved when the costs involved were realised.

One American ambassador, who has served at missions with compounds, claims that while intended to improve staff morale, they actually damage it. 'Americans who live like this constantly associate only with each other' he says. 'They live under resort conditions which represent neither those of the United States nor those of the host country. They fail to understand the country and learn its problems and attitudes sufficiently well to perform effectively in their official duties. This in turn leads to frustration, frictions and dissension.'

One of the reasons for the splendour of diplomats' houses abroad is that homes are expected to be places where people can be entertained. 'It should be borne in mind,' said the Duncan Report in Britain, 'that members of the Diplomatic Service overseas are available for duty for virtually twenty-four hours a day, and need pleasant and suitable surroundings for entertaining at home as well as in the mission.' This is acceptable if you agree that the quantity and the level of entertaining that is such a huge part of diplomatic life is necessary. 'Dining,' said Lord Palmerston, 'is the soul of diplomacy'. And it has not changed much – although one ambassador imparted the revolutionary information that he was moving away from throwing cocktail parties to dinners for fourteen or more guests.

Diplomats regard party and dinner giving and going as work. During a strike in April 1970 that involved Italian diplomats in Rome, one refused to attend an ambassador's dinner party on the grounds that parties were part of his official duties and that he would be strike-breaking if he went.

Diplomats justify entertaining on three main grounds: that social functions project a good image of the country concerned; that they are useful places for obtaining information; and that at them contacts and friends are made. 'You should remember,' says one French ambassador, 'that for better or for worse the image I project has much to do with the impression people here have of my country'. Lester B. Pearson argued that in going to parties, 'Sometimes a man in a corner . . . either under the influence of alcohol or in desperation will give away some interesting and even important information.' On the third justification, a high-ranking Asian diplomat says, 'You need to know people on a social level so that you can best deal with them on a business one.'

But so much of the social life seems to have no end product but itself. And because of the awful diplomatic tradition of reciprocity, the more parties that A gives, the more X, Y and Z will have to throw to return the hospitality.

Even those diplomats who do not agree that socialising is important, accept the system. 'It's a drag,' says an American ambassador. 'Cocktail parties are useless for conversations. The noise is such that you can't hear; you can drag someone into a corner, but it's better talking to them at their offices in the daytime. I wish they could be banned.'

They claim, however, that if a diplomat did try to opt out, other countries' diplomats would regard his actions as a deliberate snub. 'You entertain and you have to go to other people's functions or they will draw conclusions about you and your relations with their country,' one says. 'People get insulted very easily. You may say that if there are 200 people there they won't notice if you don't turn up. But they do.' Another, from the Caribbean, who had been to two receptions the previous evening, and was facing two more that night, claimed: 'It's tiresome, but you have to do it. It's particularly difficult if you represent a neutral country like me. If you attend a function given by Israel one day and not one given by Jordan a few days later, people draw implications from your non-attendance. Not going is always regarded as showing displeasure; attending is an acknowledgement of friendship and regard.'

There are a lot of excuses for celebrations, apart from the coming and going of diplomats and the arrivals of visiting dignitaries. In a major capital with 120 missions, each will have a National Day party and at least one for an important visitor. That means 240 functions simply as a starter. The number of annual events celebrated by the diplomatic corps in London is 411. On just one day, 1 October, there are these reasons for a party: Cameroon Reunification Day; Cyprus National Day; Nigeria Republic Day; Spain Day of the Caudillo (to commemorate the accession of Franco to head of state); and China Inauguration of the People's Republic.

One finds it hard to accept any of the justifications: image? There must be exceedingly few people today – in an age of mass communication and travel – who draw their impression of a foreign country from that of one man on the spot. Gathering information? Talk at cocktail parties is necessarily social and superficial; at dinners it is guarded. Making contacts? Well, yes. But influencing them? Party guests include large numbers of people whose influence will never be needed anyway. And, even if Y's attempts to influence Mr X aren't counteracted by everyone else who is giving him hospitality, it seems a little naive to believe that important issues will rest on whether X liked Y's claret. Some of the biggest party givers are the smaller countries who are not really setting out to gain anything from them anyway. The Moroccan National Day party in London in 1970 was attended by over 1,200 people, and the choice of food was such that guests were given menus: Les Specialités Marocaines included: Méchoui d'Agneau de l'Atlas, Poulet aux Olives de Fez, Couscous aux Raisins de Rabat-Salé, Pastillas Fourrés de Tétouan, Boulettes de Meknès, Kafta de Marrakech, Sardines de Safi and Thon d'Agadir; les desserts included: Muhallabia de Tanger, Gâteaux au

Miel; Briwat, Chebaquia and Griwesh; and the Friandises de Fez featured Cornes de Gazelles, Ghriba, Halawwiyatt. The birthday of the Shah of Iran saw parties for upwards of 2,000 guests in foreign capitals. A farewell party for the Kuwait ambassador in London in 1970 was attended by over 2,500 people; all the ground floor reception rooms of Claridges Hotel had to be taken over.

As for the claim that no country could take action to cut down on socialising alone for fear of upsetting others, it is clearly nonsense. It is claimed that all countries would have to agree. But if all the ambassadors who told me they would cut entertaining if they could were really serious, they could get together and stop the excesses tomorrow.

There is obviously need for *some* entertaining, and sometimes one accepts its value. In totalitarian countries, for example, it provides a safe setting for diplomats to talk to colleagues or residents without calling attention to the fact. One ambassador in Cairo, just after Suez, recalled that it was difficult to call on other diplomats without the Egyptians knowing. At cocktail parties, carefully standing with his back to the wall, he could exchange confidences.

As it is, examining guests lists, it is striking how the same names re-occur: rather like a constant stream of family celebrations. This happens not only at ambassador level. Military attachés invite military attachés; first secretaries give parties attended by other first secretaries. And often there is the same coterie of charming, but ineffective, hangers on. At big parties, even the gatecrashers seem to consist of the same professional group.

Diplomats claim that after a few years they become used to their nomadic lives. 'You complain of course,' says one French diplomat, 'but you get experienced and take moving on in your stride. You keep lists of all the things that have to be done – the letters of thanks, the parties, the housing arrangements. And you get expert at packing.' Another, Irish, claims: 'It's a bit like celibacy and sex for a priest. Because he knows he's not going to get it, he doesn't think about it. Because you know that you are going to have to keep moving, you don't worry about it.'

To an outsider, though, the constant moving, the strain of putting down new roots, adjusting to climates, languages and new colleagues, does seem to tell. The suave, controlled diplomat in public is often different in private – gulping down a third drink in twenty minutes, wondering whether his wife really offended the ambassadress with what was meant to be a mild joke, concerned whether what he has heard about being sent to Kabul is really true. And some will admit to worries. 'You never have friends, nor even your own dentist or doctor,' says one Briton. 'Then in these highly stratified societies, you start to see colleagues drinking too much or getting nervous twitches. You start to wonder – because you never notice such things about yourself.'

One notes the strain even more in wives, and in children. The diplomatic wife is a strange creature: an unpaid worker who bears much of the worry of her husband's nomadic life.

The most powerful diplomatic wife is the ambassadress. Like her husband she has a representational role; she is also 'mother' to the embassy wives. Her job is no less real than her husband's though supplied free. At a grand embassy, the ambassadress is probably briefing the cook while the ambassador is considering the wine list. She has to provide the 'right setting' for entertaining. She is always on show; her husband will brief her: 'You have to explain the government's position on particular subjects or the exact relationship with another country so that she doesn't speak out of turn or be indiscreet,' an ambassador explains. She is expected to attend promotions, open shops, give talks, and make contacts. Those of small nations regularly visit fellow nationals in hospital. A Caribbean ambassador accredited to both Washington and Ottawa says: 'When I am away from one, she will attend functions for me. When I return she knows the people and can introduce me.'

Many women confess it is a strain. The wife of one ambassador says: 'Sometimes there's no staff to help or only a tiny one and then the work is hard. But if you have a large staff, there's a different strain: you have their problems too.' A British ambassadress in a European country had to give three dinners one evening to celebrate the signing of a treaty. The first was for journalists, the second for delegates and the third for top people. For that, she says, she had the help of just one part-time cook.

Others complain the housekeeping is difficult. 'I really have to stretch the money,' says one. Another welcomed a gift of a large and beautiful piece of rock from embassy staff on moving:

'I'll be able to place it in the middle of the table instead of flowers,' she says. 'The allowance doesn't cover flowers nine months of the year.' A number of ambassadors' wives find that they cannot take the strain. 'It gets harder to do as much as you get older,' says one. 'Yet if your husband is doing well the work increases.'

Ambassadors from highly sophisticated countries sometimes find themselves forced to retire early because of their wives. This is never given as the official reason, and often there is a reluctance to admit to it. But the personnel records of many services contain illustrations. One ambassador who was willing to admit that his pending early retirement was due to this cause said that he did not blame his wife; he understood; and 'some of my colleagues, I know, had to do the same thing'.

As the senior diplomatic wife, the ambassadress is a figure to be regarded and treated with wariness by other wives. Sometimes she is hated; she is usually feared.

When an ambassador's wife is 'providing the right setting' at one of her parties, mission staff may be invited. The invitation means they are expected to help.

The State Department guide, *Social Usage Abroad*, given to diplomats going overseas for the first time, spells it out well:

When invited to the residence of a chief of mission or of a senior officer, staff members are expected to do all that they unobtrusively can to assist their hosts and make the guests feel welcome. Without giving the impression that they are usurping the function of host or hostess, they should for example:

1. Arrive at least 10 minutes early.
2. Leave promptly when the proper time comes, that is, when all guests, not members of staff, have left.
3. See that guests are taken care of from the minute they arrive, especially as they leave the receiving line.
4. Mingle with guests, introducing themselves to persons they have not met and indicating that they are members of the staff.
5. Keep alert, especially at the embassy, or residence of the consul in charge, to see that every high-ranking guest is escorted to the door and that his car is located for him.
6. Watch the host and hostess in case they need assistance.

The ambassadress sees that 'her' wives conform to all the social niceties. Like diplomats, wives have to do the 'right' things and wear the 'right' clothes. (*Social Usage Abroad* warns that gloves 'are worn for all social occasions in most countries. They should be used for luncheons, teas and receptions although they are always removed for eating and drinking'.) And she also 'encourages' them to get involved in outside work as well.

Since the beginning of 1972 wives of American diplomats at least are not forced to undertake any duties, whether it is entertaining or attending parties, or taking part locally in social or charity work. The decision that the wife is a private individual and that the Foreign Service cannot levy any duties on her was given in a State Department policy statement, the result of grumblings by diplomats and their wives. Nor, it was decided, would the activities of a wife any longer be mentioned in reports on her diplomatic husband.

But, despite that, in all services, including the American there is certain work a diplomat's wife has to do unless she is to send her husband off to dinners alone or let him throw parties by himself. And even though her extra activities (or lack of them) may no longer go into a report, it would be a naive wife who thought that what she did or did not do had no bearing on her husband's future prospects. In diplomatic services, the grapevine is as important as the official report. One comes across them running schools in North Africa, financing hospital beds in South East Asia, making clothes for institutions in Indonesia, giving tea parties in Britain and arranging bazaars in Holland.

There have been a few heroines. Polly Lukens, a young U.S. Foreign Service wife, killed in an air crash in the early 1960s, was in the Congo during some of the most violent days after independence. She helped refugees fleeing across the Congo river, feeding them, giving them clothes, and supplying beds for fifteen–twenty strangers each night.

Formal wives' organisation may mean rigid control over the amount they are expected to do. 'The wives of all agencies meet monthly under the leadership of my wife to consider and act upon matters affecting morale and to co-ordinate their participation in worthwhile projects,' wrote an American ambassador in *This Worked for Me*, a collection of the experiences and advice of

U.S. ambassadors. 'The wives join directly in and contribute directly to the work of existing national organisations such as Girl Scouts, Y.W.C.A. and philanthropic organisations. Participation in these groups is voluntary. . . .' But as wives know, social pressure and knowing what is expected makes it all anything but voluntary.

Diplomatic wives have their special problems outside of all this unpaid work. Frequent moves to new countries are often more of a strain to them than to their husbands: 'At least he's got a ready-made, familiar environment at work during the day,' says one Scandinavian wife. Diplomatic wives rarely take outside jobs. The Duncan Report felt that British wives should be allowed to do so – although accepting there would be problems if they wanted to work at, say, political journalism. Some countries ban wives working absolutely.

Wives of many diplomatic services have looked with admiration at the fighting qualities of Swedish foreign service wives. They come from a country where Women's Liberation is very strong, and where sixty per cent of housewives under the age of sixty go out to work.

'Most of us,' says a young diplomatic wife, 'now have degrees. We find the idea of just being a glorified decoration for our diplomatic husbands rather degrading.'

As a result of their efforts (which have included countless meetings) Swedish wives are now allowed to work. But, in practice, few do. The practical problems are often too great – their professional skills gained at home are not valid in a foreign country (a lawyer, for example, can't practise just anywhere), and there is the problem of their diplomatic immunity. Perhaps even more importantly, they find the climate in a foreign diplomatic community against them working. 'You can *feel* that it is not liked,' admits one who does work.

Norway has an interesting way of dealing with the situation. Wives are allowed to work up to a certain limit. When a wife's salary reaches a certain (low) level, however, the money is deducted from her husband's allowance. Consequently, there is great inducement not to work, which is exactly what the foreign service wants. It would much rather she was leading a hectic social life, helping her husband. One Norwegian first secretary's wife, who likes working as a teacher, goes out to work for just a few hours a week – but does not ask for payment.

Diplomatic wives meeting for the first time appear to have a pattern. They start conversations by listing places they have been and people they have known there in order to try to establish some sort of relationship. They are highly status conscious – the status being that of the ranking and reputation of their husbands.

At small diplomatic parties they are a sad sight. You watch them working, handing around drinks, urging people to sofas and chairs, making sure Monsieur X isn't monopolised by Dr Y. Then, as the evening goes by the men congregate in one part of the room, the diplomatic wives talk about knitting or schools in another. In small groups, they often appear over-cautious and nervous if their husbands begin being indiscreet: several wives on separate occasions could not hide their worry when husbands began confiding their unflattering views of their current ambassadors.

Several personnel officers record more problems with wives than with their husbands: 'You do get cases of neurosis,' says one. A diplomat says he is worried about his wife: 'I know she has more time to brood on the problems than I have. When I come here (his office) she sits down in a house that's too small for us and she thinks of the kids who are at a school that neither of us like.'

It is an artificial life too. One European diplomat's wife who had a baby abroad said: 'At first there were servants to look after everything. Then we were posted home, and I thought "Good God, what do I do?" '

Wives of various countries, including Britain, America, Canada and Sweden, have started diplomatic wives' associations to help with some of the problems. The British one, run by a committee of twelve in London, has no official standing but works closely with the Foreign Office and describes itself as 'primarily an unofficial welfare association'.

If wives are flown home ill, they arrange visitors. A wife going to a new country can get lists of goods she will find available locally, and the association will try to put her in touch with someone who has recently returned. It will also help in the search for accommodation when her husband is posted home, and keeps

lists of shops that sell out of season clothes for the women going
to Africa when it is mid-winter in London.

The association gets letters on individual problems. It never
involves itself in disputes between wives at posts – and that mostly
means between an ambassadress and one of the embassy wives.
But one member concedes that some of the letters are ones 'that
the writer knows we can't do anything about – but it's a safety
valve for her'.

How a wife behaves, impresses, and involves herself at a post
matters more and more to her husband's career as he rises in
rank. 'You are never likely to make the top,' admits a diplomatic
personnel officer, 'if your wife is known as a two-headed dragon
or an alcoholic or someone who doesn't fit into her environment'.
On the other hand, admit some foreign services, they have diplomats who are ranked higher than their personal abilities merit –
because their wives are rated so highly. In some services, it is
regarded as a real disadvantage for a man to marry a foreigner.
Even in the most liberal, marriage to an American wife would
probably mean the diplomat would never be ambassador in Washington, to a French woman, good-bye to thoughts of the top post
in Paris. Some services, like the Turkish, ban marriage to foreign
nationals completely (a reason why so many Turkish diplomats
are bachelors). A French diplomat, who had married an American, was already attracting hostile comments from his colleagues
– not because of her nationality *per se* but because of the kind
of parties she gave: noisy and not chic.

Just as wives are sometimes casualties of the diplomatic life, so
are children. 'Our wives and children are the people who pay
the price no matter how we try to make it up to them in other
ways,' says one Italian diplomat.

Schooling is a large problem. Generally, a diplomat has to
make the choice of sending the child away to a boarding school,
or keeping him or her with him and using local facilities. Both
are fraught with difficulties. The British have a reputation for
keeping children in England; one wife explaining why she had
sent her six-year-old away to prep school, said, 'If I didn't, he'd
have no chance at the right public school later.' Even in the British
service, however, it is becoming increasingly accepted that not
all children are 'boarding school material'. 'And,' says one wife,

'even if they are, you have the problem of what happens to them at holidays if you haven't got kind relatives.' In a number of services, including the British and German, children are flown home free to see their parents.

There are problems, too, in keeping a child at a post: despite the presence of Lycées and American Schools in some parts of the world, facilities are not always good and methods and curricula vary. When assigning, foreign services cross off family men for posts where there is no schooling. But often, when there are facilities, they are not liked. And changes of school can be frequent: one diplomat's daughter had attended eleven schools by the time she was sixteen.

At least one psychiatrist, involved with the Peace Corps and on treating patients in Washington, is convinced that rearing children overseas may leave them with serious emotional scars. Dr Sydney L. Werkman, of the University of Colorado medical school, believes: 'Overseas living fosters a mixture of fears, unusual child-care practices, special problems in sexuality and a sense of alienation.' He quotes one young American raised overseas as saying: 'There is always the feeling that you don't belong anywhere; the fear that you will become attached to your friends and then have to leave them. The large majority of children growing up overseas are unhappy Americans. They are neither one nor the other, unhappy away or unhappy in the United States, unless they enter foreign work themselves.'

Diplomats report that the disturbances often show on a return home. The boy or girl finds problems of readjusting. The talk and experiences of his friends, brought up at home, are difficult for him to follow or understand. One diplomat – not American – whose sixteen-year-old daughter is attending a psychiatrist blames it on the life: 'She told the psychiatrist she felt totally rejected. I see it now – but I didn't as she was growing up. Either she was away, or the servants were looking after her.'

A number of foreign services welfare departments report 'a fair number of family and personal breakdowns'. The Americans note an increase in the number of teenage social problems. Often diplomats are brought back earlier than intended because of this; frequently they are re-assigned to posts along the Mexican and Canadian border where their children will feel more at home.

It might seem that to a diplomat the most eagerly welcomed posting is one back home. But for most this is the assignment that is least wanted and which brings the greatest shocks, both psychologically and financially.

The standard of living falls enormously, with allowances totally removed (as in the American and German services) or almost totally (as with the British). 'You are back to reality with a bang,' says one English diplomat. 'Because allowances when you are abroad are not taxed your income at home is suddenly halved. Your way of life becomes totally different. You do live a fairly comfortable life abroad. Here you don't regard cigarettes and liquor as particularly prized commodities. The first question I get asked when I go home is whether I brought any duty free cigarettes with me. That brings you straight back to the real world.'

Another says: 'It means you live two lives – one when you are at home and one when you are abroad. And of course, it's always easier to adjust to a higher standard of living than a lower one. At home you suddenly find you've got rent and travelling and buying your own meals – here when you give a dinner party you obviously feed yourself as well and it's chargeable to public funds. And I can also charge things like a baby sitter.'

Apart from money, other adjustments may be difficult: 'I hate the business of suddenly having to consult everyone and keep office hours,' says one. Another from one of the newer nations says his main problem is that he has lost contact with his own family group – 'their problems are no longer mine, and nor are mine theirs'.

Home based civil servants in some capitals take what seems to be an almost conscious delight in deflating returning diplomats. At one period in Canberra, diplomats knew they would fare badly in trying to obtain government-owned housing accommodation; they were always placed low on the list. 'It was,' says an Australian diplomat, 'a nice way of making you pay for your sins of rich living abroad.'

Almost everywhere, though, the status evaporates. 'You get a rude awakening,' says a Canadian. 'It doesn't matter if you were an ambassador with four servants. You become just a public servant.' He pauses, and then adds: 'Till you go abroad again, of course.'

Six
The Privileged Diplomat

'Striped pants are not a garment but a
state of mind.'
Lester B. Pearson

'Diplomacy,' said Prince Bernard von Bülow, a pre-World War I
German Chancellor, is 'a first class stall seat at the theatre of
life.' The definition is still largely valid. The number of diplomats
may have grown, their power may have decreased, but their
privileges are as real as ever.

They have not been relegated to the dress circle; if anything,
the diplomat's style of life is at greater variance with that of the
mass of the people than it ever was.

The diplomat has status, privilege, and a high-style of life. His
status is reflected in the marketing man's certainty that Ambassador, Diplomat and Consul are good names for products ranging
from night-clubs to cigarettes to motor cars. Ambassadorial high
jinks merit space in any newspaper's gossip columns. At dinners,
cocktail parties, in restaurants an ambassador is always worth
having around.

A twenty-nine-year-old former inspector of the Paris transport
services proved in the late 1960s just how many privileges there
are if people only *think* you are a diplomat. The man gave himself an aristocratic name and for three years posed as a French
counsellor dealing with cultural affairs. On one occasion, unable
to pay a meal bill, he ordered more champagne and persuaded
the police to call at his home. There they found letters addressed
to him as a diplomat, and were so impressed they set him free.
On another similar occasion he telephoned a diplomat who rushed
to the restaurant to pay the bill for him.

The privileges include tax and legal immunities and the right
of ambassadors to be called 'Excellency' (and some insist on it).
At the top of the profession, the style of life will embrace a
mansion, a chauffeur-driven car and servants. The diplomat's

feeling of élitism is played down by the diplomatic theorists: '"élitist" attitudes in a foreign service are undesirable,' said the report of the Commonwealth Seminar on diplomacy. They may be, but they exist: 'You won't find one country,' admits a veteran Latin diplomat, 'where you don't find diplomats believing themselves superior to civil servants at home.' 'I'm afraid,' says a diplomatic chief of protocol, 'that we're prone to develop an attitude that we are a privileged lot and a cut above everyone else.'

Some diplomats will defend this attitude. A British consul began a lunchtime address with the words: 'You see standing before you a member of a small but determined élite.' An American diplomat who was present congratulated him afterwards. 'I feel that we have to maintain this image of ourselves as an élite if we are to continue getting the best people,' he explains. 'The material rewards of diplomacy just aren't enough any more to make up for all the crap that we have to handle.'

One British ambassador claims that the public likes to see him enjoying his privileged existence just as newspaper readers are fascinated by the larger-than-life doings of international filmstars. 'Take my Rolls,' he says. 'You could say it's ostentatious. And I suppose it is. But you know, a lot of people who complain would hate it if I drove about in a smaller car. They love to see it.'

The diplomat will also argue that all these trappings are not the important thing; they are only incidentals that attract disproportionate attention. 'I wish people would think of me as what I really am,' says one, 'just a public servant whose work happens to take place abroad.' But they are important. It is the diplomat's privileges and life-style that provides the image that helps make him so widely criticised. It is not just the job he does that is questioned; it is whether his work needs to be surrounded by so much extravagance and pomp. And, fair or not, to many members of the public, the diplomat's (unwitnessed) negotiating skills and (unseen) lucid reports, are of far less interest than the fact that he can park his car where he likes with legal impunity and that he gets his Scotch whisky at a fifth the price that the man in the street has to pay.

Often it seems, too, that diplomats go out of their way to attract the kind of publicity that brands them as inhabitants of a rather silly never-never land. The number plate on the car of the Fijian high commissioner in London reads FIJI (high commissioners are ambassadors exchanged between Commonwealth countries). The number is actually FIJ 1, but the letters and the number have been run together. In the United Kingdom, car registration letters are allocated to various parts of the country. The series FIJ had been allocated to County Down, Northern Ireland, where it was expected to come into use in 1974. Obtaining FIJI involved negotiations with the British Foreign Office, the Ministry of Transport, the Ministry of Development in Northern Ireland, and Down County Council.

Of all the privileges enjoyed by diplomats, the most prized is probably freedom from local taxation and the right to buy goods duty free. The diplomat does not have to buy licences for his dogs or television sets, for having a gun, or to shoot game. He either buys his petrol from garages where the cost of tax is deducted before he pays, or he keeps the receipts and later gets a refund (in Britain, in 1971, the refund was sixty-five per cent of the cost). The tax and duty privilege derives from the principle that a government should not try to tax people outside its jurisdiction; and although living in a country, diplomats are not subject to its authority.

This privilege is especially valuable in the case of wines and spirits, and tobacco, all luxury articles that are normally subject to heavy taxes in the country of their origin and then to heavy import duties. The saving is great. At the time a bottle of Beafeater Gin was costing $5.90 in a store in Ottawa, the diplomat was able to buy it for $1.08. In London in mid-1970, Scotch that cost upwards of £2.50 in shops was available to diplomats at 56½p a bottle, vodka was 42p against a retail price of nearly £3. Diplomats could buy a hundred large-sized, tipped cigarettes for only 3p more than twenty were costing the average Briton.

In all capitals there are a few diplomats, usually from some smaller nations, who take advantage of the situation to buy cheap and resell at a profit. A delegation to the United Nations ordered 2,500 bottles of tax-free liquor in a three month period (at about one-third retail prices). In two weeks, one diplomat in New York ordered 1,200 packages of tax-free cigarettes – making him surely the chain-smoker of all time if they were all for his personal consumption.

Theoretically, chiefs of protocol in each capital keep a watch on diplomatic purchases in order to check abuses. But one admits: 'Apart from letting them know you are suspicious, and hoping this will make them behave, there is little you can do. . . .' One Asian head of mission claims to personally check the total orders of his diplomatic staff regularly. 'I hate to say it, but you have to,' he said, 'the temptation is rather great.'

But, even forgetting abuses, is cheap liquor justified? Diplomats are vehement that it is. 'I feel very, very strongly about this,' one says. 'We get it duty free because we entertain others.' But what of businessmen and journalists who also entertain others; should they not enjoy the same privilege? 'That's rather different' – but he cannot explain why. The privilege was doubly prized in the United States during Prohibition when diplomats could still import as much liquor as they wished.

Other items are also free of tax and duty: radios and television sets, perfumes and motorcars. A silk carpet, selling at £1,300 in London in mid-1970, was available to diplomats for £400. Companies, anxious to number the Corps Diplomatique among their customers, may also offer discounts. Car manufacturers and salesmen compete for diplomatic sales: having diplomats drive their cars presents a good image. Many give parties with fine wines to introduce their new models. Mercedes Benz, whose cars are a favourite of higher ranking diplomats, arranges visits to Germany. A salesman, who specialises in selling cars to the diplomatic corps, explains they get other special treatment too: 'You have to pull out all the stops for these people. They expect it. You have to be very specific on delivery dates. The car has to be A1 and you always deliver it personally to the embassy.'

Diplomats also enjoy the right of free communications through the diplomatic bag (legally this can be of any size from a small package to a lorry-load). Major countries forbid personal use of the diplomatic bag, but this is hard to enforce. Charles W. Thayer has recalled in *Diplomat* that in Russia in the 1930s when luxuries were unobtainable, diplomatic admirers often kept actresses and ballerinas in Paris fashions with clothing brought into the country in the bag.

Diplomats of some smaller countries often use it to import duty-free goods to sell on the local black-market. A chief of protocol who knows it goes on in his capital, but confesses himself powerless unless there is a blatant and proveable case, says: 'I'm afraid that you don't sanitise some people just by calling them diplomats and shipping them abroad.'

Diplomatic bags are also used for 'smuggling' home paintings and antiques. At a symposium, held during a December 1971 meeting of the American Association for the Advancement of Science, scientists asserted that American diplomats were among those who were looting archeological sites in many countries and using the diplomatic bag to send antiquities home to the United States. In Turkey, claimed one scientist, diplomats from most foreign missions indulged in looting. Because Turkey did not authorise the exporting of antiquities, those smuggled out realised enormous prices and fortunes could be made. Another speaker, from the Smithsonian Institute in Washington, claimed diplomats and aid personnel carried out similar practices in Ecuador and Peru.

Diplomats from major powers have also taken advantage of shortages in developing countries to make money. In Sri Lanka, with strong import restrictions on foreign cars, diplomats bring in vehicles which immediately have a resale value of six to seven times the amount they have paid. A number of diplomats, notably from America and Germany, took advantage of this until the government took action. It told the diplomats they were free to import cars. But when they sold them, they had to be offered to the government stores – at the imported price minus an amount for depreciation.

The fact that the diplomat is not under the authority of the country in which he is based also means he has legal immunities not enjoyed by anyone else. Unlike all other residents of a country, he is protected from criminal prosecution and (with very few exceptions) from civil actions. 'Diplomats,' said Sir Ernest Satow, 'form the exception to the rule that all persons and things within a sovereign state are subject to its jurisdiction.' Or, to put it more bluntly, they are above the law.

There are strong arguments for the diplomat's immunity. Serving abroad, perhaps in a hostile nation, he needs special protection if he is to carry out his job safely and without hindrance. 'Just think of the possibility of trumped-up charges if it did not exist,' one German diplomat says. 'Imagine life for a Western diplomat behind the Iron Curtain. He would constantly be afraid of being locked away for all sorts of imagined crimes.'

The acceptance of a need for some special protection is probably timeless. Some diplomatic writers have suggested that the first diplomat was possibly a caveman sent by one group to negotiate with enemies. This would only be possible if he was allowed to talk – and then return home alive.

The first recognition of diplomatic immunity in Anglo-Saxon law, however, resulted from a diplomat's debts. The Act of 7 Anne was promulgated in 1708 after the Russian ambassador to Britain had been arrested and attacked by several creditors.

Immunity begins the moment a diplomat arrives in a foreign nation and applies until the moment he leaves, even if he is expelled. It also extends to the diplomat's corpse in the rare event of his dying at his post. During World War I, a French diplomat was shot dead in a London hotel bedroom. A British coroner began to hold an inquest. But this was stopped after the government agreed with the French ambassador that the body had immunity.

Privileges and immunities were long recognised by the law of nations and by reciprocal practices. In 1961, however, they were codified and completed in a Vienna Convention which was drawn up by an international conference held under United Nations auspices. This convention reaffirmed that diplomatic premises, transport and documents should be inviolable, and it divided mission staffs into three groupings, each with varying degrees of immunity and privileges.

The first group contains the 'diplomatic agents' – the ambassador, his diplomatic staff and the attachés. They and their families get full immunity and tax exemptions.

The second group consists of administrative and technical staff, including typists. They are immune from criminal actions, but not from civil ones except in respect of actions performed in the course of their official duties. They can, for example, be sued for debt. Their exemption from customs duty covers only their personal articles on first installation.

The third group covers service staffs, including chauffeurs. They are immune from criminal and civil actions only in respect of acts carried out as part of their work. A driver, taking his ambassador to a dinner engagement, for example, would be legally safe jumping a red light; driving to meet his girl-friend on his day off, he would not. (Ambassadors of small, new nations often blame their chauffeurs for abuses. 'I am afraid they sometimes behave pompously because they have immunity,' one African apologises. 'I had one who used to tear up all the parking tickets and another who went through traffic lights. I changed them.')

There is a notable exception to these varying degrees of immunity. Communist powers often have special arrangements with Western states whereby all their staffs, from the ambassador to the doorman, can claim full immunities from local law.

Immunity covers not only the diplomat himself, and his family, but also his office and home. Police cannot enter either without formal permission. Asylum is not covered in the Vienna convention; in Europe, at least, it is rare, and the majority of experts claim that embassies do not have a right to grant it. In Latin America, on the other hand, political asylum in embassies is an established custom – possibly because those in power are always mindful that they themselves may need to take advantage of it one day.

On the rare occasions British embassies are invaded by a fugitive, he will usually be ushered straight out of the back door. American embassies are forbidden under Foreign Service regulations from granting asylum to anyone beyond extending temporary protection from mob violence.

In Europe, however, there have been rare exceptions. The most notable was Cardinal Josef Mindszenty who took refuge in the American Legation in Budapest when the Soviets crushed the 1956 Hungarian uprising. He remained there for fifteen years before leaving Hungary at the request of the Pope.

Immunity cannot be waived by the diplomat himself or by his ambassador. The immunity the diplomat enjoys is held not to belong to him as a person, but to his office, and his government's permission is needed.

Countries do sometimes waive immunity. In one year, 1968, the Dutch Ministry of Justice decided there were no grounds for claiming immunity for half of the seventy diplomats who fell foul of the laws of the countries in which they were serving. In 1970, a civil air attaché at the Dutch embassy in London, obtained his government's consent to stand trial on a charge of causing the death by dangerous driving of a medical student (he was found Not Guilty).

That same year the British government waived the immunity of Mr Brian Lea, the passport officer at its High Commission in Kampala, so that he could give evidence before a Uganda Commission of Inquiry. Lea, who had disappeared for two days, claimed he was forced into a car outside the High Commission and had been held prisoner. The inquiry decided his account was false and that the kidnapping story was bogus; it destroyed both his claim and his career.

If a government refuses to waive a diplomat's immunity, the host country can declare him *persona non grata* and insist on his departure.

In the case of persistent or blatant offenders against a country's law there can be firm but discreet pressures applied on the diplomat's ambassador. Kim Philby, the British intelligence man who spied for the Russians, has recalled in *My Silent War* how his fellow spy Guy Burgess even used this to his advantage. Burgess needed to be sent home from the United States to Britain. 'Three times one day,' said Philby, 'he was booked for speeding in the state of Virginia and the Governor reacted just as we had hoped. He sent a furious protest to the State Department against this flagrant abuse of diplomatic privilege which was then brought to the attention of the ambassador. Within a few days, Burgess was regretfully informed that he would have to leave.'

That was a rather special case. Yet some diplomats do frequently abuse their right to immunity from the law. And mostly they do so with impunity. It disquiets. Often immunity means the protection of the diplomat not from trumped-up charges in unfriendly states – but from the need to obey self-evidently sensible laws that others have to heed.

Police in all capitals can give instances. In one typical case in London police stopped two Soviet diplomats driving the wrong way in a one-way street. One had almost certainly been drinking heavily. The diplomats claimed immunity. Perhaps the classic case happened in Bonn in 1966 when police tried to arrest the

Malawi ambassador on suspicion of drunken driving. He refused to be arrested. The ensuing fight lasted eighty minutes and involved ten policemen. Finally, the ambassador produced his diplomatic pass, and was allowed to go. One policeman had suffered a broken arm, another a broken thumb, and a third had a torn arm and ear.

The cases are varied: from shoplifting to assault (in one case in London, the wife of a Nigerian diplomat allegedly struck her dressmaker). Occasionally there is an especially ludicrous one: in Brisbane, Australia, the wife of a diplomat at the British High Commission claimed immunity after being charged with using a water sprinkler on her lawn in contravention of a local by-law.

Diplomats accredited to the United Nations have carried out a variety of lawless or anti-social acts. Among those officially recorded by the United States are: haphazard breaking of leases, disregarding road safety regulations (in two nights in May 1972 police recorded twenty-five instances of diplomatic cars parked in front of fire hydrants), and ignoring regulations that all drivers should carry public liability motor insurance.

The numbers are not inconsiderable. In England and Wales in one nine month period, in 1969, foreign diplomats avoided prosecution for 148 criminal acts, 130 of them for motoring offences ranging from exceeding speed limits to driving without lights.

Perhaps the immunity that causes most public aggression, however, is the diplomat's ability to park his car where he likes. A number of countries, including France, Spain, Italy and Portugal, have special licence plates for diplomatic cars. In Spain they are red or blue (alternate years) and in Portugal red on white instead of the normal white on blue. It ensures in some countries, such as France, that cars belonging to diplomats are strictly left alone by the police. In other countries their owners receive parking tickets – but, unless they wish, they are not bound to pay the fine. Most do not. The Americans are among the few who do; they have instructions from the State Department to pay – and with their own money. Communist diplomats rarely do. They claim that Western states give them too few parking spots and, so, will have to accept the consequence. The Hungarian embassy, one of the worst in London, has complained: 'Outside the British embassy in Budapest there is plenty of room for your people to park'.

In one ten month period in London the number of parking tickets issued to diplomats and unpaid totalled over 26,000. The missions that take most advantage of their immunity seem to be constant: Ghana, Hungary, Nigeria, Saudi Arabia, and Uganda. In Washington, where the worst offenders have been the Africans, Asians and Russians, the State Department has adopted a tough policy and insisted diplomats should pay fines for illegal parking. In the absence of such policies, publishing the names of the worst offenders regularly at least allows outraged motorists to vent their anger. Whenever details emerge in the British House of Commons (in reply to questions from Members of Parliament) missions receive postbags of abuse.

'This aspect of the campaign,' pontificated the magazine *The Diplomatist*, 'is most unpleasant and certainly does not help the diplomatic missions concerned to feel they are working in the happiest conditions possible'. The non-diplomat motorist who has troubles parking *his* car probably preferred the view of the London *Times* around the same date. Its comments included phrases like 'intolerable disregard' and 'an abuse of diplomatic privileges'.

Protocol

The diplomat, though not answerable to a country's laws, does have a complex set of self-imposed ethics and rules. He calls them protocol. These rules, diplomats have claimed, prevent the diplomat abroad from being a completely lawless animal.

To an outsider, though, the rules of protocol appear far more concerned with social niceties and the diplomat's status and treatment than they are with ensuring that he behaves. They should guarantee that the ambassador of Abracadabraland does not sit in the seat reserved for the ambassador from Toyland, but they will not stop him driving his car over the pavement nor smuggling the odd antique if he wishes.

Protocol, in fact, provides the stage-directions for the international diplomatic play. It tells the diplomat where to sit, what to wear, when to turn down the corner of his calling cards, and whether it is in order to *wear* decorations on his overcoat (a controversial question but bad taste, says one authority commenting on this last point).

There is a lot of it. *Diplomatic Ceremonial and Protocol* is over 350 pages long. There are diagrams showing who should sit where, pages of advice on the exchange of correspondence, and rules on when to wear white gloves and how to mourn ('when in official mourning, agents in uniform carry a black *crêpe* on the handle of their sword').

It can grind small: there is advice on what time flags should be raised and lowered, and whether to write in pencil or in ink on an envelope containing a visiting card (pencil when it is delivered by hand).

Despite all this, diplomats claim that in recent years it has been stripped of its inessentials: 'What remains,' says a western European chief of protocol, 'is both essential and sensible – and can be seen to be so. We have eliminated everything that is a hangover and which could give rise to ridicule.'

Protocol today, they argue, provides a framework in which diplomatic contacts can be carried out in an orderly fashion. 'The great misconception', a chief of protocol says, 'is that it's there to trip people up. Its purpose is precisely the opposite – to smooth the path and make things easier.' A former British protocol chief says: 'So much of it is so self-evidently practical. Take the rules on precedence for seating people at dinner. Without them, you'd just have people wandering around not knowing where to sit. Apart from anything else, the damned soup would get cold.'

It goes beyond this, however. The rules are meant to reflect the equality of all states. An ambassador considers a slight on him a snub to his country. Because of this protocol has political implications.

Each foreign ministry has a protocol section, headed by a chief who is usually a career diplomat of high rank. These sections negotiate the minefield of protocol with diplomats accredited to their countries. Chiefs of protocol are today highly conscious of the association between their work and the state of political relations between their own countries and other nations. 'What happens,' says one, 'is that a mission here looks at how well or badly or how fairly or unfairly we are treating them. How long do we take to get them visas to bring in foreign staff or to provide diplomatic licence plates for their motor cars? On things like this, they decide that they are getting generous or ungenerous treatment. And they see this as reflecting the way my government views their country and its policies.' There was a striking example of this during the India-Pakistan conflict. The Americans, who were strongly pro-Pakistan, consciously gave Indian diplomats 'second grade' treatment.

Chiefs of Protocol are the smoothest of smooth operators even in a profession that is hardly known for its roughnecks. The charm that is one of the good diplomat's trademarks is taken to its ultimate: seats are pulled back, cigarettes rapidly offered (and lit) and the opening minutes of conversations are occupied by sympathetic questions about the other's health, experiences and background. Every chief of protocol, one feels, would have gladdened the heart of Dale Carnegie.

To the diplomats within his country, the chief of protocol is a mixture of Emily Post, nursemaid and friendly uncle. He will advise on seating plans, try to pacify the ambassador of X if the ambassador for Y steals his cook, and, if diplomats seem to have time on their hands, he will try to keep them feeling busy, wanted and happy by arranging galas, dinners or concerts.

The chief of protocol is anxious not to offend. Emil Mosbacher, chief of protocol in Washington when Willy Brandt of Germany visited President Nixon, found himself with a special problem. An American moonshot, Apollo 13, was in danger because a back-up astronaut had developed *German* measles. Mosbacher rose to the occasion. Talking to pressmen, he referred to the ailment suffered by the American astronaut as '*so called German* measles'.

Every chief of protocol has to contend with what one calls 'the pathological complainers'. One explains: 'These are the diplomats who are always being victimised, and not accorded their proper status. Whatever you do, they cannot be satisfied. They are like old women.' Some individuals are notoriously more touchy than others, no matter where they are posted (I ruined one British ambassador's day by sitting on the wrong side of the passenger compartment of his car).

Certain countries also take protocol more seriously than do other nations. The Dutch, the French, the Spanish, and the Italians are all rigid in their attitudes to it. So, too, are the Communist states and, even more notably so, the smaller and newer nations. One chief of protocol also believes that in every capital it is possible to gauge the missions that will be most rigid by considering the amount of work their diplomats do: 'If you take the least busy and the most inefficient, you'll usually find the greatest sticklers for protocol.'

The most important rules of Protocol concern the precedence given to diplomats and how this is operated in practice. For several centuries there was no international agreement on the subject. The Pope, at the beginning of the sixteenth century, did draw up a list. Perhaps not unnaturally, other monarchs were not happy with his definitions of which of them were the most important.

At the top of the list was the Pope himself. Next came the Emperor, followed in third place by his heir apparent, with the king of France beating the king of Spain for the fourth position. With no acceptable agreement there were classic battles between French and Spanish ambassadors, both ordered by their sovereigns not to yield precedence to the other. In 1661 the French and Spanish ambassadors in London sent coaches to meet the new Swedish ambassador as he disembarked. The new ambassador was met by the Royal coach at Tower wharf. The struggle began when that coach moved off. The French coachman urged his vehicle into second place; the Spanish coachman decided this was an insult to his king. Both coaches were accompanied by about 150 armed men, and in the fight that resulted the French coachman was dragged to the ground, and a postilion was killed. It did not end there. The king of France, Louis XIV, threatened war unless the king of Spain apologised (which he did).

There was a similar squabble between French and Spanish ambassadors in The Hague. Their coaches met in a street too narrow to take both side by side. This time the issue was solved without bloodshed. It was finally decided to pull down a fence and thus widen the road so that neither coach would have to yield precedence to the other.

Precedence also preoccupied representatives at international conferences. Discussions over who should sit where were long and passionate. Then, at the end, there would be further negotiations over the order in which each should sign the treaty (partially solved by the invention of a device called the *alternat* by which every representative signed his own copy first).

The problem was finally tackled by the Congress of Vienna in 1815. It was agreed that heads of missions should take precedence according to the date of their official arrival in a country. This means that the longest serving ambassador in any capital is the senior. Next in the order of precedence comes the ambassador who has been at his post for the second-longest period, and so on. This rule is not international law, but it is observed by most countries. A notable exception is in Catholic countries where the Papal ambassador – known as the Nuncio – is automatically the senior.

The senior ambassador is known as the dean of doyen of the diplomatic corps and he acts as spokesman for his fellow diplomats on any collective matter affecting their rights or privileges. Because the position of doyen is special and of high status, smaller countries often keep their ambassadors at a post for a long time in order to achieve it. In London at the beginning of 1972, the doyen was the Luxembourg ambassador who had been at his post for seventeen years. In Washington in January 1970 it was the ambassador for Nicaragua who arrived there in 1943.

Rules of precedence also cover all other diplomats in a capital. Technical attachés too, for example, rank according to the time they have been there – but by custom, military attachés always rank above the other attachés.

Rules govern where diplomats rank in relation to other notables. In Britain ambassadors take precedence after members of the royal family having the title Royal Highness and certain very high state and church dignitaries; in France in official meetings the diplomatic corps is seated immediately after the head of state, the prime minister and the presidents of the assemblies.

Chiefs of protocol are often asked to adjudicate on specific cases. A British expert on protocol points out that it is not always easy: 'When someone rings up and says that he's got the Prime Minister, the Archbishop of Canterbury and the Chilean ambassador round to dinner and where does he seat them, all you can really say is that he can't: he should never have invited them together.'

Once they have been ranked, the seating follows prescribed rules, not only at table but in processions and in carriages. Take an official procession with five people in the first row, for example.

Where is the place of honour? Obviously in the centre. And with four in the front row? Then it is on the right side. In a ceremonial carriage with seats facing each other, the seat of honour is the rear right hand corner seat facing forward (all the other seats have a ranking also). And it is taken very seriously. An American ambassador who wanted to give a dinner in honour of a newly arrived fellow ambassador found he could not – because all the other ambassadors outranked the newcomer who could not therefore be placed in the seat of honour.

Chiefs of Protocol say they try to exercise commonsense as well as the rule book when advising on seating plans. 'It's much more important that you should have people next to each other who can talk than that everyone is in their proper places.'

This is a particularly acute problem today: 'The more new countries you get, the more nations that are on bad terms and not speaking to each other,' says one protocol chief. 'Precedence by itself is no good any more. Go by the book and you might get Lebanon next to Israel.' Another says: 'It is not just the countries that are fairly constant enemies. Relations between two states may be good today, so-so tomorrow and awful the day after. You have to know the present mood. On top of that there's the question of individuals – every capital has a few ambassadors who won't talk to each other.'

Farcical situations do arise, however: 'I was at dinner the other evening, and there were three people sitting together with not a language in common,' says an ambassador. Chiefs of Protocol concede it happens, but only when they are powerless: 'You have to remember that some people insist on being in their proper place. Sometimes when you see a suggested seating plan, you spot a name and have to *insist* that he must be placed higher up.'

Protocol covers more than where a diplomat should sit, stand or walk in any given situation. There are the most detailed rules on dress and decorations. Before World War I the majority of diplomats and consuls had special uniforms, part of which was generally an embroidered cap or hat. Since the end of World War II many new countries have decided against uniforms for their diplomats, but there are still nations with splendid costumes – Britain, Denmark, France, Iran, Laos, Netherlands and Russia among them.

These are worn on specified occasions, among them official ceremonies in which the head of the receiving state takes part. Some African and Asian diplomats wear national constumes on such occasions.

The United States is a major country without a special uniform. Originally, Benjamin Franklin practised his diplomacy in an old coat. He then decided to conform and devised a uniform, albeit simple. In 1817 American diplomats were given a rather more splendid court dress that included a gold-embroidered cape, white knee breeches with gold buckles, a three-cornered hat, and a sword. That remained until the time of President Jackson who decided his diplomats should return to 'the simple dress' of their fellow citizens.

Special uniforms or not, the rules of dress are always quite specific – covering day and evening, formal and informal. The kinds of shirts, ties, collars, gloves, hats, shoes, overcoats and decorations are spelled out. Formal dress after 7 p.m., for example, is ordained as white waistcoat, white starched shirt with a straight collar and corners turned back, black patent leather shoes, white chamois gloves, a top or opera or cocked hat, and a black cape or a black overcoat with silk lapels. In the daytime for official proctocol meetings that do not call for special uniforms, the right garb is a morning coat and top hat.

Diplomats of some countries are often festooned with decorations given by foreign nations. The practice developed when governments forbade their diplomats to accept cash bribes. One Portuguese ambassador's current list of decorations read: Grand Cross Military Order of Christ, Portugal; Grand Cross Piana Order, Holy See; Grand Cross, Order of Cruzeiro do Sul, Brazil; Grand Cross, National Order of Merito, Brazil; Grand Cross of Orange-Nassau, Netherlands; Grand Cross of St Olav, Norway; Grand Cross, Order of Ouissan Alacuite, Morocco; Grand Cross, Order of Al Merito, Peru; Grand Cross of Merit of the Sovereign and Military Order of Malta; Grand Officer, Legion of Honour, France; Commander, Order of the Crown, Italy; Officer, Order of the Oaken Crown, Luxembourg; Knight, Order of Leopold I and the Order of the Crown, Belgium; Knight, Order of the Star, Romania; and Commemorative Medal of the Coronation of H.M. King George VI, United Kingdom.

Portugal is one of the countries where home-agreement is needed before the diplomat can accept a foreign decoration. Others include France, Germany, Austria and Spain and those with a monarchy.

A few governments, notably the British and the American, will not allow their diplomats to accept foreign decorations except in the most exceptional circumstances ('My dogs shall only wear my collars,' George III is said to have remarked). But for those who do, the rules of protocol ensure that their diplomats will jangle in an officially-correct manner.

There is rigid protocol over calling-cards. Newly arrived diplomats send their cards to diplomats at other embassies in the capital. The diplomat needs four different sorts of cards: his official ones that carry his name, rank and address; private ones that bear only his name; ones in the name of his wife; and (except in Britain) joint cards for him and his wife.

The protocol of calling cards is fraught with pitfalls: a woman, for example, *never* leaves her card at a bachelor's house. If the card is delivered by hand (good form) the corner is turned up. 'Some people', said Wood and Serres who go into the lore in detail, 'attach significance to the manner in which this operation is effected, according to which corner, the upper or lower, is turned back etc. To avoid this convention it is advisable to fold the card along the entire left side.' The handwritten 'P.P.C.' on a card signifies 'pour prendre congé' (to take leave) – sent when the diplomat is moving posts. There are others, among them 'P.R.' ('pour remercier') to say thank you for hospitality, and 'P.C.' ('pour condoléances') to express sympathy at some personal or national tragedy.

Much of protocol is ceremonial recognition of the special status of the diplomat. In all countries, no matter how large or small, newly arrived ambassadors present their letters of credence to the chief of state. The ceremonial varies according to the country, but it is usually splendid.

The ambassador, in his full uniform if his service has one, is collected in a state car or carriage. In Spain, his carriage will be drawn by six horses. In London there will be a horse-drawn coach with footmen at the rear. His staff follow him in other vehicles, military attachés resplendent in their dress uniforms.

If the country is a monarchy, he is greeted by the court chamberlain and the foreign minister. In the throne room he bows the required number of times on the way in, hands over his credentials, and may or may not make a short speech. There are moments of chat before the ambassador presents his staff and then walks out backwards. If the ambassador does deliver a short speech, it should be confined to formal platitudes. To mention any subject of controversy is a breach of etiquette. From that moment on the ambassador can enjoy the rich assortment of his protocol privileges. A British ambassador is entitled to a 19 gun salute (his prime minister, incidentally, is not entitled to one at all – 'a quite proper state of affairs', commented one British ambassador at the time his P.M. was Harold Wilson, a leader low in the diplomatic popularity stakes).

Ambassadors also have the right to fly the flag of their country over their embassy offices and official residences. Some American ambassadors have flown a special ambassadorial flag on their cars (dark blue with thirteen white stars) as well as the American flag. British ambassadors have a special flag showing the royal arms in the centre of the Union Jack.

And should there be circumstances when flags of a number of nations are flown above an embassy, the order in which they are placed is of course determined by . . . precedence.

Seven

The Ambassadors

'The job of an ambassador is much like that of an
airline pilot – there are hours of boredom and
minutes of panic.'
J. K. Galbraith, former U.S. ambassador

The ambassador is the aristocrat of the diplomatic profession.
Among the protected, the pampered and the insulated, he is the
most so. He represents his country's Head of State; his full title
has the ring of Royal Courts – 'Ambassador Extraordinary and
Plenipotentiary', even if the 'plenipotentiary' (it means 'full-
powered') has little real significance today.

Abroad he *is* his country ('I'm Mr America here,' says one
U.S. ambassador). He presents its views, argues its case, reports
back to it. He lays wreaths, takes part in ceremonies, and lives and
moves in surroundings closer to palaces than two-bedroom apartments.

As head of his embassy, he is also a leader of men. He may
have learned, and near-forgotten, over a half-dozen languages.
The most famous quote made about him, by Sir Henry Wotton,
ambassador to James I, was 'An ambassador is a honest man sent
abroad to lie for his country'. But he will say that complete
honesty is the one essential of his trade.

The ambassador may be a full-time career diplomat, or he may
be a political appointee – either because of his exceptional suit-
ability, or because of his Head of State's need to pay off a political
debt. Those of some countries may be qualified purely by nepo-
tism and be a president's cousin or a king's uncle. A few, because
of their trouble-making potential if they are allowed to remain
at home, may be sent abroad as an ambassador to what is really
a luxury banishment.

Despite the status, the ambassador profession is a crowded one.
Today there are so many of them. In 1940 the United States had

fifty-five ambassadors; in the 1970s it now has over 120. Following World War I there were about 1,100 embassies and legations in the world; now there are well over 4,000.

According to one school of thought, in the age of the H-bomb, the need for ambassadors is greater than ever. According to another, they are obsolete. John Kenneth Galbraith himself a former ambassador, has written of the American ambassador to Britain: 'apart from making appointments for visiting brass, sometimes going along on the visit, and passing on routine messages, the American ambassador does nothing. . . . The American ambassador is an anachronism, kept alive by a conspiracy between the occupants of the post and those who eat at his expense. Intelligent men who perpetuate his myth should hang their heads in shame.'

Just what ambassadors do is a puzzlement even to many whose lives bring them into contact with them. 'There are always a number of people who ask what I do?' one British ambassador says. 'The only reason more don't ask, I think, is that they're too polite.' His standard explanation, like many of his colleagues, is to give four subject headings: interpreting his own country; reporting doings in the country to which he is accredited; trying to help his country's trade; and representing – 'being my country's presence and spreading information about it'.

Most would agree that their impact today is not large; equally they would claim that their role, though modest, is vital. 'Our modest daily accomplishments are not noted because like happy marriages, they are not newsworthy,' says one Belgian. It's easy to fall into one of the extreme camps which, on one side, believe ambassadors are sometimes still powerful enough to change history, and, on the other, that they are no more than storekeepers and messengers.

Yet at most posts the 'modest daily accomplishments' indeed look modest. One British ambassador described his role as 'smoothing the hinges: not doing positive things, but keeping in touch so that when something happens, you can go click, click, click'. Pressed on what kind of things, he instanced a visit of his foreign minister. The minister's aircraft was due to land at 9.15; his first meeting was due to start fifteen minutes later. It would be impossible to cover the distance from the airport in the time. There

was, however, a new road, not yet opened. 'Because of my contacts I was able to make two calls and get the road specially
opened.'

A number of European ambassadors in London in 1972, talked
to on the same day, instanced one example, more positive but,
bearing in mind the cost of an embassy and an ambassador,
achieved at high price. A newspaper reported that the British
Prime Minister might suggest that the European Community
summit conference due to take place in Paris later in the year
might be held in London. With the French voicing doubts about
the conference and President Pompidou meeting that day with
Chancellor Brandt in Bonn many nations were interested in the
accuracy or otherwise of the report. Their ambassadors 'phoned
the British Prime Minister's office and were told that the story
was not inspired, but was totally incorrect.

Much of an ambassador's time is spent putting himself on
show as 'M. France' or 'Mr Britain' or 'Herr Germany'. Outside those occasions his working life is often remarkably monot-
onous.

A Western European ambassador posted to North America
described his typical day as being: Into the office at 9.30, after
reading the newspapers, and then spending half an hour studying
overnight cables waiting on his desk. At ten he has a meeting
with the heads of sections where they go through telegrams, share
information, and discuss what should be done. He deals with
papers until a business lunch. There is usually a visitor in the
morning (today a journalist) and one in the afternoon (this day a
businessman). Evenings are usually 'diplomatic dining around'.
He visits the foreign ministry rarely because 'most of the stuff
is done lower down the line'.

An ambassador in London opens his diary at what he says is a
typical week: Monday, visitor for coffee; giving lunch; afternoon
visitor. Tuesday, courtesy calls morning and afternoon (he is new
and calling on other ambassadors); a lunch; and a dinner in the
evening as guest of honour. Wednesday, two courtesy calls; lunch
at the embassy; dinner party. Thursday, visitors morning and
afternoon; a guest for lunch. Friday, four visitors. Saturday, Ascot.
'In between,' he says, 'I prepare my reports. And you always
find that your senior colleagues are queued up to consult you.'

Ambassadors as urbane and intelligent individuals impress more than the work they are called on to do (although there are occasional exceptions like the Italian who was receiving visitors at 10.30 a.m. after a late night – in bed, giving them an opportunity to admire the beautiful purple of his sheets).

Any diary will show large numbers of lunches, dinners and cocktail parties, often two or more an evening. One African still in tails after a morning reception, strode back into his embassy obviously highly delighted. He then reported a rather nondescript, brief conversation he had had on a landing with a local notable. 'And this,' he concluded, 'is what they say is just drinking whiskies.'

This is not to claim that ambassadors are without any impact. The way an ambassador behaves, the way with which he carries his messages must necessarily have some importance. He may have to be skilful in explaining an unpopular policy, sympathetic in listening to a minister's fears. But it remains that the crucial factor will always be the *content* of the messages.

An ambassador's task may simply be to keep some lines of communication available between his own government and an unfriendly one. Llewellyn Thompson was U.S. ambassador to Moscow during a period that included the Bay of Pigs, crisis in the Lebanon and the U–2 incident. Even keeping a surface dialogue going was difficult. On one occasion months after pilot Gary Powers was shot down in a U–2 reconnaissance plane, Khrushchev trampled on Thompson's foot at a Kremlin reception, saying: 'If I do that to you, I ought to apologise. Your government ought to have apologised.' 'The Soviet Union,' Thompson replied, 'spied without apology on the United States.' By this time, other guests were gathering around. Anastas Mikoyan intervened: 'Maybe it was Mrs Thompson's fault – women are always starting something,' he said, facetiously. 'Yes, it was all my fault,' Mrs Thompson agreed, 'and let's not talk about it any more.'

American officials point to the fact that during this period America and Russia reached the first of a series of agreements for cultural exchanges, and that as a result of the ambassador's work the two countries kept talking on a range of subjects, laying the foundations for later agreement to ban atmospheric nuclear tests.

An ambassador may still try to make policy on minor matters. 'Sometimes,' says one American based in Africa, 'I say I'm going to go ahead and do this unless you tell me not to. Then they have to sort out whether to overrule you. But it's something that can't be done often. It's too easy to lose credence – and your job.' Another believes some effect on policy can be achieved by asking for instructions at the last moment. 'Say I fix an appointment two weeks in advance. I wouldn't tell them at home until two days before. If necessary, I'd blame it on the man I'm seeing – say that he'd asked to see me. This way, there's less time at home for too many to get involved, and your view gets more taken into account.' But these latitudes do not apply to major topics: 'No ambassador can *ad hoc* on things like Berlin or the Common market or on bases in Panama,' says a French diplomat. 'There the instruction would be most precise.'

Ambassadors work hard on the reports they send home: the style is at least as important as the content. One of the best compliments one can pay of another is that he 'writes well'. There is infinite care to combine the facts and the interpretation with fine writing, although in some cases it simply means over-long messages.

The content of reports appears to range from the abysmal to the brilliant. Reading one ambassador's report on the British political scene, it was hard to believe that it could not have been bettered by a young newspaper reporter. Others impress. Kim Philby has referred to the embarrassment caused during World War II by the Spanish ambassador's despatches of 'quite exceptional quality' (British intelligence had access to the Spanish diplomatic bag). 'As we had no doubt that the Spanish Foreign Ministry would make them available to their German allies, these despatches represented a really serious leakage. Yet there was nothing that could be done. There was no evidence that the Duke (of Alba) had obtained his information improperly. He simply moved with people in the know and reported what they said, with shrewd commentaries of is own.' (Without detracting from the Duke's skills, it should be noted, however, that this constituted a very special period of time.)

Even though there are temptations to report what the foreign ministry and the minister would like to hear, the amount of sometimes unwelcome objectivity is impressive. Long before British Labour leader Harold Wilson talked of a united Ireland, diplomats had been stressing this was the only long-term solution.

Some of the ambassador's time may be spent as a direct publicist or propagandist for his country. This can involve praising his nation's products. Esther Herlitz, as Israel's ambassador to Copenhagen, spent much of her time extolling avocados, oranges, frozen dates and egg plants. 'I couldn't cease from my labours on behalf of the avocada until Danish television had done a programme on how to serve them, then I knew my work was done,' she said. 'I could now turn my attention to the egg plant.'

It may mean opening exhibitions, dining industrialists – and, at its simplest, an ambassador praising his own car. At an extreme it can mean an attempt to 'interfere' in the internal events of the host country.

At one time Irish diplomats attempted to make use of the lobbying powers of the large Irish community in the United States to win support for their country's policies.

During the 1972 American election campaign, Israel's ambassador in Washington gave an interview with Israel radio which, to most, was seen as a call to the Jewish community to vote for Richard Nixon. 'I cannot recall any other president who undertook such commitments towards Israel as Nixon in the Moscow summit,' he said. (Later he claimed the quote was taken out of context and the Israeli prime minister made a statement saying Israel was neutral. But by then the message had been given.)

More normally, however, ambassadors spend much of their time in the publicity and propaganda field reacting to events – as apologists rather than instigators. This is particularly so of representatives of unpopular regimes. The South African ambassador in London protests to the British Broadcasting Corporation that a documentary film is malicious; the Greek ambassador criticises the London *Times* for a leading article headed 'A more complete tyranny in Greece'; the Dominican ambassador writes a long letter to the *Financial Times* extolling the virtues of his president after the paper queried them. Meanwhile, in Rawalpindi the British high commissioner is apologising to Pakistan for a *Times* article on the Muslim religion, and in Beirut the Soviets

protest that the showing of a film containing torture scenes during the Stalin era will harm relations between the two countries.

Whatever they do, ambassadors are made to feel important.
They are eagerly sought after as guests at events. Local dignitaries covet their presence. In Australia, different States compete
with each other to entertain them. And they like this, just as they
enjoy the circles within which they move. 'You are dealing with
quite important and interesting things – basically with what makes
countries tick,' a Western ambassador says. 'This is enormous fun
– just the stimulus of being next to the centre of things.'

They dislike 'amateurs' who do not play the game according
to the set rules. One ambassador, frequently given the task of
transmitting his country's anti-American views to the State Department, is constantly annoyed by the tartness of the Americans.
He is a professional doing his duty; the job of American officials
is to be equally professional, accepting the views impersonally.

They dislike Governments who do 'unprofessional' things. 'The
worst thing,' one British ambassador says, 'is being put on the
carpet by the foreign ministry for something your country should
not have done and over which it – and you – are in the wrong.
Things like your government imposing a trade restriction on
some commodity and not notifying the other government even
though there is an obligation to consult, or flying an aircraft
through their air space without permission. You get a feeling
you've been let down by your own side.'

They also dislike 'gimmicky' politicians. 'During Robert
Kennedy's time,' says an American, 'you'd get messages fired
off to about 900 people, saying "tell us what the young think
about x". We'd all jump because we knew it was Bobby doing
his youth thing. Now no one would pay any attention to it.'

To do these things, ambassadors cost money – a lot of money.
In 1970 the British ambassador to France was being paid £9800
a year, receiving an allowance of £26,755 a year, and the embassy was costing over £1 million a year to run (and he has since
received a pay rise). The British Chancellor of the Exchequer,
told the House of Commons in December 1971 that the British
embassies in Paris or Bonn cost more to run than Buckingham
Palace, and the total cost of all aspects of the British monarchy
were little more than the cost of the embassy in Washington.

To cut the apparent cost, ambassadors are sometimes accredited to more than one country. Britain recently decided on its first London-based ambassador – a departure that seemed more exciting than it proved. The head of the West African Department became ambassador to Chad while retaining his Whitehall desk 3,500 miles away. Previously is was covered by an ambassador who had to serve five central African states, and was based in Yaoundé. It proved little more than a courtesy appointment, a special arrangement to meet a particular problem, because the former ambassador in Yaoundé recommended his successor should have fewer countries under his umbrella.

But for some at least, it brought visions of courtesy ambassadors being exchanged but staying in their own countries. 'Such an arrangement carried out internationally,' said one cynic, 'would at least cut out the time-wasting of socialising and the trappings that surround their presence abroad.' One of these trappings is 'making calls', a tradition that, to an outsider, appears ridiculous. A new ambassador is required by diplomatic etiquette to call on other heads of mission and his wife on their wives, although some ambassadors in capitals with a very large corps now take a harder line and call only on a number of their colleagues. Even so, the number rarely falls below thirty, and calls are returned. Even diplomats and ex-diplomats have called it an anachronism. But it continues, and it has to be stressed because of the vast amount of an ambassador's time it consumes and because it is a notable example of a diplomatic practice that has no end product but itself.

Biddle Duke, former U.S. ambassador to Spain and El Salvador, has claimed that calling on the 120 ambassadors resident in Washington 'is a useful exercise'. One newly arrived ambassador in London deep-enmeshed in paying his calls, admitted that afterwards he would not be dealing with more than about a quarter of the ambassadors involved. But calling was 'the done thing and I think it's essential. It's no longer *de rigueur* here to call on all, but one must be careful not to give offence. If one is too selective in the process of choosing which countries to call on, it may be taken amiss.' When ambassadors return his calls, he gives them tea or coffee if it's morning, a drink if the time is after noon. Making all his calls, he estimated, would take him about a year.

It is also like painting the Forth Bridge: by the time calls are finished, there are more to make because new ambassadors have arrived. In one brief period in London in 1970, fifteen new ambassadors and high commissioners started work and all set out on their calling rounds. Yet even those who complain continue with the ritual. In diplomacy, it is hard to scrap an obsolete part of the machine. J. K. Galbraith said of the practice: 'Though tedious, it is for many members of the profession a valuable alternative to unemployment.' In a letter to President Kennedy, he called it 'an incredible waste of time', and in his diary, 'endless and futile'. Yet, in his own words, he did 'struggle on nobly' and finished them.

Making calls is perhaps the most obviously ludicrous of the traditions and trappings of the protocol of ambassadors, although it is far from being the only one. Ambassadors are lined up to see visiting heads of state. An Asian ambassador, who in a short period of time, had been summoned to meet the Japanese emperor, the Grand Duke of Luxembourg and others he could no longer recall without effort, complained that the only purpose was 'to shake their hands. And that took most of a day each time.'

The standard of living for ambassadors in many countries is of the height that could otherwise be enjoyed only by a millionaire. There will be a huge and elegant house, servants, a chauffeur-driven large car, and perhaps the use of an air attaché's aircraft. The transition to this wonderland existence can begin immediately on arrival in a new country, with their staff specially rounded up to meet them. It continues with the ritual involved in presenting credentials to the head of state.

The ambassador's residence may range from splendid to magnificent. The American ambassador's home in Buenos Aires occupies 42,000 square feet – and is described as being 'as big as the Museum of Natural History'. The British ambassador's residence in Washington has the elegance and pomp of a long-gone age with its cut glass chandeliers, dark panelled walls, silent servants and swimming pool and tennis court nearby. The summer residence of the Russian ambassador to America has thirty-five rooms; the American ambassador in Moscow occupies a massive mansion.

The Spanish ambassador's residence in London, an imposing building on the corner of Belgrave Square, has marble floors, enormous oils, wall size tapestries, antique furniture, silver cigarette boxes dotted everywhere, and a dining-room for fifty people.

It is not just ambassadors from larger nations. All live well, and in the richest, most luxurious areas. The home of the Moroccan ambassador to London in the early 1970s had its own Moroccan pavilion.

At the grandest residences there are silent butlers of the type who can estimate the cost of a visitor's suit – accurately – in three seconds without staring. As you leave, they stand immobile, umbrella outstretched for you to take as you pass.

Not surprisingly, ambassadors behave like men born to enjoy such privilege. Even in private, in the most relaxed settings, they keep their aura. At a small dinner party, taking place quietly and unofficially at a continental pavement café, a group, including the British ambassador, sat with jackets off, ties undone. But the chief of staff was still called, 'The Ambassador'; the group still waited for him to give permission for them to smoke.

As with the making of calls, some ambassadors will act apologetic – they don't really like it but. . . . 'I feel crazy being called Excellency at every turn,' one says. 'But the communists and the new nations are very insistent on the practice.'

Admit it or not, ambassadors love their status. The British Labour Government, under Harold Wilson, took a slightly harder line than predecessors in giving lesser ambassadors knighthoods. One who had not received one (although his predecessors in the post, serving under a different government, had) bemoaned: 'I don't mind for myself but the servants don't understand. They try to pretend it hasn't happened; they call the Ambassadress "Milady" and me "Excellency" or "The Ambassador".'

The special status can exist right through to death. If an ambassador is unlucky enough to die at his post the funeral service traditionally includes military honours.

In private, some ambassadors will debate whether all this privilege should not be scrapped. 'Sometime,' says one Spanish ambassador, 'someone is going to have to question whether it's appropriate for us to be in large mansions with servants, pursuing a pattern of life which is no longer related to that enjoyed by anyone else around us. When diplomacy started, other people were living like it. Now there's a great gap.'

Another, a Canadian, agrees, but adds: 'How you alter it, I don't know. Entertaining people in hotels and clubs just isn't the same. So you have to have a plant. The trouble is that the plant we use now is out of all relationship. There is no longer any comparison between the lives of the people and the lives of the diplomats.'

Entertaining and being entertained takes a large part of an ambassador's time. Sir Douglas Busk, a former British ambassador, estimates in *The Craft of Diplomacy*, that in the course of a year the British ambassador in Paris will give beds to the extent of 250 'house-guest nights', meals to not far short of 2,000 persons, and drinks or teas to another 1,800 – not counting the annual reception in honour of the Queen's birthday, which will average 2,800. In a very small embassy the total would probably be 20 house guests, 500 meals, 900 for drinks and teas and 400 for the Queen's Birthday Party.

Wise diplomats formulate and practise their own eating and drinking rules, and they boast a drunken ambassador is rare. One practises a policy of never drinking *after* dinner; another rations himself to one drink per party – 'I have this ability to hold a drink'. Another insists on straight tomato juice; a fourth, rations drinks, and always leaves a third of his food on the plate, and tries to get out of a reception in 25 minutes 'although you have to gauge what is a respectable time after you arrive'.

Nevertheless, socialising is punishing ('it's the drip, drip, drip of drinking night after night, not the big booze-up' one says). 'I now try to be selective,' another says. 'You can't go to three receptions a night unless you want to be a corpse.' One ambassador and his wife, about to leave their post looked ill after three weeks of farewell parties given by fellow ambassadors, and confessed they 'felt awful'.

The man who reports, negotiates and represents is also expected to be something else: a manager of men. Apart from diplomatic qualifications, he should be able to lead and run his own embassy. This management role is a difficult, and yet crucial one, in an age when embassies are often mini-Governmental setups.

In theory, there is no doubt about the ambassador's authority over everyone at the mission. In the American service it has been reaffirmed in letters from Presidents Eisenhower, Kennedy and Nixon, and in Canada, in 1970 in a series of review documents, *Foreign Policy for Canadians*. These stressed that 'the Government has decided that heads of post abroad must be given clear authority over all operations at the post in accordance with approved operational plans; and the head of post must represent and be accountable for all departments' interests in his area of jurisdiction.'

Some ambassadors would claim that in more recent years the position has improved: the Kennedy letter of 1961, for example, was hailed by one U.S. ambassador as 'solving' the problem of directors of larger aid missions who negotiated direct with governments ('the governments were happy to talk with them because they were the guys with the cash'). But even if the ambassador has the paper authority he still has to enforce it. An American ambassador summed up the problem this way: 'Under the various presidential letters you have all the authority in the world – provided you don't exercise it. What can you do, for example, if you think there are too many other agency people at your mission? Except in the case of misconduct, you can't go up to someone and say, "You are not doing a damn thing; go home". You have to negotiate with his agency in Washington. And the fight can go on for a long time.'

If there are tense relationships between the foreign ministry and another department, an ambassador will sometimes go out of his way to ensure he does not 'interfere'. One Canadian immigration attaché got drunk publicly on several occasions, once rolled over some tables, and on another occasion molested women. His behaviour was widely known – except in the immigration department at home which, because the ambassador kept quiet, was the last to hear.

Even over his foreign service staff, an ambassador's management capabilities are limited: 'I can't dismiss them; I can't alter their pay; and I can't dramatically alter the jobs they do.'

One ambassador believes there are only two ways of trying to deal with the control problem in practice. 'An ambassador does have certain things going for him; with his own staff he does write an evaluation of each man. It becomes a document that can never be destroyed. So a damning report is something any man wants to avoid. And he does control cable facilities: a telegram can't be got out without him knowing. But of course he can't control other lines of communication. I remember an officer concurring with a cable and then writing to say he disagreed. It's only luck you hear of it. I threw out one man who did that. I told his agency I wouldn't have a liar who concurred at a public meeting and then went behind my back. I'm not saying that we should close lines of communication, but it's a question of loyalty.'

Another pointed out with representatives of home agencies an ambassador had one weapon: 'If you think money is being wasted, you can keep making that obvious in your cables.'

In replacing members of his own staff, an ambassador often feels he is not given a wide enough selection or that the candidates are not described candidly enough: 'Usually we're presented with a *fait accompli*', one complains. 'The system doesn't give us enough alternatives.'

At the same time, the ambassador is regarded as the head of the family to his mission staff. But too close a contact is ruled out by the rigid social structure of the foreign service and of a mission. The ambassador and his wife are at the top, high above anyone else. *Social Usage Abroad* devotes a page to the responsibilities of staff to their chiefs of mission.

There is a great gulf between the ambassador and his diplomatic staff. A young Australian likens him to 'a king on a small island', and a Spanish first secretary says that being at an embassy is 'like being in a submarine, and the ambassador is the commander'. The ambassador to his staff is like a Victorian father. Staff don't mind this; the status of the ambassador is part of their profession, admired both in itself and as a goal (just as the courturier dresses of an ambassador's wife at a major post are a spur to foreign service wives). What they do want is an ambassador who backs them, has some power in the system and knows of their existence.

Sometimes they also want to keep him out of the way – 'Our last ambassador went off for days shooting and fishing,' says a British head of chancery. 'That was good because it kept him out of the way. The trouble with this one is that he is around too much.' A French diplomat agreed: he felt every ambassador should have a healthy outdoor interest, and he envied his colleagues at another mission whose chief was a golf fanatic.

Pampered and praised, ambassadors often believe they are more loved than they actually are. One prided himself on his contact with local people and particularly with the large local staff. When he left there was a collection among the local staff. It raised less than $8. His diplomatic staff, quietly, made it up to a considerably larger amount – and preserved his illusions.

Not all the world's ambassadors are professional diplomats by any means. Many of them are direct political appointees. America, which fills many of its most attractive posts this way, is the best-known example. But other nations use political appointees too – sometimes infrequently and for sensible, practical reasons. But in other cases they are used regularly, often as part of the 'spoils' game – in return for political support or financial contributions.

The number of such appointees may depend on the government in power or the reigning foreign minister. Washington for years was regarded as a political appointment in the Australian service, but was then switched to one for career diplomats. A recent Spanish foreign minister believed in a number of political appointments; his successor was much more in favour of using members of the diplomatic service.

There are strong arguments for using some politically-appointed ambassadors. Overall, a few of them help to break through the excess caution which permeates most diplomatic services. A high-powered political ambassador – like, say, Lord Cromer, appointed to Washington by British Prime Minister Edward Heath – has the great advantage over the career ambassador of enjoying direct access to his own country's leader. (For that reason, Lord Cromer's predecessor John Freeman, appointed by a Labour Government, was rightly or wrongly regarded as not enjoying this special relationship once Heath came to power.) He will also find it easier to make unpopular reports than a career man.

Another advantage is that he can more easily, openly, represent his *Government's* views (which are sometimes different from those of his country as a whole). Christopher Soames, as

British ambassador in Paris, for example, could make speeches strongly in favour of Britain's entry into the Common Market – a step not favoured by the opposition nor the mass of the public (his utterances made the anti-Common Market *Sunday Express* say he 'should stick to the job at which he is so good – passing canapés at cocktail parties').

But the bulk of politically appointed ambassadors are not men of special capabilities, placed in posts to which they can bring special advantages. '*If* they were,' one career ambassador says, 'it would be great. But some of them are clots, laughing stock . . . they make you shudder.'

Diplomats of many nations argue that there is a little sense in a system that says that a good businessman or engineer or newspaper magnate necessarily makes a good diplomat, a job that calls for basic qualities, experience and training. 'No one,' says a Spanish ambassador, 'would expect I could replace a man at the top of, say, the engineering profession. Surely, it is just as nonsensical to think that man could do my job.' In pre-Castro Cuba American ambassadors were men without diplomatic experience and without knowledge of the language.

A number of countries, claim American career diplomats, are sent a procession of 'third rate political hacks'. Tiny Luxembourg, at least, rebelled. After a succession of political appointees, it hinted it would be displeased with another. It then received a career man – although that situation was soon changed again. (The famous Perle Mesta, ambassador to Luxembourg from 1949–1953 and the inspiration for 'Call me Madam' earned herself the nickname of 'Perle Harbour' among U.S. career men for her antics.)

John Foster Dulles once told a press conference: 'I would be very sorry if there was any rule that because a person contributed to a political campaign fund, he was thereby disqualified from being an ambassador.' And, of course, there is no such disqualification. The result is that political appointees at times occupy every Western European post and several other pleasant ones. In Spring 1970, about thirty per cent of the ambassadorial posts of the U.S. were held by political appointees. 'You won't find one in Upper Volta, or places like that,' says one career ambassador. 'They're after the nice, civilised spots.'

An American political ambassador normally gets an experienced professional assigned to him as deputy chief of mission or counsellor, and often another professional or personal assistant 'to keep the ambassador informed of diplomatic usage and to reduce his diplomatic gaffs to a minimum'.

The number two job is a key one. It can be pleasant, but more often murderous. One deputy, whose ambassador flies half across Europe to catch a show or a party says: 'I have two problems. The first is knowing where he is. Then, when I do, it's keeping him on the track I know the U.S. is committed to following. But he wants to mark his presence on the post. Often he tells me what his position is on something – and I know he's not in possession of all the information. I'm in a hell of a ticklish situation. I have to dispute it with him, though all I'm trying to do is see he gets the facts he should have had in the first place.'

Apart from paying off political debts, a major factor is that in some capitals only a millionaire can do the job. John D. Weaver in *The Great Experiment*, commented: 'If Congress were to forbid the President to appoint an ambassador to London, Paris or Rome unless he happened to be a millionaire, outraged commoners would storm the barricades, but no one seems to care when in effect, the same limitation is imposed by a Congressional combination of modest salaries and miserly allowances.'

It is not just Americans who need wealth to fill some posts. It happens with many of the smaller nations. Kuwaiti ambassadors in Beirut, Cairo and London are expected to entertain visiting nationals. Cairo is a relatively cheap city, but in the other two capitals at least it means that the ambassador has to reach deep into his own pocket. Every summer 10–14,000 Kuwaitis visit London. Because Kuwait is so small people know each other, and expect hospitality abroad. On Saturday alone, the ambassador invites between forty and fifty to lunch at his own expense. He is not forced to do so, but if he did not he would be criticised widely at home.

But this is less disquieting than what is happening with the most major powers.

The ambassadorship of Walter Annenberg in London illustrates many facets of the American practice. Annenberg, whose newspapers and fortune backed the Nixon bid for president,

can fairly be said to have bought his post. His period of ambassador proved flamboyant from his arrival – starting when he was
accused of 'queue-cutting' when handing his credentials to the
Queen ahead of other ambassadors. To protect him from bad
publicity, he needed two personal assistants.

He has lived in style, spending on his residence in London, a reputed £400,000. Veteran Paris journalist Sam White referred to
his 'interior decorating exploits' as constituting 'one of the latter
day wonders of the Western world.' One of the more dramatic
features is the chinoiserie wallpaper, showing birds and butter-
flies fluttering around trees, which was stripped off the walls of an
old house in Ireland, dry-cleaned in New York, touched up in
Hong Kong, stuck on canvas and placed in the garden room.

Annenberg is a good example of the kind of ambassador the
system can produce: ostentatious, sweet but naive, having to be
watched by an anxious following wondering what he will do next.
But that said, it is worth considering whether the job merits
anyone more qualified? The task of the American ambassador in
London is mostly non-existent. He does not have to woo the
British Government; it is the British that have to do the persuading and this is done at the Washington end. What Annenberg
has done with his wealth is act as a superb publicist: his
paintings, including works by Monet, Picasso and Van Gogh,
were loaned to the Tate Gallery for the public to see them; when
an Englishman's garden was wrecked by vandals and the Englishman died trying to right the damage, Annenberg offered to see it
was restored; he gave £40,000 to improve Chequers, the British
Prime Minister's country home; $10,000 to St Paul's Cathedral;
and financed a book on Westminster Abbey. 'One thing I will
say for him,' admitted one detractor, 'is that he's the only foreign
ambassador in Britain whose name is known to the people here'.

Ambassadors are expected to have all the qualities of a good
diplomat, only more so. And ambassadors should behave *like*
ambassadors: a retired Dutch ambassador's farewell tribute was
that he behaved like a swan – 'elegant and serene on the surface,
but underneath paddling like hell'. A French diplomat commented: 'If someone said that about me I'd be very happy.'

A key quality needed is moral courage. Part of this involves an
intellectual honesty: 'You do need guts in a lot of places – guts not

to mind being unpopular with the government to which you are accredited,' says an Australian. 'There's often a temptation to tone down your instructions, and not say things as firmly as you should. It's part of the normal desire to be liked.'

There's an equal temptation to report in a way that will bring liking back home. For American diplomats, this was particularly so during the McCarthy era when stands unpopular with the Red-hunting senator called for great courage.

A French ambassador confessed that during Gaullist days he was sometimes castigated by superiors for being 'unpatriotic' because of the nature of his reports. In the early 1970s one Arab ambassador in London was notorious among his colleagues for slanting his reports in an anti-British way that would find most favour at home. Equally as tempting, sometimes, is to make no judgement at all, or to hedge all bets – so that the reporting ambassador can never be held to have made mistaken judgements.

The need to please, fortunately for diplomats, is not so great as it once was among the Greeks. By the fifth century they had established a system of inter-state relationships with diplomats chosen by the popular assemblies. The assemblies, if then displeased by the diplomats' reports, could jail them – or even order their execution.

Physical courage is also a quality needed today by ambassadors in many parts of the world. The kidnapping of diplomats, though concentrated in Brazil, Uraguay, and Guatemala, has spread as far afield as Bonn, Ottawa and Buenos Aires since 1969. Murders and murder attempts have taken place in Istanbul, Stockholm, and London.

Embassies have always attracted lone protesters and eccentrics including claimants to defunct monarchies and advocates of incredibly complex plans to save the world from disaster. But in recent years missions in many capitals have also been the centre of increasingly militant demonstrations and 'invasions'. A number have now installed entrance doors that are opened electronically from inside only after the visitor has been vetted.

The kidnappings proved that it is almost impossible to protect a diplomat. The kidnappers have also been in a situation where they cannot lose: either, in return for their kidnapped victim, they obtain concessions from a government; or, if the government refuses, by killing their victim, they prove to the world that the government concerned cannot protect the diplomats within its care. One feature of the kidnappings has been an escalation in the ransom demands: a kidnapped U.S. ambassador in 1969 was exchanged for fifteen prisoners; the following year the price for a kidnapped West German ambassador was forty.

In August 1968 revolutionaries shot and killed the American ambassador to Guatemala during an unsuccessful kidnap attempt. But the epidemic of kidnappings began the following year when Charles Burke Elbrick, the U.S. ambassador to Brazil, was held for three days, confined in a bare room measuring ten feet by three in Rio de Janeiro. The kidnappers, who released him for fifteen political prisoners, maintained later that they had 'nothing personal' against Mr Elbrick but that, as an ambassador, he was the representative of 'big capital interests of the United States'. There followed a rash of kidnappings: in 1970 alone they included a Guatemalan foreign minister, the Japanese consul general in Brazil, the U.S. military attaché in the Dominican Republic, the British trade commissioner in Montreal, the U.S. labour attaché in Guatemala, and an unsuccessful attempt at a U.S. consul in Buenos Aires (who was shot in the shoulder escaping). One Government, that of Guatemala, made a stand that year. After the German ambassador, Count Karl von Spreti was kidnapped, they refused to accede to the kidnappers' demands for money and prisoners. The ambassador was murdered.

Although governments have met to consider answers and safeguards little has emerged except there is little that can be done. In one meeting, of the Western European Union – an organisation then consisting of Britain and the six members of the European Economic Community – in 1971 a report was adopted on the possibilities of international action. One suggestion examined was the W.E.U. members should declare in advance how they would react to cases of kidnapping. But the conclusion was that countries could not say in advance how they would react in individual cases, and that in the last resort it was not possible to prevent kidnappings.

There have also been killings and attempted murders. In 1971 the Yugoslav ambassador in Stockholm died eight days after rightist Croatian separatists fired five bullets into him. Later in the year the Jordanian ambassador in London escaped an assassination attempt when his car was fired upon; shortly afterwards in Geneva a bomb, apparently intended to kill the Jordanian ambassador there, blew up in the Jordan United Nations Mission office, hurting four people.

Other attacks have been numerous. Some of those in one year, 1970, included: bombs hurled at a U.S. information service library in Dacca; a time bomb found in a ground floor lavatory at the U.S. embassy in Athens, and, in another incident, two people killed in a vehicle in the embassy car park, apparently while carrying high explosives to the embassy; a bomb explosion outside the residence of the British ambassador to Argentina; a guard outside the home of the British ambassador to Chile shot in in the leg from a passing car.

In addition, there have been 'invasions' of missions. In the same year these included thousands of young Cambodians sacking the North Vietnamese and Vietcong embassies there; Iranian students occupying the Iranian consulate general in Munich; Ambonese in The Hague occupying the Indonesian Ambassador's residence, holding the ambassador's family at gunpoint; and Arab students taking over the Jordanian embassy in London 'in the name of the Palestine Liberation Organisation'.

Diplomats have faced their dangerous situations with a notable courage and calm.

In Spring 1970, a number of American diplomats in South America asked the State Department to adopt a policy of no ransome in order to stop the kidnapping.

A British journalist, Roy Perrott, of the London *Observer*, was with the British ambassador in Uraguay, Geoffrey Jackson, a few weeks before he was kidnapped early in 1971. Perrott talked with Jackson about the chances of his being kidnapped. 'His wife, Patricia, was at a garden table, musing over a pair of secateurs and the drinks tray. I rather wanted to talk about the Tupamaros, on or off the record: how to understand their strange invulnerability, for instance. "You must come and see the roses," she said, exhibiting an old-fashioned type of nerve that had seen good service on the Khyber Pass, the Crimea, and elsewhere. It was a little undignified to notice danger, she seemed to say. "We have to take security seriously but we try not to fuss about it," the ambassador said, "otherwise life becomes impossible." The Jacksons were both relaxed with, I thought, a bit of an effort showing through. He walked me over to the vegetable garden, ignoring the gunman visibly posted in the shrubbery, and I showed him how the side-shoots of tomato plants ought to be pinched out. "I don't think they're getting anywhere," he said. "Meaning the Tupamaros."'

Similar 'stiff upper lip' attitudes can be seen elsewhere. Another ambassador, the subject of kidnap and murder threats from local extremists, is accompanied everywhere by three police body-guards. At night, his residence is floodlit and guarded. He insisted on taking me for a long walk through his extensive wooded grounds. The guards were ordered not to follow. The grounds were a killer's paradise. He was obviously more concerned about my reaction to his temporary estate: a proud gardener, he wanted it to be liked. What did he think of his guards and the threats: 'Well, if the government here believes it's serious, I'm glad to have them. They become pets really. Now let me show you what I hope to do over there. . . .'

During violent demonstrations in Zambia, over British plans to sell jets to South Africa, the high commissioner was sitting inside his residence sipping sherry. A brick came through the window. 'I hope,' he said, looking at the glass, 'this doesn't cloud my sherry'.

All this endears, as does their attempt to develop the reputation of dry wit – which is perhaps an understandable counter-reaction to the hours they have to spend conversing in over-polite phrases.

Adversity can bring out the best: a French ambassador to Moscow is reputed to have made an official protest to the Soviet foreign ministry that he was not followed by the secret police as were his British and American colleagues. This, he complained, was a slight to France's status as a Great Power.

Often, they are still 'characters'. A former British ambassador to Ireland once met a man in a local pub. Thereafter he referred to him as 'my Irish poacher' – and used him as the source of the 'views of the people', certain he had really got down to grass-roots views which he could report to balance those of officials.

Sir John Pilcher, Britain's ambassador in Tokyo until 1972, once told the wives of foreign V.I.Ps a story involving a geisha who farted as she knelt to serve a samurai tea (the point of the story was that, respecting the discipline of the tea ceremony, the samurai did nothing until it was over when he cut off her head). But it stunned his guests into silence.

Another ambassador came across a small crowd trying to burn his country's flag. It was soaked in oil, and wouldn't light. He went up to them on foot, unrecognised, made sympathetic noises and then advised petrol would be more effective (it was).

Students demonstrating at the British high commission in Kuala Lumpur as a protest against possible British arms sales to South Africa wanted to burn the Union Jack. It hangs from an upper storey and cannot be reached from outside. It was reported by the London *Sunday Telegraph*: 'So, in the middle of the fracas, one of the students telephoned the High Commissioner, Sir Michael Walker, and politely asked if he could have a flag for burning. Ever mindful of his duty to encourage British exports, Sir Michael no less politely replied that he was afraid he hadn't one to spare and that the students must buy one.'

Forced to deal with, talk with, and sit next to bores, ambassadors can be verbally vicious in a quiet way. One British ambassador, told by a visitor who refused to leave 'I hope you don't mind me staying here all night drinking your best claret,' replied: 'But it's not my *best* claret.'

Another, finding himself at a formal dinner next to a dim and rather dull woman, spent part of the evening talking about his days in Egypt, and convinced her (successfully, he claimed) that the reason the pyramids had not shrunk was because there is no rain.

A Canadian sat next to Russian leader Kosygin's daughter at a dinner party. She knew he had served in London, and wanted to talk about student protest in Britain. 'It's terrible the way they are behaving,' she said. 'Can you tell me why?' The ambassador replied: 'It's very simple. The students believe that the police are collecting information about them and building dossiers. I'm sure you'll agree that if this happened in any country, students would behave the same.' He reported afterwards that there was a rapid change of conversation. Some have suffered because of their wit. An American ambassador who was allegedly responsible for the classic phrase 'Dull, duller, Dulles,' ended up in a secondary post in Asia.

Sometimes an ambassador can be unintentionally funny: like

the Spanish Ambassador in Taipeh who, in 1970, in a fulsome pro-Chiang Kai-shek anniversary message, said that the mainland of China regime was about to fall in the not too distant future, and that Mao and the communists were doomed.

Just how closely ambassadors group together with colleagues depends on the size of their country and the place to which they are accredited. High commissioners in London keep closely in touch with each other, meeting regularly – but this is a purely practical system because of the need to discuss topics that affect them all. Representatives of large countries in major capitals will probably see more of local government representatives than of their colleagues, although some capitals are notoriously 'incestuous'.

In large capitals, there is an increasing tendency for ambassadors from many countries to form themselves into small groups. The Arabs, the Asians, the Africans and the Latin Americans all form their own blocs and appoint their own – unofficial – 'doyen'. This can lead to complications. In the early 1970s the 'doyen' of the Latin Americans in London was the Dominican ambassador – except, that is, as far as the ambassadors from Chile and Mexico were concerned. Their countries, alone among the South Americans, recognise Cuba, whose ambassador had been in London longer than the Dominican. Apart from providing extra opportunities for social gathering, it is hard to know what such groups do.

Ambassadors remain individuals and, frequently, highly intelligent and highly political ones. Often they disagree with the instructions they have to carry out. Yet resignations are not common. In fact, one finds that although ambassadors feel there must be some point at which they would resign rather than carry through their orders, they regard the possibility as a doubtful one. 'I have never been faced with it,' says an ambassador. 'But I think every diplomat must have at the back of his mind: where is that point.' Another says: 'I went to the trials of the Vichy leaders after the war; I admit I felt some sympathy with them.'

When there is talk of resignation among Western diplomats, it concerns people rather than principles. Two British ambassadors told me that they would have resigned if George Brown had continued at the British Foreign Office: 'I would rather go than serve under the man,' one said.

Resignations and revolts against the home government are much more common among ambassadors whose countries are volatile and subject to constant changes of power. The coup which overthrew Prince Sihanouk as leader in Cambodia in 1970 forced ambassadors to take stands for or against him or the government which ousted him. Cambodian ambassadors in Cairo, Moscow and Dakar and to the United Nations in New York rallied to the exiled prince, and in Prague the first secretary of the embassy took over the embassy in his name, locking out the ambassador, a supporter of the new government. In London, the Cambodian ambassador Samroth Soth decided to support the new regime 'absolutely'. 'It is a personal question for every ambassador to decide,' he said. 'It's a heart-rending choice, very difficult, but one must make it, and I have.'

Latin America provides its share of resigning ambassadors. Venezuela's ambassador in London resigned in 1970 in protest at his government's decision to shelve the border dispute with neighbouring Guyana for twelve years. Argentine's ambassador left at about the same time, to become minister of interior after the coup; but only to resign that post because of disagreement with his government over the possible return of former President Peron.

The Bangladesh situation also brought crises of principle for some Pakistan diplomats: the deputy high commissioner in Calcutta quit to become head of a Bangladesh mission in Spring 1971. So did the Pakistan ambassador in Poland – after first withdrawing his embassy's funds from the bank.

Western resignations are rare, but not totally unknown. The head of the British Foreign Office disarmament department, in 1970, asked to be moved from his post as a protest at Britain's decision not to outlaw the use of CS gas.

It is highly volatile nations, too, that are most likely to dismiss and recall their ambassadors. It is rarely for personal conduct, although the Sierra Leone high commissioner in London in early 1971 was dismissed after allegedly entering into a 'bigamous' marriage. Coups are again a major reason: Sudan's coup and countercoup in 1971 led to purges of ambassadors in Britain, Yugoslavia and Italy.

Even in less explosive situations, however, an ambassador needs to be well thought of by his own and the foreign government. The American ambassador in Chile in 1971 had to be moved because he so alienated the Chilean head of state that official dealings almost ceased. The Greek regime has had problems both ways. A host country has to agree before a specific ambassador can be posted there. Greek ambassadors acceptable to the host country have been recalled to Athens because of sending unfavourable reports. This has happened with civilian ambassadors to Britain and France. On the other hand, attempts to send ones more acceptable to the regime itself have sometimes failed; in 1969 the Greeks wanted to send a General to represent them in London. Because of protests in Britain, they were forced to drop their request. Most tragic is when a government uses an ambassadorial post to ease out an opponent – as happened with Alexander Dubcek, who was sent as Prague's ambassador in Ankara before being totally stripped of any power.

Even if ambassadors survive to enjoy a normal retirement – as most do – they have a problem. Because their lives have been spent being rootless, the question is where to settle. Some ambassadors stay in capitals which they know; European hotels house permanent American ex-diplomatic residents. For British ambassadors, who retire at sixty, there is always a chance of a company directorship or a government appointment to head an institute or to sit on a committee. Although the standard of living must drop (gone are the huge houses and servants) pensions are as high, or higher than the salaries many middle-class professionals earn while working. During the last years of service many buy houses to which to retire: in England the Cotswolds, the West Country, and the Home Counties are favoured. Provence in France is a special favourite for many retired diplomats.

For many, though, retirement is not a pleasant prospect. One ambassador, enjoying the high living standards that go with the job, said: 'I know people tell you they haven't any private income. But honestly I haven't, and neither has my wife. We haven't saved anything. I'm not sure how we'll manage.'

French diplomats have at least one status advantage. They are allowed to keep and use their ambassador title after retirement. But says a British ambassador sadly: 'In England you are just a retired Englishman. . . .'

Eight
Diplomats Abroad: Trade and Consular

TRADE

'Exporting is fun'
Harold Macmillan

Today's diplomat needs to display interest in trade – or else. It has become, for many nations, the single most important aspect of his work. 'The name of the game,' says a British diplomat, 'is Sell, Sell, Sell'. Though diplomats overall may be criticised and their work condemned as outdated, the commercial side is as 'in' and as revered as peace and dieting.

Ambassadors rush to volunteer how much time they spend trying to help improve exports. With diplomacy under attack, it has become the great justification for their existence. Men whose predecessors would have had contempt for commerce gladly open trade fairs, entertain importers, chat-up a post office official in charge of a stamp printing contract, or work the conversation at dinner round to the merits of their country's aeroplanes, canned food or fashion.

Even diplomats from countries which have a separate government trade service dealing with export promotion stress the amount of effort they spend in preparing the way for commercial agreements and in supplying economic reports that will be of help to trade. Australian diplomats, who have always left commerce to the men from the Department of Trade, point out they now concentrate increasingly on economics in European countries (because of the Common Market), in Japan (its principal trade partner) and in relations with communist China.

Bright young graduates who might in the past have put themselves forward for diplomatic services often now opt for the overseas trade agencies when the choice exists, and trade commissioner services have been known to have up to a hundred candidates for each vacancy. 'Once,' says a trade service diplomat with glee, '*they*, the diplomats, walked with kings. We were carpet-bagging salesmen. That's all changed.'

It is not politic for a diplomat in any service to attack the trade role. But that does not mean that many do not feel it degrading. 'It really is a rather nasty thing to have to deal with,' admits one American ambassador. A department head believes: 'If I asked all the heads of posts in my area, without warning, to tell me the volume of trade between the country in which they're based and here, there would be quite a few who couldn't answer. And some of them would say. "That's not my field".' At a meeting in Canada of diplomats to discuss integration with the country's trade service, one stood up and said he was not keen to sell lino – and he would not expect his trade colleagues to open a cultural exhibition either. Some older ones distrust the 'jargon' of trade and economics. A British diplomat received a note from home, telling him not 'to use incomprehensible terms like "liquidity" in your letters'.

The French make it clear that diplomats dealing with trade are a different class. In many countries' embassies, a commercial man may be the second-ranking officer and, thus, take over temporarily in his ambassador's absence. A high-ranking British diplomat specialising in commerce recalls having to call on a French ambassador on such an occasion: 'When he received me, he made it clear that he thought we had sent the butcher's boy.'

Even those whose views are not extreme believe that some services, notably the British, have swung from under-emphasising trade to completely over-stressing it. And many would question the practical value of much of the work now being forced upon diplomats.

An increased emphasis on trade in the conduct of diplomacy is, in many respects, a return to the past. The Venetian diplomatic service, from which modern diplomacy grew, was in its origins a commercial machine. Britain's diplomatic agents in the Near and Far East had trade origins, with organisations maintaining envoys who were half official and half commercial.

When ambassadors and ministers became personal representatives of sovereigns, they shied away from commerce which became synonymous with a lowering of their status. The Germans, rapidly followed by the Americans, began to change that. Commercial horse-trading joined political bargaining, and energies were concentrated on securing concessions for home traders. By the end of the nineteenth century, the American State Department was also supplying businessmen with details about foreign markets that had been collected by diplomats.

Nevertheless, up to the beginning of World War II diplomats would generally have considered it no part of their role to know anything about commercial or economic matters. 'My predecessor here fifty years ago,' says a British ambassador, 'would have been *horrified* at a suggestion that he should. It would not have been much worse than asking him to serve in a shop.'

Today's diplomat is expected to get deeply involved in economic reporting, in helping formulate and negotiate commercial policy and in some – where there is no separate trade service – with the 'nuts and bolts' of straight export promotion which can range from finding import agencies for exporters to arranging sales drives at local stores.

The increased emphasis on this side of diplomatic work is a reflection of both need (countries *have* to get out there and sell) and of the fact that the borderline between politics and economics and commerce becomes increasingly difficult to draw. On the latter, for example, Britain's application to join the Common Market was argued in terms that were economic and commercial, but the issues were political. Italy's decision to recognise communist China had more to do with trading opportunities than ideology: the political decision to do so was quickly followed by the sending of a fact-finding mission to investigate ways of increasing trade.

As to need, even the United States has had to give commercial diplomacy a new importance as the traditional surplus in the American balance of trade has disappeared. Trade policy initiatives have been aimed at the communist bloc. Ambassadors are exhorted to get involved with the thirty-plus United States Chambers of Commerce overseas, and the diplomats on route to posts attend conferences with businessmen to discuss their wants. In the field, officers supply background information and advice, help businessmen make contacts and (unofficially) in certain countries advise on whether bribes are needed.

Perhaps Britain and Japan are the countries that have most made commercial diplomacy a god. Britain, because of the loss of its role as a great power and its balance of payment problems, has stressed commercial diplomacy in a way that has had repercussions on the discussion of the role of other foreign services throughout the world. Its diplomats are much more deeply concerned in the detailed work of export promotion than those of other countries. The amount of involvement is unique, although some diplomats claim that other foreign services may be forced over the years to progress in the same direction.

In the early 1970s 384 of Britain's diplomats overseas were commercial staff; they were helped by another 400 locally-engaged commercial men. In assessing the staffing costs of the diplomatic service's involvement with trade – £10.4 million by 1970 – the service estimated that a third of each ambassador's time was being taken up by commercial work.

While the luxury of embassies is now something for which British diplomats feel obliged to apologise, trade offices can be praised for their lavishness. After all businessmen expect and need to see offices like the British Trade Development office in New York – huge, and gold carpeted, ashtrays illustrated with parcels wrapped in Union Jack paper.

Japanese diplomacy, it might be said, *is* trade diplomacy. Its foreign policy has, since the war consisted almost entirely of promoting and expanding trade, although the Japanese hate their reputation as 'economic animals'.

The Supreme Export Council sets exporting goals; individual firms, the trading houses which co-ordinate the export efforts of many small and medium size companies, the semi-governmental Japan External Trade Organisation JETRO (with trade centres and offices) and diplomats combine to help realise them. JETRO has European bases in Düsseldorf, Hamburg, Paris, Milan, London and Vienna. In Düsseldorf there are permanently 1,500 Japanese businessmen representing one hundred companies, and it has earned itself the name the 'Tokyo of Europe'. In countries where there are no trade representatives, Japanese diplomats get even more actively involved. 'The Japanese,' says a British businessman, 'seem to plan it all like an invasion'.

In more recent years, there have been hints that Japan might retrain some of its trade-conscious diplomats in pure political work (in preparedness for Japan taking its place as one of the major powers), a reversal of the trend in other countries. But the need to increase the percentage of exports to parts of the world other than the U.S., easing dependence on that market, means an undiminished drive. Politics still takes very much second place. To sell to China (and by the early 1970s to become that country's main non-communist trading partner) Japanese executives happily take part in periods of self-criticism, attacking their own country, praising communism. After negotiating a trade pact in 1971 a group of them issued a joint communiqué with the Chinese. The Japanese Government, they said, had brought about a revival of militarism, and they endorsed the view that Formosa was part of China. Diplomats see nothing odd in it: it helps keep Japan's trade balance healthy.

With two distinct functions involved in the trade field – economic analysis and commercial policy and negotiation on the one hand, and export promotion on the other – the major question is whether diplomats should handle both.

It seems to be generally conceded by all countries that they are the men for the first job; the information gathering, assessment, reporting, and negotiating skills required are basic to all diplomacy. All that may be needed is some specialist training grafted on. A diplomat from Ireland, a country with a highly impressive overseas trade service, the Export Board, says: 'Although we don't get involved in day to day commercial matters, we do try to keep a longer term watch on it. We concentrate on trying to forecast trends or developments or problems that might arise that could have a bearing on trade. And of course we get deeply concerned in discussions on things like tariffs.'

German diplomats too carry out a reporting and negotiating role, although the big industrial associations play a major role in export promotion. By 1971 there were twenty-nine German Chambers of Commerce in twenty-seven countries throughout the world; 'Without them', says a German diplomat, 'embassies would be flooded with requests for help and information and we just would not be able to handle it all'.

In countries where there are no representatives of the industrial associations, German diplomats get more involved in the nitty-gritty. And German diplomacy overall is well geared to trading opportunities; in Latin America, for example, Germany has long realised the future economic advantages of sending up and coming young people to Germay to train and to study.

The British expect diplomats to deal with both functions, and argue that they are closely related. To promote exports the officer needs to know the general economic situation and prospects of the country. And in some countries he also needs to be able to advise on the stability of the regime, a political judgement that a diplomat is best qualified to make.

Even some who accept this argue that there should be exchanges of staff between diplomatic services and business to ensure they both understand the same language. But companies have been more prepared to accept staff than to loan out their own, and the numbers exchanged have been pitifully small: in February 1971 there were just two businessmen on loan to the British diplomatic service. This was blamed not only on the hesitancy of business firms, but also on the meanness of the British Treasury which was not prepared to finance a sufficient margin of manpower in the diplomatic service for it to have men available for loan.

Other countries have tried a similar practice but generally without much success. The British Duncan report cited Sweden where, it said, work with the diplomatic service is 'a recognised part of a business career, and likewise service in business . . . a recognised part of a diplomatic career'. In fact, it is not quite like that. Sweden has a separate Trade Commissioner service which operates its own offices throughout the world, and staff for this service does consist of businessmen who join for a three year period and then return to commerce. But the interchange between the diplomatic service proper and outside is minimal; in a ten year period only about ten diplomats have gone into business for a period, and officials cannot recall one businessman who has been loaned to the diplomatic service. In neighbouring Norway, where the idea has also been raised, diplomats have been reluctant to move either to industry or to home ministries. 'Anyone at my level,' says a first secretary, 'would think twice about doing it. It could be a good way of getting rid of someone quietly. There is no assurance that you will be brought back.'

Some diplomats are not unhappy that the attempts at interchange have largely failed: 'Businessmen brought in are too concerned with their own specific interests,' one Briton says. 'They don't realise that it's overall trade that we have to expand. They still think of the one industry they know.' Another claims: 'One problem is that they can't accept that even exporting must take a second place to political considerations when necessary.' The Americans, who have long discussed such a scheme, have come across another major obstacle: 'The great fear,' says one official, 'is that a businessman borrowed from a big company could find himself helping the rivals of the firm he was going to rejoin, and therefore face a major conflict of interest.'

On the positive side there has been a move towards some specialisation among diplomats handling trade. The Americans have introduced a stream of diplomats with economics backgrounds. In the British service a diplomat who takes, and likes, a commercial job and handles it well is likely to find it followed by a similar one at another post.

Nevertheless, there are countries that argue that export promotion calls for men with backgrounds and personalities that are totally different from those of most diplomats. 'What's needed,' says an official in Ireland, 'is people with the potential to be good managers. And while diplomatic services still want academics, we need them a bit extraverted because the business of selling is people and not sitting behind a desk and writing reports.'

Some also wonder whether the diplomat is not too gentlemanly for the world of international business. German businessmen, for example, have a reputation for being more concerned with getting results than being regarded as nice people. One English diplomat in Western Europe complained that German firms moved in on importers handling British goods. 'They tell them that they are having to spend too much on advertising the products they handle. Then they say, "Take our goods, and we'll do all the advertising for you. . . ."'

But the diplomats argue that beneath the smooth exterior they can be as tough as the toughest businessmen. One English first secretary in a small country was conducting a long-term campaign to persuade the nation's airline to change over to British planes. He had had one setback. The airline, during initial negotiations, had been offered on lease a frustrated export order, a Caravelle, by the French, at a low price. 'They got the contract for two years,' he said. 'We pointed out though that their running costs would be enormous. Now I get the information on what the costs actually are from someone I know inside, and the figures are proving us right. I keep bringing this up and reminding them whenever I get a chance to chat to a minister, the airline, or any of its shareholders.'

Another English diplomat, concerned with air travel agreements, spends much of his time trying to persuade the country in which he is resident to allow more charter flights by British airlines. Sometimes, he says, he makes use of technicalities to exert pressure. 'Say something about one of their charter flights isn't exactly right. I'd wait until their 'plane had been flying for about sixty minutes, and then call them and say that we won't let it land unless. . . .'

A number of countries have decided trade should be a separate speciality. Shortly after World War II Norway set up an Export Council, a semi-official body like the Japanese JETRO, funded by taxes on exports. It has its own offices in major capitals like Paris and in other important cities has attachés on embassy staffs. The Australian Department of Trade has always been a strong one, operating independently at home and abroad. Its men at missions come under the ambassador (and don't hesitate to use him as a 'front man' in important matters when necessary) but report direct to their own home department. Countries like Sri Lanka also second men from the Trade Ministry.

An excellent example of an independent Trade Service and the advantages of a separate agency is the Canadian. This is now over seventy-five years old and by the beginning of the 1970s it had about 250 officers at seventy-five posts, some of them purely trade, but at others with officers attached to embassies. They claim to have a flexibility that the diplomatic service does not, being able to assess officers and operations on a cost benefit basis. They can open and close offices pragmatically, without getting involved in the political implications which are always considerable if a country wants to close an embassy.

One of the officers was moved into Alaska because of the possibility of business being generated by the oil industry there.

After six months, during which time he operated from his house, he had been responsible for several million dollars worth of business. But his assessment was pessimistic: the big decisions, he said, were made in the United States. He was moved out on the grounds that keeping him there, with an office and staff, would waste money in view of a minimal return.

The service also claims to match men to posts in a way that a diplomatic service never could. First the requirements of the particular job are analysed: what kind of academic background is needed, what age level, should the man be married, what special skills? One post in Teheran, for example, needed someone with an engineering background and a knowledge of oil field equipment.

The unique feature of the Canadian system, claims one officer, is that the trade diplomats can function more as overseas representatives of industry than of government, and that the normal civil service bureaucracy is removed. 'Ninety per cent of the cases I deal with,' says one officer, 'are handled on a direct basis with individual companies. They come straight to me, or I make a direct approach to them if I hear of something I think might interest them.' He admits, though, that if his country was larger and its companies more geared to exporting, direct contacts would have to be decreased.

Whoever handles the trade promotion side, it breaks down into two categories – responsive, when the officer simply answers requests from firms, and initiative, when he goes out looking for trading opportunities. The work involved is new, and sometimes strange, for the traditional diplomat. Responsive work includes supplying background information on local trading conditions, providing status reports on firms and advising on import agents.

They are proud of exports they have initiated, no matter how small the value. One Briton, on a briefing tour of factories at home, went to a small factory making sweets. 'I thought they'd go down well here because everyone has a sweet tooth. So I saw a few people and they have been selling happily ever since.' Another Englishman, in a post too small to have a diplomat handling commercial work full-time, said 'I came across a man here who rides for a hobby. He wanted a piebald, and he couldn't get one. I made some inquiries, got the name of someone and 'phoned him. It was only £700 but £700 is £700.'

Diplomats claim, however, that they are forced to spend too much time on the responsive side instead of being able to devote themselves to seeking new trading opportunities. Often they do things that business could easily handle itself, like finding an import agent. 'The trouble,' says one, 'is that we're like the girl who can't say "No". In our case if we turn down some request for help – even if it isn't going to help the balance of payments one damn bit – the firm is going to start yelling to its M.P. or local newspaper about diplomats not helping the export drive.'

Diplomats in the commercial field get themselves heavily occupied in helping and guiding businessmen on trade missions, preparing itineraries, giving briefings, and sometimes accompanying them. They also concern themselves with industrial fairs (a growth business: in one recent year the British government supported participation by British firms in 239 of them). And they become deeply involved in promotional weeks. Today the world is full of British Weeks, French Weeks, Swedish Weeks, Israeli Weeks, Japanese Weeks. . . . The aim is a large scale promotion of consumer goods in a target area. The basic sales drive is backed by publicity, supporting events, and much gimmickry. The British mount them on the most massive scale, and have sent military bands, London buses and policemen, replicas of Big Ben and Eros, Beefeaters and copies of English pubs. They can be expensive: a Tokyo British Week in the late 1960s is reputed to have cost £1 million, and another in Vienna soon afterwards £300,000.

Diplomats help organise them but they are sceptical and sometimes bitter: 'The theory is simple enough,' says one. 'With the gimmickry you create a Christmas selling situation outside the Christmas period. Then, the theory goes on, some of the goods continue to find a market. The trouble is you can never assess the result. You don't know how long the effect lasts. Nor do you know how much you are being deceived by local storekeepers: they're not likely to say anything to dissuade you when they are going to get short-term extra sales because of your flags and bands.'

Another says: 'What hurts is that political diplomacy is now branded as being of debatable value because you can't judge its results. But Trade weeks! Well, can *you* think of a more unscientific way to export?'

The sceptical diplomats received some supporting evidence

from Miami storekeepers who, in the early 1970s, brought the cancellation of a British Week there by refusing to order more British goods. One store president said: 'We've had British Weeks and Israeli, French, Italian, Bavarian and Swedish Weeks. You name it, we've had it. The public aren't interested any more. What they want is value for money, and imported goods don't have speciality value any more.'

Diplomats are equally concerned about the parts of the world in which they are forced to concentrate their commercial work. Almost a quarter of Britain's commercial diplomats, for example, are in Europe. 'I would have thought this was the one place where industry could stand on its own feet,' argues one.

A colleague instances the work of British commercial diplomats in Germany. 'That's a country that is near, its language is easy to learn and in any event English is widely understood. Can you really believe that we need to have commercial diplomats there? Can industry really argue that without us they wouldn't be able to sell anything? If they couldn't – and I'd love to tell them but I daren't – they shouldn't be in business.' The place for commercial diplomats to be, argues another, is in countries that are not easily accessible to businessmen and where there are language and other barriers.

One sympathises with diplomats. It had been decided that they should emphasise their trade role, but the decision-makers seem never to have thought it through.

Many diplomats feel that the modern world has decided that businessmen whose collective views in this field are of crucial importance are figures of more than human qualities who can make no mistakes. The diplomats themselves, who cannot publicise their views, find them less than perfect. Asking them to talk about businessmen is to open floodgates:

'Why can't they do something about after-sales services; it's no good my helping sell their product if a few months later everyone is yelling they can't get it repaired. . . .' 'If you talk to businessmen, you might tell them that advertising counts abroad as well as at home; sometimes they advertise once but never follow up. People don't buy on quality any more; they buy on what they see advertised in the newspapers or on television. . . .' 'They visit once and then cut themselves off; there's no continuing con-

tact; and then they wonder why importers are losing interest. . . .'
'Delivery dates are broken so often.' Stories of businessmen flying
in without warning on Sunday afternoons and then complaining
missions are not geared to help them are common.

A diplomat whose job includes sitting on a committee primarily
composed of businessmen, which allocates large sums of money
for export promotions, says: 'I confess I'm a bureaucrat. In my
profession we need a document even to change the towels in the
washroom. But we do gather facts and do list options. On these
committees I see hundreds of thousands of pounds being spent
purely on impulse.'

They can cite ludicrous examples of business practices. To take
two from a major British market, Ireland: there are English firms
which sign their letters to Irish companies 'Home Sales Manager',
a phrase calculated to drive any Irishman into the arms of the
I.R.A. One very large English company handles Eire from its
Southampton office. The reason is that if you add together the
populations of Eire and Southampton it totals the average sales
area for the company.

And, sometimes, businesses are openly dishonest. One diplomat
recalls a firm which wanted an agent abroad. 'I inquired around
and found six I thought would do, and arranged appointments.
Their man came over to conduct some interviews, and that was
the last I heard of it for a while. Then the firm came here and set
up its own office – in opposition to the agents. They'd got the information. I suppose you'd call it industrial espionage. There
was nothing I could do. But when the word got around it didn't
help my relations with firms here one bit. . . .'

CONSULS

'We are the Cinderellas of the diplomatic service.'
A consul

If commercial diplomacy is fashionable, consular work certainly
is not. The work is of accepted importance, but the status is that
of the poor relation. 'It's not new for us to be thought of as the
diplomat's humble brother,' says one. 'But that doesn't make it
any the less hurtful.'

In one respect, of course, consular work is a lowly occupation: its officers are not negotiating international agreements, talking with presidents, or writing despatches on the changing political climate in China. Their work is much more humdrum: helping visiting nationals who have been involved in accidents or have ended up in the local jail; arranging to fly bodies back home; dealing with visas and passports.

Yet to most residents of any country it is this mundane work that most directly concerns them. The ordinary citizen may never set foot in a foreign ministry or see a political diplomat; in a world where foreign travel is common, he has a good chance of needing the help of a consular officer.

In most countries today the consular service, which was originally a separate one, is combined with the diplomatic service, and officers are interchangeable. 'At the top, though,' admits one official who sits on British promotion boards, 'there's still too damn much of dishing out consul-general jobs to failed political diplomats as a sop for not having been made ambassadors.'

Some of the work is carried out in the consular sections of embassies, but additionally there are independent consular posts. America has about 260 of these; British ones absorb the energies of nearly 500 full-time members of the service and almost 2,000 locally engaged staff.

These independent posts are divided up into consulates-general, consulates, vice-consulates and consular agencies. Between the first two there is little difference except size, consulates-general being traditionally posts established in more important areas. Vice-consulates are posts, headed by a career officer, answerable to the consul-general or consul in whose area they fall. Consular agencies are small sub-offices run by a local man, sometimes a retired career officer or a businessman. They usually work in return for part or all the consular fees they receive and sometimes also get a small allowance. Many countries rely on them heavily. Denmark, for instance, had 472 in 1970 (compared with 280 career diplomats in the country's foreign service).

These 'honorary' consuls are occasionally strange figures. In 1972, the Honorary Consul General for San Marino in London was Sir Charles Forte, the hotel and restaurant magnate. Brazil's man in Manchester, England at the beginning of the 1970s was a private detective who had one room above his offices devoted to his consular work. It was decorated with the Brazilian flag and photographs, and piled high with Brazilian magazines. His main task, he explained, was flying the Brazilian flag on national days and also seeing it was flown from the local town hall. His job stemmed from the fact that he was a student in Brazil with a number of the people who later came to power. He received no pay, but the privileges included invitations to local social events including the annual Lord Mayor's dinner.

Consular work has been expanding at a vast rate in recent years. Despite that, services of many nations have been ordered to slim. In just one year the United States closed ten consulates in countries that included Yugoslavia, Ireland, France, Switzerland, Canada, England and Austria. Those of many countries complain that, with increased workload and staff cuts, services are overburdened.

The problem is not that consular services do not need to be reduced in size, (they do: like embassies, consular posts have got out of hand) but that the politicians will not properly accept that this should also mean reducing the range of work with which they deal.

Perhaps the greatest problems for all consular services have been brought by the worldwide increase in travel. There are more visas to be issued; American foreign service employees now process and issue two million a year. And there are more people needing individual help. 'There are not only more travellers today,' says a Japanese consul, 'but they're not as experienced as those of the past. They're much more likely to run into trouble and have to come to us.' Many of the requests for help range from what has been called 'the trivial to the preposterous'. In a short period of time the consular section of one small mission in Europe dealt with a caller who wanted the embassy to buy his Great Dane, a visitor who broke into a meeting on the Common Market to ask for £50, and a young man who had just arrived and had found he had left all his traveller's cheques at home.

Money is a constant problem: the British Foreign Office gets requests for help home from about 2,000 tourists every year, repatriating when money cannot be obtained from other sources such as a bank or relatives, though passports are impounded and returned when the money is refunded. 'They don't come in and say they're very sorry and need help,' says one consul.' They're not at all apologetic. They just hit the counter and say "I want money".' A Spanish consul says that he sometimes has to lend money out of his own pocket to people who have lost their holiday money at the local casino, and complains that one man has still not paid him back.

Holiday areas are obviously the worst and sometimes posts there have to be reinforced during the peak travel months. A consul in one complains he is expected to be on call twenty-four hours a day, seven days a week, acting as banker, doctor and travel agent. Another, an American, objects to 'jobs like being asked to rush around to the local nightclub to rescue an idiot who has spent too much money on champagne for hostesses and can't pay the bill.'

Some consular services have a reputation of being tough with such visitors, among them the Dutch and the French who help, it is said, 'only those of its citizens unable to crawl'. But other consuls complain it is hard to say 'no' – because the disgruntled visitor is then likely to complain to his political representative or to newspapers. A British official says: 'You know that if they write to their M.P., he will take them seriously. No M.P. is ever going to tell a voter that he ought to grow up and not expect services like this. So we have to keep on supplying them.'

Sometimes one sympathises with the tourist, and agrees that a consul has been over-bureaucratic. A Briton in Yugoslavia with his wife received a telegram saying the woman's mother was seriously ill. Their return air tickets were of no use because they were for a charter flight five days ahead. 'Our fare back to England was about £90. As we only had £75 I telephoned the British consul in Split and asked for a loan of the difference. They refused the loan saying that I would have to telegram relatives in England and ask them to cable the money to me. As telegrams between Yugoslavia and England take at least a day to arrive, and banks are closed at the weekend, I should not have received my money for five days. Were it not for a very kind German who lent me the money, my wife and I would have been seriously delayed in getting back to England.'

Yet these instances make the footling cases no less real nor common. What consular services should be doing, they argue, is refusing to handle these, and concentrating on cases of real need – people whose money has been stolen or who have been assaulted or have been involved in accidents.

The travel growth has also created other work at both ends of the age range – with the young, drugs; with the elderly, illness and death abroad.

The young constitute one of the biggest problems. Some countries have grown increasingly reluctant about allowing the entry of long haired 'hippies' who they think will not be able to support themselves. An American vice-consul was summoned to the airport to talk to one young man who was being refused entry and was refusing to answer questions. The consul talked to him for a while, explaining the problem. Finally the young man agreed to co-operate; he reached in his pocket and brought out $1,000. 'But why,' said the consul, 'didn't you show them that before? You would have had no problems.' 'Because,' said the young man, 'it's none of their fucking business'.

Mostly though, consular officers do not get called in until after the young have got into trouble. Often this concerns drugs. In mid-1972, 934 Americans were being detained abroad for drug offences, the highest number ever and nearly six times as high as the figure four years before. Nearly half were in jails in Mexico, Canada, West Germany and Israel.

Once they are charged, there is little the consular officer can do, except visit them in jail, advise them of their rights, and suggest local lawyers. 'We can't say to the authorities "Hey, this is an American citizen; send him home." Yet this is what many of them expect.'

Another, British, agrees: 'They just won't realise that when they're abroad they're responsible to that country's laws. The first thing they say when you visit them in jail is "This wouldn't happen at home", but they're not at home.' Consular services have gone in for preventive work, issuing warnings. In Spain, where seventeen Britons were in jail for drug offences in mid-1970, the British ambassador personally signed pink and blue pop art posters circulated in the country. They begin: 'This is an open letter to British visitors to Spain. It has just one thing to say – stay off the hash. Don't smuggle it, don't peddle it, don't carry it for others.' And it ends: 'The game is simply not worth the candle. We have too many young people in jail already; please don't join them.'

In Kabul, Afghanistan, a note posted in the waiting-room of the British embassy reads: 'At dawn on Monday 22 February (1971) the eightieth person to be sentenced to death for possession of opium was shot by firing squad at the Lashkay firing range at Rezaich, Iran. Under the reinforced Anti-Narcotics Act anyone convicted of smuggling, peddling, or possessing more than ten grams of heroin, cocaine, morphine or two kilos of opium or hashish is subject to death by firing squad. No foreigner has yet been convicted under this law; but there is no reason why foreigners should be excluded from being sentenced to death for it. DON'T RISK IT!'

The State Department has published warnings, pointing to cases like that of a young American who was sent to a work camp after trying to smuggle marijuana into an Eastern European country. During the twenty months he served, he developed tuberculosis.

The elderly present a different, but an equally increasing, problem. For America it is most acute. Many of its country's travellers are middle-aged and old, and a large number die abroad. In one year, in the late 1960s, the total was 6,000. The consular officer cables details of the death home, and waits for burial instructions from the family. If the body is to be sent home, he arranges it.

Consuls also get deeply involved in accidents and tragedies, helping identify bodies and notify relatives and – more satisfyingly – helping survivors. In one not uncommon case a woman consul spent days looking after four Australian youngsters, badly injured in a road accident, visiting them in a Dickensian hospital with iced water and beef tea. (This, she says, is one of the rare occasions on which she was thanked for her help; 'mostly people say nothing; in this case the mother of one said how grateful she was, and that made up for so many instances in the past.')

Sometimes the tragedy is on a far larger scale. Three thousand people died in an earthslip in northern Italy in 1963. An American consular officer and an Italian member of the consulate drove from Venice for an on-the-spot check. The services of the consulate were offered in co-ordinating and transmitting requests for more help. The officers then began checking the site and hospitals to see if any survivors were American tourists. One couple were; the wife needed moving to a hospital with greater facilities. The officer arranged this with the American military. He then began notifying the relatives of Americans who had been killed.

Consular services are also asked to trace as many as 1,000 lost nationals a year. Normally, the search they adopt follows a set pattern. An officer will check with relatives of the missing person who are known to be in the country. If relatives or friends at home can supply an itinerary, inquiries will be made at places he was due to visit. Checks will be made with local immigration authorities. Co-operation from them may be poor – as in some communist countries. It may be good from others – but difficult because either records are bad or because there might be as many as 200 ports of entry through which the missing person could have entered or left. If this does not find the man, consuls generally have to give up the search.

Occasionally, though, a consul will go far beyond the routine. An American consul was asked to look for an American student who vanished in central Africa while descending the M'Bomou river. The student had been alone in a dugout canoe. Later a local fisherman reported he had seen him. The consul travelled 2,700 miles over rugged roads and trails, on foot through jungles, savanna and marshland. He then returned to the capital to borrow the only helicopter in the country. From it, he spent days inspecting numerous islands in the river that might have held a survivor. Later, when a friend of the student arrived from home, he conducted a third search. All were unsuccessful.

In another case a U.S. consul in Ecuador, Harry M. Lofton, set out to look for two Americans reported missing after setting out to climb Sangay volcano, the most active and dangerous volcano in the Andes. Lofton led a search party into the Sangay wilderness. From the last remote hacienda, the base of the volcano was two days away – one on horseback, eighteen gruelling hours on foot the next. At the end of the first day the party came on one of the missing Americans, barely conscious, suffering from frostbite and exposure. He and his colleague had reached the top of the volcano and spent a night there, increasingly dazed and weakened by sulphur gas, lack of oxygen and exposure. Then they had started mistakenly down the 'impossible' wrong side of the volcano. One of the two, realising the mistake, had turned back in time. The only chance of finding the second man appeared to lie in trying to track him from the top. Lofton and two Ecuadorean climbers, with Indian packers, started upward. Still two-thirds of the way from the top, the Indians stopped and would go no farther. Ice walls, constantly falling boulders and lava, and swirling gas and hot ash made progress increasingly difficult and dangerous, but the three men finally reached the top. There they found traces of the two Americans, and followed the missing man's tracks down the wrong side until the tracks disappeared. Mist and snow and gas limited visibility to three feet; continuing the search was impossible.

After that other consular functions, such as looking after resident communities of his own nationals seem routine. Consuls can register births and deaths of their fellow countrymen and some British consular posts hold warrants allowing them to perform valid civil marriages. American consuls cannot do this, but may witness a wedding. Consuls also, traditionally, have the task of caring for their country's seamen. It dates from the time when sailors were waifs of the world and needed to be under the protection of the consul. Today the work is largely routine, involving such things as safeguarding ship's papers for a day or so while a ship is in port, and, processing and signing on or discharge of a seaman who is a citizen of the consul's country.

Occasionally it can be more hectic. In Okinawa the captain of an American ship radioed his shipping agent that he was carrying two 'crazy seamen' in irons. He wanted them removed under guard when the ship put into Naha. The shipping agent notified the consul, who went aboard with a psychiatrist. They found the sailors handcuffed to their bunks. The foreign-born captain told the consul in heavily accented English that the sailors were crazy and had threatened his life. The sailors told the doctor the captain was mad and carried a pistol in his belt. The doctor and consul concluded nobody was insane, but all were suffering the strains of a serious personality conflict, probably compounded by a language barrier. Arrangements were made by the consul for the sailors to ship out of Naha on another vessel.

Consular officers today are also expected to play a part in wider diplomatic activities. Even the mundane role of issuing visas may be linked to attempts to secure a political advantage. One American ambassador expects consular officers to watch out for applicants who can be of use to the embassy. 'People come to the consular section because they want a service. The Embassy can get something in return from them if it organises itself to tap these potential resources discreetly and methodically. The most productive areas are applicants for non-immigrant visas, who usually come from the more affluent sectors of society, and local Americans seeking passport service. A university student may know a great deal about developing attitudes among the student population. He may be a means, either now or after his U.S. experience, of providing an "in" to local youth groups. A rancher from up-country should be well informed on economic conditions in his area, rising political figures, and peasant unrest. A relative of an important official may be a means of creating a favourable impression on that official.'

Spanish consuls have a particular problem because of the large number of exiles from the Civil War still living abroad. This means that much of their work necessarily has political implications. One, who took over the office in Mexico (where Spain is not *officially* represented) concentrated on wooing exiled nationals. And he persuaded them – with some success – to pay visits to Spain again.

They are also – especially in the British service – expected to concentrate more on trying to promote trade, a development many resent, claiming they are neither properly equipped, nor trained for such a job, and that the rest of their work is not being cut back to make it possible.

Yet there are strong reasons why the consular officers should be deeply involved, not only in commercial work but in other non-traditional functions. A number of consular districts cover areas so rich and prosperous that as commercial and exporting centres they are more important than some whole countries. As the man on the spot, with local status and contacts, the consular officer should be better placed to do an adequate job than the diplomats at the embassy, far removed in the capital. Apart from seeking export opportunities, the consular officer can also do a major public relations job. He will give speeches; but more importantly because he should be known as an important figure locally, how he acts and reacts can have a large propaganda effect.

One American principal officer at a consulate, covering a large district with many towns separated by difficult terrain, used offensive techniques, taking the consulate out on tour. 'Apart from earning the appreciation of many people for saving them a time-consuming trip to our city, we gathered data on how things were going in the back country,' he said. 'It was instructive and amusing to chat with the little people as well as the local big-wigs. The bootblack, the charwoman, the fruit vendor, were often as informative as the mayor in commenting on such elementary problems as family, food, employment, schooling etc. . . . We seized upon the opportunity to show films in places where this was a novelty and where life in America was little known.'

A post can feed its embassy with detail on trends in the area, intelligence including particularly biographic details of local notables, and reports on groups such as students and labour. Their keenness, and their worth, in this respect may be determined by the mission's attitude to them. Many embassies treat subordinate posts like poor relations. Others encourage them.

One ambassador's 'encouragement' was what he personally called 'hard but effective'. When visiting posts, he tests officers to see whether they are making useful contacts with local notables. 'Well in advance of my visit I ask the principal officer to stage an appropriate function, at my expense, that will enable me to meet key people from a designated list of target areas. I have the consul introduce me to every person present, and I judge by the warmth and friendship of those introductions how well he really knows his contacts – and how well he's doing the job I've set him to do. Deficiencies show up quickly. When they do, a private discussion with the officer concerned on the importance I place on consular influence is sufficient stimulus to bring about a better programme of representation on his part.'

Although consular officers and diplomats are part of the same service, and interchangeable, those who have spent a large part of their lives in consular work are easily indentifiable.

They are blunter, and their speech more direct, less diplomatic: 'I recall these two girls,' says a woman consul. 'They'd been picked up drunk. I found they'd been travelling on this Danish ship, lying on their backs all the time, satisfying the crew. What did I do? Well I gave them a lecture. One of them was quite stunned. "*My mother* never spoke to me like that," she said. More's the pity I told her.'

They also seem more willing to bend rules, concentrating on achieving a practical result. One consul recalls a national of his own country who had married a local girl. The couple had twins and soon after, the women had left him, returning home. 'He came to see me. His wife had taken one twin and left one with him. That kiddie was pining and his doctor said the children really should be together. He wanted to know whether there was anything he could do.

'Well I knew he wouldn't get far legally. So I told him that as I saw it all he could do was kidnap the child – but for Godsake not to quote me. I knew there was one of our ships in port at that moment, and I suggested that he went and had a word with the captain about getting out afterwards.' What happened? 'Oh, I never knew. That's one of the troubles with this job; you often don't hear the ending. I like to think he had the sense to do what I suggested.'

They also believe that even if the diplomat has the status they do the work. 'It's true,' says one. 'If you don't believe it go and see how many memoirs have been written by ex-diplomats and how few by ex-consuls. You'll find diplomats keep diaries to publish the moment they retire. Consuls don't. They're far too busy.'

Nine

Diplomats Abroad:
Defence and Propaganda

DEFENCE ATTACHÉS

'In every land and language, the term military
attaché is only a synonym for a spy.'
Monat, *Spy in the U.S.*

Defence attachés, along with ambassadors, share the distinction
of being the only diplomats whose names first have to be cleared
with the receiving state. This convention is a testimony to the suspicion with which they are traditionally regarded. Occasionally
they will even hide on the diplomatic list under an assumed function. One North African defence attaché in London, with a high
military ranking, is listed as a public relations adviser, and is
described as 'Mr'.

Once in a foreign country, any special restrictions on diplomatic movement or surveillance will be directed primarily at
them. They are regarded as 'spies above spies'. Some rather like
the image; in the age of 007, being a licensed spy adds a touch
of glamour. One British service attaché, on leave, announced himself at neighbourhood parties with the cry: 'Your resident spy has
arrived.' He then assures you privately – as will all his defence
attaché colleagues – that he does not actually do anything clandestine; that his diplomatic role is no more sinister than that of a
cultural attaché trying to arrange an art exhibition.

And he is probably telling the truth: as a spy the military
attaché has been downgraded. There is still sometimes clandestine
activity, but the espionage focus has swung to those professional
intelligence officers who, in diplomatic lists, will hide behind
much more innocuous titles like first secretary (information) or
simply second secretary. (Four known such operatives at one
London-based embassy recently carried these secretary rankings.)

The heyday of defence attaché as spy during recent years was the period of World War II and the years immediately after. During the war, Professor Alfred Vagts has pointed out in *The Military Attaché*: 'spying became so much the work of service attachés that spies and attachés grew to be almost indistinguishable.' He instances the case of an American sent to the Vichy embassy as an assistant naval attaché who 'did not know which end of a boat went first'. 'Now,' says a high-ranking Western counter-espionage officer, of espionage carried out in his country: 'It is primarily civil; the military have become pretty innocuous.'

That said, it would be a pity if the image disappeared. For the actual work of a defence attaché is nowhere near as glamorous. Nor, in most countries, is the job considered to be an upward step on the military promotion ladder. And, just to make the attaché's life even less desirable, generally he does not fit in well with diplomats at an embassy.

The defence attaché has existed for about 150 years. Before then, collecting information about a country's armed forces was the task of ambassadors and other diplomats, thus earning *them* the spy label. Developments in weaponry and the increased speed of troop movements brought by the railway made countries increasingly interested in military information. To satisfy mutual interests, governments began exchanging military experts. These had two advantages over non-specialists: for the sending country, they could better judge what they saw, and for the host country they were more easily controllable in their activities.

Today the service attaché has four functions. The first is information gathering and reporting (normally by fully overt methods). The second is advising the ambassador on military matters. The third may involve either helping sell or buy arms for his country. And the fourth is a wide representational and liaison one – from attending functions in full-dress uniform, to arranging exchanges of military personnel, to making sure that a visiting general gets the appropriate treatment.

Defence attachés are not members of their country's foreign service, but are officers from the armed forces, temporarily attached to missions, and usually subordinate to the ambassador. Their attachment is normally two to three years. At large missions there may be separate air, naval and army attachés. The one considered senior will normally be called defence, armed forces, or military attaché and will handle over-all reporting as well as his army, navy or air role.

As in all diplomacy, the numbers of men involved have grown. Every nation has eagerly sought to place them at missions. 'No embassy and few legations,' Professor Vagts has written, 'seem complete without at least one of them, even when their usefulness has sometimes seemed dubious.' In the early 1970s there were over 200 service attachés, advisers, and assistants attached to sixty missions in London including those of Mexico, Nepal, Sudan, Zambia and Thailand. In the late 1960s the United States had 400 officers serving abroad as attachés or assistant attachés, Britain had nearly 160 at 63 missions (apart from 200 people at the British Defence Staff in Washington) and France 119 in 58 countries. Germany and Japan, countries which for a decade after World War II opted out of the military attaché game, had resumed the practice. Germany had 58 serving in 28 countries, and by the early 1970s had seven in London and ten in Washington including the assistant attachés. Japan had six resident in Washington.

Sometimes it is hard to know what they do. 'They look lovely on ceremonial occasions,' says one diplomat, for once able to enjoy the role of condemning overstaffing. 'But I hardly think much would be lost if at least half were sent home.' Ellis O. Briggs, retiring American ambassador, told the Senate that in the late 1950s in Athens he had seventy military men attached to the embassy. 'Had I been able to deploy them for three hours every morning in full dress uniform, playing leapfrog across the Acropolis, that would have made as much sense as most of the attaché duties they solemnly declared they were engaged in.' In the early 1970s the United States had one military attaché based in Dublin, Ireland. His role, it was explained, was that of being 'representational'.

Military men and diplomats are not natural neighbours. Service attachés complain that their function is misunderstood by the diplomats. 'They feel that all we have is a cocktail-drinking and sword-carrying role,' says a Finn. An American agrees: 'There are still far too many ambassadors who don't take service attachés seriously, and like us around just to put on our bright uniforms and walk behind them.'

The service attaché finds himself not only serving in a strange land, but surrounded by diplomats from another service, whose backgrounds and ways of working are totally different. An English diplomat claims: 'They just don't fit in. They are used to being told to do something, saying "Yes sir" and going away and doing it. Then they come into this disorganised world of diplomacy where you never know what you are achieving and you never know the end product.'

And as part of his watching and reporting role, the military attaché may start forming political judgements – something not likely to endear him to diplomats who regard that as being their expertise. In Japan all watch for signs of the growing power of the military – something most defence ministries believe will come, but over which diplomats often feel they are hysterical.

He often feels he is the best informed man at the embassy on what is actually happening in a country: 'We travel about more than anyone else,' one South American says. 'The political man is in the capital and rarely goes outside. We travel broadly and go to more functions and have a much wider knowledge of the country.'

The image is not helped by the sometimes glaring differences between the 'ideal military attaché' and the man who actually holds the job. Describing the ideal man, a Western Defence Ministry Intelligence Director, says: 'He should be well trained in his own speciality. He has to have staff training. He has to be a man who, when he sees something, knows what it means. He's using his subjective judgement for us, so we've got to know that it's good judgement. He should have been around long enough to be experienced. But he should be a man on the way up – someone who is going to end up a high ranking officer.'

But it is not always quite like this, for two reasons. The major one is that in many countries accepting a temporary assignment as an attaché is not a good step career-wise. The offer usually comes when the officer is in his early forties; acceptance is normally not compulsory. If the officer does accept the job, he cuts himself off from his own service at a crucial time in his career. 'You may, in your new job, have an ambassador enthuse over you,' one military man says, 'but that won't have much impact'.

The second is that attaché posts are often given out to officers as a pre-retirement present. It constitutes their last tour of service. Many services say they are trying to change this practice – but admit that pressures to give a man nearing retirement a cosy posting are strong. There have been attempts in some countries to make an attaché posting more attractive. In the American service this seems to have had effect: overall United States attachés are now universally regarded by military men as being the second most efficient in the world (the Russians are usually regarded as the best, both for the men chosen, their training, and their knowledge of languages).

Before going abroad, military attachés are prepared in a series of briefings that include the country's people, culture and history. There may also be language training. The foreign ministry will explain the political situation; intelligence will go over what is known about the country's military forces, personalities, and equipment. 'We also,' says one seriously, 'make sure he's okay on the diplomatic things like eating at big dinners.'

Once abroad, the defence attaché's information-gathering role applies to both friendly and unfriendly countries. 'Basically wherever you are,' one European says, 'what you want to know is how strong they are, what they've got, what their plans are, and the power politics of their services.'

In friendly countries the main task will be assessing what material, from a mass available, needs to be reported. Local defence ministries even send some attachés monthly returns on their strengths, and will answer questions. A wealth of other information is on hand from parliamentary reports and in journals and magazines, particularly technical ones. 'You still, though, have to assess the accuracy of what you're told,' one Canadian says. 'The military here would never tell me a deliberate untruth; our relations are too close. But they might just put the emphasis on what they want me to believe.' Another, English, says: 'One thing you always have to remember: *everyone* has a secret.'

At the other extreme, military attachés in unfriendly countries, such as Western ones behind the Iron Curtain, will have to make the most of a little. 'All you can do,' says an American, 'is travel round as much as they'll let you and try to make up your mind whether what's being published and what you are being told is the truth.' In such situations, the spy-epithet abounds. The west brands communist attachés; Iron curtain countries, western ones. (The Russians do it with more style; could the west ever equal the *Pravda* description of an American naval attaché that he 'roamed our land like a wolf'?)

Much depends on what is meant by spying in any given country. Is stepping outside the role of attending parties or gratefully accepting a carefully-arranged excursion to a military installation *en masse* with other attachés, espionage? In the eyes of many countries when done by a representative of a rival power, the answer is that it is.

In their reporting role, military attachés share a common problem with diplomats: they often feel cut off ('it becomes pretty damned easy to think to hell with them back home; they don't care about me') and they wonder how far to report in such a way that will be honest but unwelcome. 'People most want to read what they want to believe,' says one 'and the military man isn't exempt.'

Too great an emphasis on organised visits to military installations and on socialising, has been criticised. Major General Sir Kenneth Strong has complained in *Intelligence at the Top* that Britain knew too little about the French armed forces before World War II. The military attaché there – 'like our other service attachés' – was 'largely occupied with activities with very little military value: conducting V.I.P.s, laying wreaths, appearing at official ceremonies and meeting socially with the French. It is true they were invited to various military exercises, but these were usually stage affairs and gave little opportunity to judge real military efficiency.' Such men still have their modern counterparts.

The attachés also have nitty-gritty but time-taking jobs carrying out liaison work – dealing with the exchange of military men, making arrangements for visiting ships, getting permission for a military aircraft to overfly a country. There may also be more offbeat roles. American military attachés have been much involved in disaster relief. In 1963, the earthquake in Skopje, southern Yugoslavia, in which more than 1,000 died, brought immediate needs for medicine, food, blankets and temporary housing. American help centred on the embassy, with the military attachés dealing with the logistics of getting the relief airlifted in.

The British military attaché in Dublin has what is probably a unique job in the service attaché business. There are, according to unofficial estimates 7–8,000 southern Irishmen, serving with the British forces. The attaché looks after problems that arise concerning their home affairs. A soldier may be injured in Hong Kong, and his mother has to be told and flown out. He may have to be informed of trouble at home. A pregnant girl may be trying to trace him. And there are Irishmen who come home on leave and don't want to return. One called at the embassy to ask for an extension to his leave – because he hadn't 'finished' his honeymoon. Others desert, and decide later they want to return after all. They get travel warrants to get him back.

The Irish law forbids recruitment for foreign armies and, not unnaturally, particularly for the British Army. The military attaché again has an odd role. He doesn't seek recruits. But if someone seeks out information about joining, it is perfectly legal to give information and advice on where they can join.

A major role for many today is involvement in arms sales. Most of the trade today in arms is official government to government sales, and the total volume at the beginning of the 1970s was estimated at about £2,000 million a year and likely to double within five years. Four countries dominate the business, the United States, Russia, France and Britain. Others involved include China, Israel, Belgium, Germany, Sweden and Canada; their share of the market is small, although China's has been growing. A third of the arms go to developing countries.

Arms selling is closely linked with trade and political diplomacy because it yields foreign earnings and is also regarded as a way of exercising influence. Defence attachés look out for opportunities or for developments that might lead to arms needs, and they contribute to the advice that helps determine whether arms *should* be sold to a particular nation at that time.

One attaché sees his job in this field as 'being an antenna for possible sales. If I get the word they're looking round for a minesweeper I pass it back. Or you might go further, and try to forecast what they'll be wanting in the future like, say, radar, and alert people to that.'

British service attachés are expected to get even more enmeshed in the arms selling process than others. In some areas of the world it is regarded as their main function. They are expected to seek out opportunities and also to help sales teams who fly out from Britain. They are fed with defence sales literature. One of them says: 'I try not to keep ramming things down their throats here, but I do make them aware of what we've got to offer. For example, I've got a man coming over this week to talk about a new form of mine we are flogging on the market.'

Of their advisory role, British attachés especially often complain that exporting considerations take priority over defence ones: 'We are too damned shortsighted,' says one. They feel particularly strongly about the sale of computers to the Soviet Union – in modern warfare, they point out, computers are an essential part of weaponry.

French diplomats take arms sales very seriously, again for foreign exchange and political reasons. Sales give power and prestige to the country's diplomats in many parts of the world. In areas like French West Africa, which the French hold as their arms preserve, there have been diplomatic battles as Britain has tried to break in.

Arms can also be tried as a means of diplomatic pressure, though not always successfully. France withheld Mirages to punish Israel; the United States withheld Phantoms to try to force Israel into an interim agreement which would reopen the Suez Canal. France which, by 1971 had the third biggest armaments industry in the world, enjoys one unenviable reputation in an unsavoury business: that of being willing to sell to anyone. A fifth of its Third World exports in 1971 went to South Africa. Oddly, the two main Communist countries seem to have the best ideological record, if such a thing is possible when selling arms. Whereas, say, Britain has supplied arms both to India and Pakistan, China will supply Pakistan and not India, the Soviet Union, India and not Pakistan. As part of their wooing of Africa and the Arab world, both stay out of the Israeli and South African market.

An attaché's function can also be arms buying. An Israeli defence attaché in London for two years had the main task of trying to persuade Britain to sell Israel Chieftan tanks (unsuccessful because of a ban on selling arms to countries involved in the Middle East conflict).

Military attachés in all capitals are perhaps the most easily definable of the groups among diplomats. They are also the most closely knit. One French attaché says: 'There is this feeling of *camaraderie* among us that you don't get with others. I suppose the reason is obvious: we're all distinguished by uniform, our common training and, whoever we are, a common aim – the defence of our own country.' Another, Israeli, says: 'Take twenty tank men from twenty countries and they'll have things to talk about.'

This feeling can extend to the local military's relations with the attaché. One military attaché in a friendly country suddenly found that because of events that nation's and his own had become distinctly unfriendly.

'I usually lunch in their G.H.Q. mess every week, and I went along as usual. The atmosphere was what I'd call embarrassing for a while. Then after the third round of drinks, one said: "This thing we're not talking about, may do us a bit of good – we may get a bigger army just in case we have to go to war with you." Then the bad atmosphere disappeared. They now joke about my place as a spy.'

They are also, collectively, easily the most avid of socialisers within a diplomatic corps which as a whole is hardly known for its reticence to throw or attend parties. There is a continuous stream of dinners and entertainments.

They take it in turns to host lunches for the rest of the defence attaché group, offering their colleagues specialities of their country. The Soviet supplies Russian food and vodka and Caucasian wines, the Finnish delicacies like reindeer meat. The most swinging of them also compete to give the most varied and talked-about parties. At one, the Belgium defence attaché got his fellow attachés – including a French admiral and an Italian Lieutenant-Commander – to come dressed like habitués of Chelsea's King's Road. The buffet dance went on to dawn with onion soup in the early hours. The following day – Tuesday – was a working day.

One attaché, not denying the stress on the social side, thinks he can rationalise it: it is because the defence attaché's job is only a temporary one. After a short period of diplomatic privileges and immunities, glittering parties and dinners, it is all over. He makes the most of it. Diplomats around him can spread it all over forty years.

'Opinions are stronger than armies.'
Lord Palmerston

On 14 July 1961 Sir Harold Nicolson recorded in his diary that he had watched a television interview with Yuri Gagarin, the Russian astronaut who earlier that year became the first man to circle the earth in a satellite. 'He certainly possesses great propaganda charm, and will personify Holy Russia for many millions. How can a country be a menace when it has as its hero a man with so entrancing a smile?'

Today propaganda diplomacy is a mixture of this gentle approach and of the hard sell; some is aimed at achieving immediate effect, some at obtaining longterm results. It is now recognised as an essential arm of foreign policy. The ceaseless war of words and culture absorbs the energies of thousands of diplomats and the expenditure of millions of pounds. Ironically while the military attaché's role is largely passive, that of the propaganda diplomat is totally aggressive.

The apparatus is comparatively new, and constantly growing. The aims are broadly constant: to persuade others that the nation concerned is peaceful/friendly/cultured/technologically-advanced/special/has the best language/propagates the most sensible policies/boasts the ideal way of life.

The methods range from simply feeding out information to organising elaborate events. Students are imported, potentially valuable foreigners fêted, exhibitions mounted, plays and ballets exported, books subsidised, radio broadcasts beamed, and schools opened. None of it is altruistic; it is all meant to achieve results.

Propaganda, with its role of appealing to public direct, is one of the diplomat's more recent functions. For older diplomats it is still sometimes regarded as a distasteful one. The French early realised the value of exporting their culture. And the Soviets practised direct appeal to the masses from the beginning (at their first diplomatic negotiations, with the Germans in 1917, communist diplomats headed by Trotsky threw pamphlets from the windows of their special train and urged troops to overthrow their masters).

But in most countries distaste made propaganda diplomacy a late entrant. The Americans, for example, refused to become involved until Pearl Harbour. The British attached press attachés to more important missions in the 1920s and created foreign broadcasting and cultural machines in the 1930s. But the apparatus was more of a token than an operative machine. World War II made propaganda a necessary – and suddenly moral – activity, although in the early years afterwards only Moscow felt it worthwhile continuing with it as a foreign policy weapon.

Even today, diplomatic services deeply involved are reluctant to use the word propaganda; they use less openly repugnant (and less accurate) ones like 'information services' rather as some people talk of 'passing away' instead of 'death'. And there is always, from diplomats, an almost unconscious assumption that it is the 'other side' which engages in blatant propaganda; what their country does is simply transmit the truth.

The two main divisions of propaganda diplomacy are information and cultural work. The first includes disseminating news and views to journalists or broadcasters or through publications. Cultural is wide-ranging including mounting exhibitions, sending artists and scientists abroad and promoting a language. Some countries, including Britain, keep them separate; others consider them so close as to be undistinguishable.

Diplomats working in propaganda will have different emphases depending on what their country hopes to achieve. Both the Americans and the Russians are 'selling' competing ideologies, to each other and to other nations. 'This means,' says one, 'that you need to get across not only that you are right, but that the other is wrong and his way of life doesn't work – a kind of constant "better than you" approach.'

French diplomats battle to prove the supremacy of the French culture and language. Canada tries to project itself as a bicultural nation which is a separate entity from the United States. Britain sees it primarily in terms of helping exports. South African propaganda is much directed at justifying apartheid, stressing 'the advantages' it gives to black Africans who are not turned into 'pseudo Europeans'. Small powers see the major role as making their voices heard at all. When Guyana became independent, its first ambassador in Washington saw his information task as making people realise his country existed. He spoke at meetings, went on television. He seems to have been successful. 'When I first arrived, sometimes at receptions I would be introduced as the ambassador from Ghana and my letters went to the Ghanaian embassy. When I left some of their's were coming to me.'

Countries differ in the way they organise their propaganda diplomatic machines. There are four basic methods adopted. The first, and most common, is to give both information and consular work to regular diplomats. The second is to use a separate agency for some of the work, though allowing the dipomats to retain policy control. The third is to keep information under the control of a ministry of information, while letting diplomats handle cultural work. And the fourth is the reverse of this – diplomats handling information, and another body dealing with cultural work.

Canada is an example of countries adopting the first approach. A diplomat argues: 'Both information and cultural work are governed by foreign policy needs. Information is an integral part of embassy work. And much of cultural work involves negotiating agreements over exchanges of people or events – a natural diplomatic job.'

America adopts the second method. The State Department retains direct control of educational exchange programmes and of cultural presentations sent abroad. In the field, both information and cultural work is carried out by officers of the United States Information Agency who operate in over a hundred countries. But they are under the authority of the ambassador, and at home the State Department advises the policies the agency should follow. An U.S.I.A. officer claims that the great advantage of a separate agency is that operatives are specialists. 'The man handling information will probably have a background in that work or in journalism, and the one dealing with culture is probably an academic. So you get people who know their job.' Sweden practises a variant of this system: officers for press and information work are recruited separately and not integrated with the diplomatic service. But they work at missions, and rise in the ranking scale to counsellor level. Exceptional ones can be made ambassadors. A third method – information directed by a separate ministry – is much favoured in countries where control of the press is regarded as a government function. Spain is an example of a country using it, and the Information Ministry has its own men at larger missions.

The British adopt the fourth approach, making a sharp distinction between information work – a regular diplomatic activity – and culture which is the responsibility of the British Council, a body independent of the Foreign Office but government supported. There are representatives of the Council in about eighty countries, and in about a quarter of them they are on embassy staffs and are called cultural attachés. Although diplomats, particularly at smaller missions will be expected to help with cultural work, British Council staff never deal with information.

The British see a political advantage in the method: it publicly displays division between the cultural officers and the regular diplomats who, admits one, 'after all, are always a bit, well, sinister'. It makes cultural work look more altruistic and not subject to political pressure. But, in reality, there is great pressure from the British Foreign Office and from ambassadors. Often the Council likes to settle in a country and begin a longterm process of building up a reputation and influence. The Foreign Office, on the other hand, sees culture as a policy weapon in a constantly shifting international scene where priorities and the countries to be wooed change. 'What you get' says a British ambassador, 'is the inbuilt immobility of the British Council coming into conflict with what we'd like them to do at given moments of time.'

What happens in such events is a 'discussion to reach a workable compromise'. The Foreign Office can use as a lever the fact that the British Council is now almost totally reliant on government funds, and diplomats have great power when it comes to suggesting allocations of resources for overseas operations each year. 'That,' says a British Council man, 'is their weapon when they are arguing that their ambassador somewhere thinks it would be nice to do something cultural there, and the Council knows that that place should be low on its priorities.'

Other examples of 'interference' were revealed in a British House of Commons Expenditure Committee report on the British Council. The report claimed that British ambassadors had queried one in twelve (eight out of ninety-six) Council appointments in a five year period, three of them so vigorously that the Council had felt compelled to cancel them. The Committee recommended that ambassadors should no longer even be consulted. The Committee also criticised the methods by which a former Foreign Office assistant under secretary was appointed Director-General of the Council in 1968. The choice of an ex-diplomat seemed a 'strange one'. The post was not advertised. The committee called it another instance of an 'excessive degree of influence' by the Foreign Office over British Council appointments.

The Foreign Office also keeps a watching brief on cultural exports. 'One or two' plays, according to one diplomat, are found unsuitable for shipping abroad – not so much for political reasons, but because they do not display 'a good picture of the British way of life'. (The State Department exercises a similar, but more direct, control. And if anti-Americanism does seep through, politicians will spend hours finding out why.)

In the field, diplomats handling information work will increasingly concentrate on trying to reach people through 'selling' information to newspapers, news-agencies and broadcasting networks. There is a lot of activity: every embassy in Washington, for example, has at least one man liaising with the press. 'It's both a responding and a selling job,' explains one. 'If they have questions, you try to answer them. But, more importantly, you try to get publicity for certain things that are happening, and some understanding for your policies.' The diplomats are backed-up with a flood of material from home: the U.S.I.A. send out thousands of words a day from Washington for local distribution to newspapers and magazines. There are also photographs, cartoon-strips, pamphlets and magazines. Printed information propaganda ranges from the clumsy to the sophisticated. In the first comes such efforts as 'Pakistan News Digest' with blatantly propagandist stories – sample opening 'The Indian puppet regime in occupied Kashmir...'. In the second are Soviet propaganda newspapers, sold in the West on a reciprocal arrangement. The British circulated 'Soviet Weekly' is a readable selection of soft-sell material that includes news, record reviews, chess notes and a question-and-answer column dealing with such queries as 'How much does the average Soviet family pay for such things as rent, heating, lighting and telephone?'

The cultural diplomat works in a much more hazy field. Where the specialist information man has to get used to talking to journalists and knows such things as the importance of deadlines, the cultural man, if not actually an academic, will have a scholastic bent.

The nation which concentrates most on cultural diplomacy is France, spending each year between £40 and £50 million (compared with Germany's £20 million and £12 million in Britain). France was the first modern nation to recognise the advantages of cultural programmes with other countries, and today it is high-powered and highly respected. Its cultural attachés (always attached to embassies) enjoy a higher status than those of other nations, and the post of head of the Cultural Affairs Division at the French Foreign Ministry is an important one in the service, hotly competed for by very high-ranking officials.

A key objective of French cultural diplomacy is the promotion and protection of the French language. This is a major element in French foreign policy; France regards its language as an instrument of prestige and power, a way of asserting leadership of Western Europe, and a sign of its independence from the United States.

Diplomats are involved at many levels. At the United Nations in the 1960s they lobbied support from thirty-eight countries to win absolute parity for the French language with English. Cultural attachés in foreign capitals try to negotiate, and then enforce, agreements by which French becomes the major second language taught in that country's schools. Huge efforts go into maintaining French in French-speaking areas like parts of Africa.

The apparatus is massive. There are about 30,000 teachers of French and other subjects now working abroad, two-thirds of them in North Africa. French is being taught at 100 lycées, 55 institutes and 141 cultural centres, either completely or partially run by the French government. In addition there are subsidies to private schools, most notable the Alliance Française which has about 200,000 students.

Other countries also lay great stress on teaching. About thirty per cent of the British Council's budget goes into education and the teaching of English; the Americans have 130 'binational centers' which are joint enterprises between the host government and the United States. These offer English and other courses at minimal fees to about 250,000 enrollees a year. The Germans encourage their language through the Goethe schools. In recent years Japan has joined the cultural language battle with exchange programmes, designed to bring scholars and intellectuals to Japan, and with funds to help in the study of Japanese abroad. At the United Nations, Arab states have pressed for their language. Arab ministers taking part in the opening General Assembly debate give their speeches in Arabic on the advice of the Arab League.

It remains though that it is France's cultural diplomats who tackle the task with most frenzy. This is partly because they fight a losing battle with English, and partly because they still like to regard it as the main language of diplomacy. One French cultural attaché has been given to describing English as 'a communications medium distantly related to the language of Shakespeare'. It has gone as far as insistence that the successor to U Thant (not fluent in French) as secretary general of the United Nations must speak French. France pressed for the man who succeeded, Kurt Waldheim, who had a good command of the language, unlike his main rival, Max Jacobson of Finland.

English has all the advantages. It is the mother tongue of 309 million people (French is the first language of only sixty-three millions and is not even in the top ten spoken languages). It is the most used for communicating facts, and therefore is the international language of science, technology and economics; an inquiry by the Association of French speaking universities showed that it is used by ninety-seven per cent of the world's scientists. It is the language of most computers, the main language of Japanese and German salesmen, the predominant language in the United Nations, and is used internally in non-English speaking countries, as for example in nuclear factories in Brazil. It is spread by *Time* Magazine, movies and American business, and receives incidental help from propaganda broadcasts by the Chinese and Russians – in English. Franglais has invaded the French language, and words like beatnik, baby-sitter and hamburger finally achieved listing in the 1971 edition of *Petit Larousse*.

English has also largely superseded French as the diplomatic language in many parts of the world. French became the unofficial language of diplomacy during the eighteenth century when Latin was found wanting. Today even non-French diplomats regret its downgrading; it is, they say, the perfect diplomatic language because of its precision and clarity.

France, with the richness of its arts, also concentrates on overseas exhibitions. Exhibitions generally are a major part of cultural diplomacy. Some of the most striking are those which the east and west exchange. They are chosen to produce the image that the country wishes to achieve in the other. A 1972 Russian exhibition in the United States – 'Soviet Union: Arts and Crafts in Ancient Times and Today' – had a soft-sell approach. (The exhibits, explained a Soviet embassy first secretary, 'symbolise the friendship between all nations of our country'.) America in return sent an exhibition of gadgetry, from kitchen appliances to cars – a collective message of what the consumer-starved Russians were missing.

People are also exchanged: from students to ballet companies and jazz bands. France and Germany have mutual exchange programmes that embrace people from scouts to mature students.

Diplomats recommend local people in politics, industry, arts, science and labour who should be invited to their country. One American ambassador explained that his aim in making the choices was to find people not pro or anti the United States but 'those on the borderline who might be described as searching for an acceptable ideology'. Another says that one prime consideration for choosing people for the grants 'is the effect the choice of any one individual will have on expanding the Embassy's contact opportunities'. A third stresses he searches for the possible grantee's 'potential influence' in his country. Some missions persuade returning grantees to form themselves into associations.

Other image-making efforts include providing libraries abroad. Many countries do this on a large scale. Even tiny ones seem to feel it worthwhile; the Formosan embassy in the Vatican has one that includes a spacious reading-room. It was opened because the ambassador was concerned about the shortage of Formosan reading material in Italy, a not very surprising state of affairs. There is also what is the most purely propagandist part of the cultural machine, overseas broadcasting. Although the actual work is not carried out by diplomats, it is part of a country's overseas representation apparatus, and is controlled, or influenced, by diplomats and foreign ministries. After World War II, for example, it was at the insistence of powerful American diplomats that the Voice of America adopted a tough anti-communist line.

Programmes are beamed to and from the West and communist countries, into the Arab territories and Israel, and into Asia, Africa and Latin America where the transistor radio audience grows rapidly and where millions can be reached who cannot read. It has been called, accurately, the war of the airwaves. Although there was some radio diplomacy before World War II, by Britain and France and by Mussolini, it was Goebbels who made it an integral part of total diplomacy. The tone of radio diplomacy today ranges from the shrill to the friendly persuasive. Today's main practitioners (with 1969 broadcast hours a week in brackets) are: America (2,401), Russia (1,866), China (1,391) Britain (726), West Germany (705), Egypt (597), Albania (469). There has been great growth, and development, in the last two decades. In 1950 Britain headed the table (with 643 hours a week) with Russia and America second and third and Australia fourth. China's overseas broadcasting amounted to only sixty-six hours a week, and West Germany's was nil.

In Britain, overseas broadcasting is carried out by the External Service of the British Broadcasting Corporation. In 1971 there were thirty-nine foreign language services (including Swahili, Arabic, Chinese, French and Polish) and what is known as the World Service. The latter is broadcast for people whose first or second language is English and operates programmes of news, current affairs, plays, sport and music twenty-four hours a day, seven days a week – an effort, it is claimed, 'matched by no other country'. The strength of the British services, it is claimed, is that they are carried out by the B.B.C., an independent corporation.

The official U.S. overseas broadcasting arm, the Voice of America, comes under the U.S.I.A. It has a reputation for being more aggressive than the dispassionate-sounding BBC services. Forty per cent of its programmes are beamed at communist listeners. In addition 'private' radio networks have been much used, notably Radio Free Europe (for a long-time C.I.A.-

financed). Radio diplomacy has its counter-attack side: the jamming of foreign broadcasts.

Additionally, many countries make widescale use of film and recorded television material in friendly foreign countries. The U.S.I.A. for example, produces documentaries and newsreels and has over 7,500 projectors dotted about for showing films or for loan. The Agency spent nearly $250,000 and three years on a one-hour long film 'Vietnam, Vietnam', directed by John Ford. The film, showing the U.S. side in the controversy, was then shelved because of the change in attitudes and events since filming began.

Most countries run film shows at their overseas embassies. Sometimes the missions find it hard to attract large enough audiences. One Irish diplomat, in charge of the invitations, found the perfect solution. The invitation card promised: 'We will have drinks before the show, in the middle, and at the end.'

There is also a 'black' side to propaganda, close to espionage and subversion. Newspapers can be secretly subsidised in return for adopting an acceptable line: an English language newspaper the *Eastern Sun* in Singapore closed in 1971 after documentated Government accusations that it was financed by loans from communist intelligence sources in return for accepting instructions on editorial policy. The American C.I.A. has carried out the same kind of operation. And demonstrations meant to look 'spontaneous' and thus create favourable publicity for a cause can be organised. Soviet diplomats in London in 1971 produced documents that almost certainly proved one such case. There had been a Jewish demonstration at the embassy. Its cause (Jewish prisoners in Russia) was just. But it was secretly organised with the help of the Israeli embassy in London. One of the documents was the request to the Israelis for £644 48p to cover demonstration expenses.

Ten
Embassies and Espionage

'Intelligence is probably the least understood and
the most misrepresented of the professions.'
Allen Dulles

All nations spy. And, to a greater or lesser degree, all make use
of their embassies for some part of their espionage activities.

At a Soviet mission, up to seventy per cent of the 'diplomats'
may in fact be spies; Western ones never approach these figures,
but the number of intelligence officers on the staff can still be
considerable, and others on the diplomatic list may be drawn in
from time to time.

It is an embassy activity that no country is keen to admit or
publicise. Spying is not a nice word. Even the Soviet Military
Encyclopaedia has two entries – one 'military intelligence' for
what the Russians do and 'espionage' (with its sinister tone)
for what capitalist powers carry out.

A Canadian diplomat, John W. Holmes, in a lecture has presented what might be regarded as the Western line:

> It might be useful . . . to emphasise to any of you who may be
> confused on the subject, that diplomats and spies are different
> breeds, different professions, and they don't mix with each other.
> The diplomat is under strict instructions to keep away from skul-
> duggery. He gathers his information legitimately from newspapers,
> taxi drivers and at the very worst from a foreign cabinet minister
> whom he may have assisted towards mild inebriation.

Spy trials, both east and west, however, have shown how
closely intermingled is the world of the embassy and the work of
the spy. Eight English and five American diplomats in Moscow,
for example, were connected with Oleg Penkovsky, the Soviet
intelligence officer who fed information to the west. On one
occasion Penkovsky passed film concealed in a box of sweets to a
child to give to its mother – the wife of a British embassy attaché.

On another occasion a British embassy reception for the Queen's birthday was used as the contact point to hand Penkovsky a letter of instructions. The truth is that all nations spy according to their means, utilising the most suitable methods – and using embassies as espionage bases in one good method for many sound reasons.

Embassies and spying are closely linked in another respect. Because of the conversations that take place within missions, and the documents they hold, the buildings are targets in the audio-surveillance war. So too are the communications between embassies and home offices. The staff are also a focal point for the intelligence services of the host country. The British Radcliffe Committee on Security in 1962 said: 'The maintenance of security in the Foreign Service is in many ways more difficult than in the Home Civil Service. The staff are dispersed all over the world in relatively small units, and, operating in foreign countries, they are subject to attack by foreign intelligence services on a scale far greater (particularly behind the Iron Curtain) than is known in this country.' If the Russians ever had a similar committee report, it could say just the same.

It is in the nature of intelligence services that their size and budgets, and scale of operations are secret. The largest are certainly the Russian and American. The Soviet apparatus consists of two agencies – the K.G.B. (the Committee for State Security) and the smaller and less powerful G.R.U. (the Chief Intelligence Directorate of the Soviet General Staff). Both have men at missions, and the K.G.B. also has its operatives on the staffs of Tass and Pravda abroad and organisations like Intourist and the Moscow Narodny Bank. The Americans have nine major intelligence-collecting agencies, but the most important are the National Security Agency which intercepts messages to and from embassies and the Central Intelligence Agency, created in 1947, and with a staff estimated at 15,000 Americans and several thousand foreign agents, and a budget of probably over $600 million. C.I.A. men are now an integral part of U.S. missions.

Other important, though smaller, ones are the British and the French, both of which are highly regarded, the British more so. Israel is particularly respected in the world of intelligence. Experts from other nations talk of her two great coups: knowing the locations of all Egyptian planes before the 1967 Six-Day war, and learning the main details of Khrushchev's famous de-Stalinisation speech before other nations, including the United States.

The most spy-ridden capital in the world is probably Vienna – at least according to the Austrian Minister of the interior in 1970. He estimated, perhaps even proudly, that with 50,000 secret agents (half from the West and half from Soviet bloc countries) that the city was the espionage capital of the world. Vienna is certainly used as a clearing house and a handing-over point for material – sometimes from one nation to an unfriendly one via a third party. By accident, I was admitted to one meeting when a Soviet was handing over information from the Poles to an Austrian for transmission to Israel (both parties thought I was with the other).

But the actual spy-centre, certainly of Europe, is probably West Germany – a country regarded by the Soviets as an easy one in which to operate. In one year, 1970, West German counter intelligence captured over 750 communist spies, but it was reliably estimated that many thousands remained. The Russians have had notable successes there. A freelance photographer in Bonn managed to obtain from the secretary of a foreign ministry official nearly 1,000 secret papers before he was revealed by a defector; an important member of the German intelligence agency B.N.D., Heinz Felfe, was a double-agent who fed the communists details of agents operating in the East.

It is widely believed that countries spy only on their enemies. But it is not true. Although a large intelligence agency will direct the major part of its work towards its natural enemy – as for example, the U.S.A. at the U.S.S.R. – it will also seek secret information about the plans and intentions of even its closest allies. The United States, for example, knew before the Suez invasion of 1956 what Israel, Britain and France were likely to do. American intelligence had been spying on all three nations, possibly mainly through the interception of those countries' radio messages.

French intelligence is directed at the British and the Americans as well as the Soviets: the British at the Irish and vice versa; the Soviet at their fellow communists; and Egyptians at other Arab States.

Intelligence networks may also be unofficially *allowed* to operate in a clandestine way in a foreign country, as long as that
country feels the target is not its own nationals. A classic instance
of this is the operation of South African intelligence in London,
directed from the embassy, which concentrates on its own 'dis-
sident' nationals and anti-apartheid organisations. It has long
been allowed to function and has even been given some co-
operation. In return British intelligence expects information.

Espionage, like reports from diplomats, constitutes only one
part of a country's total Intelligence, a word that covers all the
material gathered by a nation from all sources. Intelligence
divides neatly into two components: that gathered openly, and
that collected clandestinely, the espionage part. The overt material
comes from diplomatic statements, from books, technical publications, newspapers, official reports, and radio and television broadcasts. Everything openly available is scrutinised by experts in
case it may be of use. Even novels are studied; they may point to
changing attitudes, or reveal small, but interesting, detail. Intelligence experts in the West estimate that perhaps ninety per
cent of all their Intelligence material comes from open sources.
The Russians, who have the advantage of western specialist journals and easily-obtained reports and papers, probably gather
ninety-five per cent of their information this way. In addition,
great volumes of material are collected by the cameras and monitoring devices of spy planes and ships and satellites.

The value of openly collected material is probably even greater
than its proportion. But countries regard it as not enough. It may
not be sufficient within itself, and much of the time it can contain
built-in deception – the purveyors knowing it will be picked
up. Because of this, the clandestine side (espionage) is regarded
as vital. Espionage is not new: the Chinese were practising it
before the birth of Christ and basically the methods of deception
and the types of agent have not changed much over the centuries.
The man spying for the British on Benjamin Franklin at the time
he was heading a mission to secure French assistance for the
colonial cause passed messages by placing them in a bottle in the
hollow root of a tree – what today's spy book addicts will recognise as 'dead drops' or 'dead letter boxes'. The basic problem –
obtaining secrets that the other side wishes to preserve – is also

timeless. But here priorities in the type of material sought may differ. The Americans are most interested in the military equipment, capabilities and policies of the communist world. On the political side, there is great attention paid to building up the information which will help policymakers judge accurately what the Russians or the Chinese will do *if*. Though obviously interested in the military side, much of Soviet espionage is directed at trying to obtain scientific and technological secrets. It was significant that when, in 1971, the U.K. ordered home ninety Russian officials and named fifteen others not allowed to return, the clandestine activities of the majority of them appeared to have been in the realms of industrial, scientific and weaponry technology.

A scientist and businessman whom the Russians thought they had recruited in the United States (he had actually informed the F.B.I. of their contact and was working under its instructions), later described the information which interested the Soviets. 'They basically wanted scientific and engineering reports. They consider, I think, that their technology is not up to ours, and I think this is what they really want. They don't need to know troop movements and things like this as the espionage people did during World War II. They want technology, new weapons, faster airplanes, rockets, things like this. They wanted proprietary industrial processes such as the oxygen steel process as installed in this country. They wanted details – what size pipe is used, the pressures, the operational details, so they could duplicate. They wanted this machine for applying constructional materials. They wanted records of classified technical meetings. There were several classified technical meetings or conferences during this period, and they asked me to go and get the proceedings or to order the proceedings later and to pass it on to them.'

There are reasons for this: the Russians, though operating a closed society which shuts its scientists and technologists off from contact with the rest of the world in all areas even vaguely related to defence, still needs to keep up with developments in the west. Much of the information they have to seek by espionage means could be discovered quite easily, and legally, by their western colleagues.

Whatever it seeks, espionage grinds small. Attachés visit bars used by journalists hoping for snippets of information. A chauffeur is persuaded to keep numbers of cars that visit his employer's address. In London one target was the office where details of car ownership are recorded. An official was asked to check lists of numbers to see whether they were kept in the routine files or in the special section, with restricted access, where intelligence men's vehicles are registered. In another a Soviet diplomat tried to obtain a Defence Ministry internal telephone directory.

'Clandestine intelligence,' says one officer, 'often means lots of bits, mostly routine, rarely of obvious importance.' It has been queried whether the vast effort, manpower, money and skills expended produce anything worthwhile. Some of the most valuable information, it is pointed out, has come from men like Klaus Fuchs, the atomic spy, who voluntarily fed information because of his Communist convictions, or from Penkovsky, so anxious to give information that he continued trying to make contact even after the Americans disregarded his early approaches (they were afraid he was acting as an agent provocateur). But the importance of reports from agents, lies in obtaining specified detailed information, in the chance discoveries, and in corroborating overtly-obtained material.

At operational level, espionage collection involves an intelligence officer and the agents he recruits and controls. The officer may be what the Soviets call 'legal' or he may be 'illegal'. Legals are officers who work from embassies; illegals are those who infiltrate a country, living there totally like nationals, probably working under the cover of some business. Western intelligence officers publicly refer to the practice of operating with illegals as a Soviet one, but other countries use it too.

It exists both to duplicate an embassy-based spy system (a vital precaution in case of the severance of diplomatic links or even war) and also to overcome some of the inherent disadvantages of legal espionage. Under the illegal system, a staff intelligence officer of the country concerned is trained and conditioned to pass himself off as the native of another country. He will firstly live abroad in that nation for a number of years, doing nothing untoward. Then he will be recalled for specific training for his assignment and sent off again, supplied with all the necessary papers and background. One notable illegal was Gordon Lonsdale, central figure in what the British called the Portland spy ring. He was a Ukrainian whose background was built up in Canada and whose spying activities took place in Britain. Another was Colonel Rudolf Abel who operated in the United States for nine years and, after being caught, was exchanged for the American spy 'plane pilot Gary Powers.

The system, developed by the Russians in the 1920s, has the advantage that if an illegal is caught, he cannot be directly tied to the embassy, thus lessening the degree of harm caused to relations with that country.

Legals and illegals have their own separate communications systems. The illegal is often supplied with a radio set, bought in the country to which he is assigned, and then altered by experts. Although it will then be equipped for sending messages, it will look like any other radio (because they are available internationally Japanese sets are often used). Illegals have a communications problem in that illicit radio signals can be picked up by the monitoring services of the country in which they are operating. However, messages can first be taped and then played over at fast tempo so that the operator is never on the air long enough for his location to be pinpointed.

An Israeli spy, Eliahu ben Shaul Cohen, who so successfully infiltrated Syria in the guise of a Lebanese of Syrian descent that he almost became deputy defence minister, sent coded reports almost daily for nearly two years until he was arrested in 1965. He chose as the location for his clandestine transmitter a site in the diplomatic quarter of Damascus. That way, his coded signals were just one of many in the area that the monitoring services picked up. His scheme worked until the day the Syrians decided to check new Russian equipment and ordered all missions to stop broadcasting. Only Cohen's signal remained, and he was traced, tried, and hanged.

Except in emergencies, legals and illegals have no contact. Money and materials are relayed to the illegals via the embassy diplomatic bag – delivered to the embassy and then passed on by 'dead drop'. But there are also illegal courier routes in operation. The illegals will usually stay in a country once they are placed there; legals are constantly moved around like the diplomats they pretend to be.

Compared with their illegal colleagues, spy-diplomats at missions have one disadvantage. They are under surveillance, and often followed. The Soviet press attaché in Ottawa in the mid-1960s complained: 'I'm followed all the time, night and day. I'm followed when I go out fishing and when I take my wife and three-year-old child out for ice-cream. Sometimes one police car follows me, sometimes there are three. Sometimes when I'm lost I ask them the way.' But the number to be watched in some countries can be huge (one explanation as to why the British expelled 105 Soviets was that surveillance had become impossible with so many Russians in London; 'much of the time we didn't know where most of them were', one officer said). Experts say that it takes eight people to mount day and night surveillance of one man.

All spy diplomats are trained in losing those following them. They also frequently wander to no set pattern, visiting places for purely legal reasons, so that observers cannot identify any special area that interests them.

Despite this problem (and the associated one of diplomats sometimes being restricted in the distance they are allowed to travel) embassies have many advantages as bases for spying. They offer 'cover' to foreigners – who ostensibly are in the country as ordinary diplomats dealing with politics, trade, culture or information. The embassy building is immune from raid or search and houses radio and cipher facilities. And the diplomatic bag provides a safe and regular means of communicating documents and the money to pay agents they recruit.

Intelligence officers in embassies may be listed in the diplomatic list as first, second or third secretaries or attachés. In larger missions they may be given counsellor rank, useful at least in the British service in explaining the decorations accumulated by an intelligence man that would hardly have been awarded him as a low-ranking diplomat.

The Russians also give counsellor 'cover' to intelligence operators. Royal Air Force Chief Technician Douglas Britten, jailed in 1968 for twenty-one years for passing information including codes, was recruited and 'run' by a counsellor in the cultural section at the Russian embassy in London. The officer in charge of the British spies George Blake and William John Vassall also held counsellor rank on the embassy staff.

In Soviet missions, the man in charge of legal espionage – the *rezident* – used to be the military attaché. Today, although the defence man will be a G.R.U. officer, he never holds this top-position: it would make identifying him too easy for rival intelligence organisations. This does not mean Soviet service attachés do not spy. In 1971 the assistant military and air attaché at the Soviet embassy in Tokyo was caught trying to buy from an American G.I. the plans for missile and radar systems.

In Western services at least, the intelligence men are under the ambassador. President Kennedy's letter of 1961 stressing the authority of ambassadors over mission staff was in part the result of C.I.A. activities emanating from embassies getting out of hand. Usually today a C.I.A. man will tell an ambassador what he is doing and will show him his reports. But he will not explain how he plans to carry out his assignment (which may involve bribery, blackmail or bugging) nor give the sources for the information contained in the reports.

The relationship between diplomats proper and the intelligence men is often a fraught one. Diplomats concede that agents now look and act more like other mission staff than they used to, thus making their cover more plausible and their presence less openly embarrassing. (Even the K.G.B. men who once had a reputation for looking like screen heavies are now much more sophisticated.) But many ambassadors do not want to know about them. Overall there is a feeling that what they do is not 'nice'; to the diplomat their presence always represents a potential embarrassment. In any event, as far as the diplomat is concerned, the material they collect is very much second rate compared with what he gathers and interprets. For Communist countries, on the other hand, espionage is an integral part of 'total diplomacy'.

The basic job of any legal officer is to recruit and run agents, almost always nationals of the country in which he is based. These networks of agents form the basis of clandestine intelligence operations. The intelligence officer's control, guidance and support of the agents within his network, may be exercised direct or through intermediaries. In British parlance the intelligence officer's embassy office is the 'station'.

Information gathered from agents goes first to the intelligence officer who then carries out a preliminary assessment for accuracy and use. If he considers it valuable, it is transmitted home. At large key-embassies there may be several officers, each with their own agents reporting to them.

The 'cover' of C.I.A. agents is often quickly broken by local people. In 1962 a naval captain, Charles R. Clark Jr, who was naval attaché in Havana from 1957 to 1960, talked of the C.I.A. during questioning by the Senate Internal Security Subcommittee. He said that at Havana there had been 'a considerable number' of C.I.A. people in the embassy. But their cover had been 'terrible'. He told the hearing: 'Everybody in town who had any interest in it knew who they were. . . .' At missions where there is a large contingent of intelligence men, they will be isolated in a specially secure and restricted part of the embassy – it in itself a pointer to local staff who they are.

The cover of a mission does, however, provide the intelligence officer with a legitimate and easy access to potential agents. At receptions, parties and on visits he can concentrate on establishing contact with likely candidates, some of whom will have been invited at intelligence's request.

During the social conversation at a reception, the intelligence officer may say he is sorry that they cannot talk more; perhaps they could meet again, possibly for a meal. All countries use this method. A Polish radio telegraphist in a military establishment, Adam Kaczmarzyk, executed in 1969 for spying for Britain, was recruited at a film show at the British embassy in Warsaw.

The pattern of initial contact, recruitment and assessment is illustrated by cases on F.B.I. files of Americans who pretended to be co-operating with Communist intelligence agencies after being approached by them.

One man, an executive of a machinery and equipment company, was approached by a Russian employee of the United Nations International Children's Emergency Fund on the excuse that the Soviet was seeking equipment for undeveloped countries. Another, a State Department employee, had to call on the Czech embassy in Washington in the course of his work. During one visit he was invited to a reception by one of the diplomats. 'We had a very pleasant social discussion, and during the reception he (the diplomat) suggested that we should get together at a later date, and become a little more acquainted and perhaps have dinner together, and so forth.'

A third was assessed over a four year period. At first he was asked 'for simple reports and for things that were not highly classified'. They checked his background at the same time. 'They obtained all my biographical data, where I worked and schooling. They had photos of me from magazine articles. They had photos of my family. They tried to develop a personal friendship where we talked about everything. We went to lunch and to dinner. And they gave me vodka and . . . other items . . . .'

The intelligence officer will ease his new agent in gradually, building up his work, giving him small assignments and errands. It is part of the testing process, and is also designed to ensure that later the recruit finds it difficult to refuse more major assignments for fear of being betrayed to his own side.

Intelligence officers occasionally get agents who work for them for ideological reasons. But they form the smallest proportion, and perhaps surprisingly, these agents are often distrusted. 'The unpaid agent,' said Kim Philby, 'is apt to behave independently, and to become an infernal nuisance. He has, almost certainly, his own political axes to grind, and his sincerity is often a measure of the inconvenience he can cause.'

Much more preferred are agents who can be bribed or blackmailed or both. The intelligence officer is always seeking people in debt or living beyond their means. Money and sex are a powerful combination. The British spy Harry Houghton who supplied the communists with information from the Underwater Weapons Research Establishment was recruited while at the British embassy in Warsaw, Poland. First the Poles inveigled him into blackmarket currency transactions and then compromised him with his Polish mistress. Homosexuals are universally considered a security risk because of the opportunities of compromising them (Vassall had his behaviour recorded). Anyone with relatives behind the Iron Curtain is particularly susceptible to pressures.

'The search,' says one veteran western operator, 'is for weaknesses. Once you find them, you start applying pressure. This is best done by stages.' Often a combination of pressures will be tried. In one American case, a man the Russians were interested in was subjected to four. First they told him they had located relatives in Russia. Then they obtained handwritten reports from him which later could have been used for blackmail. They had him implicate himself by performing minor assignments. And they also offered him money and his firm contracts.

Offering sex – followed by blackmail – is an age-old technique. Because of the attempt to convey the impression that such methods are practised only by *them*, there are sometimes delusions about the use of this by one's own country. Allen Dulles, being questioned on television in June 1963, was asked how widespread was the use of sex in espionage.

> Dulles: I think it is world wide. As long as there is sex, it is going to be used.
> Question: Does American intelligence ever use sex as a bait to get information?
> Dulles: I don't discuss those matters very much.
> Question: We at least don't use it as widely as the Soviets do?
> Dulles: No, we certainly do not. We recognise the existence of sex and the attraction of sex, though.

That, probably, conveys the true picture: the west does practise the same methods, but perhaps not *quite* as much or so unpleasantly.

In controlling and operating his agents, the diplomat-spy will use all the techniques of espionage: messages that mean something else; false-bottom containers; ciphers; Minox cameras; radio transmitters; 'dead-drops'; and 'live-passes'.

At Oleg Penkovsky's trial it was revealed that he had been given a set of picture postcards with English addresses. If he changed his place of work, one card would be posted – to Mrs N. Nixon in Berkshire, England. This would contain a view from the Kotelnichesky Embankment and carry the message: 'I am having a pleasant time and have even found that I like vodka. Moscow actually looks this way and you should see the size of the streets. I will give you all the details on my return. With love, Dick.'

'Dead drops' are the passing over of material without making personal contact. The material is usually hidden in a container such as a can or cigarette packet, or (after being reduced to microdots) in a hollowed out battery or pencil or coin. This is then left by the diplomat or his agent in a prearranged place such as a tree root or at the base of a sign post for collection by the other.

A scientist/businessman, John Huminik Jr, working under F.B.I. guidance after being approached by Soviet spy-diplomats in the United States, told the Committee on Un-American Activities the procedure he was told to adopt.

Now what Revin (one of the Soviet diplomats involved) wanted me to do was to photograph material, classified documents, et cetera; put the film in a beer can or a cola can; take it to the predesignated spot at the predesignated time and place it there. Then I was to go to a telephone booth and mark a specific page on the phone book with a number ending in three zeros, for example. Revin would then check the booth and he would know that the drop was 'loaded'.

Revin would then himself, or have one of his associates, 'unload' the drop. Then he would mark the book in the phone booth with numbers that would tell me that he had 'unloaded' the drop. Now the way this worked, for instance, if the drop was at 11 o'clock at night, I would go to the area, place the can with the film in the predesignated spot, and cover it with leaves. A half hour after or fifteen minutes later, I would go into a specific phone booth, maybe miles away, and put the numbers on a certain page. Then I would go home.

Revin would go check the book and he would see that the numbers were in the page. He would then unload the drop. Then he would drive all the way across town to the booth that was assigned to me and mark another number on a specific page, which told me the next morning that the film had been picked up. If the numbers were not on my phone book, then I was to go back and get the material because this meant he could not get it for some reason. So it is very elaborate; it protected him from being directly involved with me. If he saw something suspicious in these areas, he could leave the material there, making it very difficult for the F.B.I. to apprehend him in the act of getting the film, because they were always deserted areas. You could see clearly that there was no one there.

He also described 'live passes' – ones where information is handed over personally – in which he was involved:

One was at the Riggs Plaza shopping centre in North-east Washington. I went on December 2, 1965, to a phone booth and pretended like I was making a phone call. I then went back to my car and waited. Valentine Revin drives up in his car, goes into the phone booth and pretends like he makes a call. He gets into his car, and I follow. He leads me on a chase for maybe forty minutes through the city, going all over the city, I don't even remember. We were driving so fast we both should have gotten tickets; it is a wonder the police didn't catch us. He wanted to go fast because nobody could follow. If you go fast, you can usually tell if somebody is following.

We finally ended up in Silver Spring near the Sligo Creek Parkway. We pulled up to another stop sign, and a Volkswagen starts up about a block away – another Soviet vehicle. Then we go down along a three mile or four mile road that has no access roads. The Volkswagen goes ten miles an hour, and we go sixty. Pretty soon we leave the Volkswagen, which blocks up the road so if the F.B.I. were following they could not get by. Where the stop sign is he opened his hood as though he were having car trouble. I walk up and throw the stuff in his front seat, and that was it.

The spy diplomat also schools his agent in how to abort meetings if he believes he is being watched or followed. Methods that have been used to cancel face to face interceptions include transferring a newspaper from one hand to another, taking out a handkerchief, and fumbling with a tie. All indicate that contact should be avoided and the diplomat and his agent simply walk past each other. Methods are also detailed for cancelling meetings further in advance. One that has been used involved the agent going to a prearranged telephone box and drawing a circle around the first name in one specified alphabetical section. Sometime later, his controller visits the box and checks to see if the meeting has been cancelled. If the name has been ringed, it has.

There are two sides to the espionage activities of every country. There is the attacking arm which seeks to obtain material illegally, and the defending one which tries to prevent others doing the same as far as its own nation is concerned.

This applies in every part of the work. Intelligence officers from nation A try to enrol diplomats from nation B whose own intelligence officers have tried to ensure that any such attempts will be unsuccessful. Country A tries to see what is inside embassies, intercept its radio messages, tap its telephones and plant electronic surveillance devices in its offices. At the same time country B is guarding the building, encoding the wireless communications, using scrambled telephones, and seaching for bugging devices.

Because one of the easiest ways to obtain information is to

ensnare a diplomat as an agent to spy on his own country, vetting plays a major part in all diplomatic services. In Britain, for example, they undergo 'positive vetting', the highest form of security checks for civil servants. But in all services, vetting has never been totally successful in finding all security risks, some of whom have later turned to spying. During a series of special checks during one year in the late 1960s, the American State Department found nineteen homosexuals who had got through the security procedures and joined the staff. All resigned on being confronted with the fact. Western experts point to the difficulty of reconciling personal liberty and the amount of checking that can be carried out. But even in Russia, where this is hardly a problem, risks get through. And, in the west, the most rigid checking procedures of all are probably those adopted by the National Security Agency, but there have still been failures. Psychiatric consultants and lie-detector tests are used. In 1960, however, two of the Agency's cryptologists defected to Russia, and subsequent investigation revealed twenty-six 'sexual deviants' working on the staff.

The next point of attack, and defence, after the diplomat is the embassy itself and its contents. The British diplomatic service spends about £5 million a year on protective security; the deployment of security guards to embassies costs about £1.25 million a year. The Americans use Marine Security Guards to make physical security checks at night and to control who enters and leaves outside working hours. There were about 1,000 of them overseas in mid-1970. There may be as many as thirty-five at a major embassy. Depending on the country in which they are based, they may be armed – as they are, for example, in Italy, France and Germany. In some countries they can only wear arms within the embassy, not on the streets. Officials stress their role is to protect classified material and communications – 'not' says one, 'to turn the place into a fortress or have a shootout if demonstrators try to invade a mission'.

In addition there are regional security officers; one, for example, covers France, another Italy and Malta, and a third North Africa. They check and advise on security measures to be adopted – the kind of locks, gates, fences. In many missions particularly in communist countries, closed circuit television is widely used. The regional officers are professional security men, many of whom have worked in military intelligence. Much of security involves constant small precautions – such as destroying all confidential waste (including carbons), and seeing doors and drawers are locked. At each embassy there will be a post security officer – not a professional, but a diplomat who has had special briefings.

Embassies are laid out on a zone system, with the highest security for the most sensitive zones, such as the communications centre. In the most sensitive, only specific mission staff will be allowed entry.

Closely linked with physical security is the classification system. There are five broad classifications: top secret, secret, confidential, restricted and unclassified. A distribution classification may be added. For example, the State Department has three special classifications within the Top Secret band for especially sensitive material – *No* distribution, Exclusive distribution and Limited distribution. The first is not restricted as it seems; an average ten copies are made of each 'No distribution' message.

The classification of material is important because it determines the amount of effort which should go into its protection – where it is kept, what kind of locks shall be used, and who shall be allowed access. In all services there is a tendency to over-classify, in order to play safe. The result is often the over protection of too much material. Classified material will be kept in a zone inaccessible to locally engaged staff, no matter how well they have been checked.

The other espionage activities all involve surveillance – of the wireless communications, telephone conversations, or of activities within offices.

The most important of these by far is radio interception. Wireless communication is widely used in the diplomatic service, even though its use (unlike courier services) is not a right under international law. The embassy should, theoretically, have the permission of the host country. Some countries object to diplomatic transmitters within their capitals, but such transmitters are not hard to conceal and with modern systems aerials are easy to disguise. Every large American embassy has its own transmitter. The British Diplomatic Wireless Service provides links with about seventy embassies, and is being extended. The British receiving station, in north Buckinghamshire, has huge aerials covering ninety-four acres of ground, and overseas relay stations are in St Helena and Darwin. The British Foreign Office will not specify the missions involved because in some cases permission of the governments has not been sought.

The important point, as far as espionage is concerned, is that all radio messages can be intercepted. The process does not even break any national or international law. Because of this messages are encoded, and if they are to make sense to the interceptors, have to be decoded. In one recent year forty-four per cent of State Department's messages were in code and, perhaps more surprisingly, so were eight per cent of those of the United States Information Agency.

The world of codes has its own language. The overall term for the field of codes and ciphers is 'cryptology'. Cryptography is the side of the work that has to do with devising and protecting them. Cryptanalysis, on the other hand, has to do with breaking them. In a code, a word, a group of letters or numbers, is substituted for a whole word or phrase. For example, bxfd or 1749 could stand for one word such as 'enemy' or a group such as 'it is believed that' whenever it appeared in a message. A cipher involves one symbol – either a letter or number – standing for a single letter. For example 'c' could mean 'z'. Today, with complicated ciphers, the same symbol can represent a different letter every time it is used. For greater security, a message can first be coded, and then turned into cipher. Today most messages are ciphered and translated automatically: an end to the days when diplomats used to cipher laboriously with the aid of the manual.

Vast resources are poured into the field. The countries with the best codes and ciphers are the United States, Russia, Britain and France. It is unlikely that, as a rule, Russia and America can break each other's codes, notwithstanding a claim by Khrushchev in 1959 that the Soviets had intercepted messages from President Eisenhower to Prime Minister Nehru of India. 'You're wasting your money,' he said during an American visit. 'You might as well send it (the information) direct to us instead of the middleman, because we get most of it anyway.'

For highest security, a cipher in which every letter is represented by a different symbol every time it is used, can be utilised *once* only and then destroyed. Because code-breaking depends on finding some pattern in the ciphered messages being studied, this makes it unbreakable.

But for practical reasons this cannot be used for the mass of information transmitted each day, and many codes can – and are – broken. A number of countries have code-breaking agencies, among them Britain, Germany, France, several Latin American, some Arab, Japan and Israel. But, again not surprisingly, America and Russia have the largest and most lavish organisations. Little is known of the Soviet, though it is conceded by Western experts to be 'excellent'.

In America, the code-making and code-breaking agency, the National Security Agency, has its headquarters on an eighty-two acre site at Fort Meade, Maryland, and it is much more secret than the C.I.A. Even the directive of 1952 establishing the agency was classified, and its sheer existence was not publicly acknowledged for five years. Then, in 1957, the *United States Government Organisation Manual* said that the Agency 'performs highly specialised technical and co-ordinating functions relating to the national security'. Its 'technical functions,' David Kahn says in his detailed study *The Code-Breakers*, 'basically consist of intercepting, traffic analysing, and cryptanalysing the messages of all other nations, friend as well as foe.' By 1960, N.S.A. reportedly employed 10,000 people at home and at least 1,000 abroad, and was spending about $380 million on its overseas interception network and another $100 million at headquarters, making it probably the largest intelligence agency outside Russia.

Every audible transmission of every country, twenty-four hours a day, is intercepted. Computers are widely used to support experts trying to break codes, and N.S.A. probably has more computer equipment than any other installation in the world. Of the agency's success in code-breaking, Kahn thinks this probably ranges from being able to read all messages in a given system to total failure. Two N.S.A. defectors said after fleeing the United States that the agency solved codes of more than forty nations in the world (that would constitute half the world's total nations then) and that they included Italy, Turkey, France, Yugoslavia, U.A.R., Indonesia and Hungary.

Because the protection of codes is so vital, cipher rooms are especially guarded in all missions. At the American mission at the U.N., the code room has a three and a quarter inch steel door and guards on duty outside. Defectors to the West have indicated the precautions taken in Soviet embassies. In Ottawa the cryptographic keys were kept in a sealed bag that was placed each night in a steel safe that was within a suite of rooms, closed by double steel doors. The white opaqued windows had iron bars and steel shutters. In Australia, the key to the safe in which cipher documents were kept was stored in an envelope sealed with wax and a signet and locked inside another safe. In the 1960s the Soviet embassy in Washington had chemicals at hand which would eat through a thick pile of papers within seconds. Perhaps the most dramatic illustration of how closely a nation guards its codes, however, was in Ottawa in 1956 when the Soviet embassy was on fire. The Russians let the flames gut the building rather than allow foreigners inside.

One still gets bizarre examples, however, which show that security can be less than total. J. K. Galbraith provides one. While in Toronto, he asked that a cable from Washington to New Delhi be repeated to him through the Toronto consulate. 'It arrived in code; no facilities existed for decoding. They brought it out to me at the airport – a mass of numbers. I asked if they assumed I could read it. They said no. I asked how they managed. They said when something arrived in code, they 'phoned Washington and had the original message read to them.'

Telephone conversations are also intercepted. Although scrambled telephones have so long been a basic feature of spy books and films, it is not generally realised how many telephone lines are not 'safe'. Lord George-Brown talked frequently to the British representative at the United Nations in New York before hearing from his permanent under secretary: 'This open-line telephoning to Hugh Caradon must be giving the Russians and lord knows who else a tremendous bonus.' (As a result, a direct, secure line was installed.) The majority of lines to embassies are still not scrambled.

The most modern, highest priority scramblers (there are ones offering a lower degree of safety) are today highly secure. The State Department has such lines, for example, to missions in

Seoul, Paris, Geneva, London, Bonn, Berlin, and Rome among others. Apart from a safe line to the United Nations there is also a secure photocopying transmitting machine. On lines other than these diplomats assume they can, and perhaps are, being overheard. The amount of caution to be exercised depends on the country. Certainly a diplomat posted to an 'unfriendly' power takes it for granted that his telephone is bugged. So do diplomats in a number of nations with a reputation for the practice, such as France and Italy. One British ambassador says: 'I adopt the system of either saying nothing worthwhile, or deliberately planting stuff in the conversation that I want them to know.' An American diplomat in Prague reportedly used to drive the communists crazy by talking Eskimo over the telephone on a tapped line. Again, tapping is a technique used by East and West. Communist countries in Oslo in the mid-1960s set out to check whether their calls were being monitored. Over the telephone they exchanged messages about a proposed demonstration outside the U.S. Embassy. The demonstration was fictitious. But at the time they had said it would take place, they were able to note that there was a large police guard around the American mission.

Another line of attack consists of the whole range of audio-surveillance, ranging through telephoto lenses, infra-red light to illuminate darkened rooms, directional microphones and 'spike' microphones that pick up the vibrations in walls made by speech in a room. Those vibrations can then be 'translated' back into speech. A laser beam directed into a room, and bounced back will be modulated by sound waves of speech in the room and can then be transformed into sound.

The equipment constantly changes and becomes more refined. It means a continuous battle between the attackers and the defenders. 'You find a more sophisticated way of doing it, and then counter equipment comes along. Then your device has to get more sophisticated and so on,' says one expert. 'It never stays still.' The most common form of audio-surveillance attack is simply the planting of microphones. It has become an almost traditional part of the intelligence battle. Sir Anthony Eden, visiting Geneva in 1954, was warned that any meetings in his sitting-room would be overheard. 'It was suggested that as a precaution I should accompany my talk with some "noises off", such as beating on the tables, which would confuse any would-be listeners,' he recalled in his memoirs.

Such unsophisticated counter measures could hardly be expected even to 'confuse' the listeners today. After his arrest Greville Wynne, the British businessman who acted as an intermediary with Penkovsky, was played recordings of his conversations with the Russian. Even though they had turned on the radio and television before talking, the Soviet intelligence men had succeeded in separating that sound from their voices which came across clear. 'At the time we thought we were safe, but we were wrong,' Wynne said in his account, *The Man from Moscow*.

Planting microphones in missions has been a serious business. In 1947 British experts reportedly found six in the British embassy in Moscow prior to the arrival of the British foreign minister. In 1964 the State Department announced that experts had found forty microphones which had been embedded eleven years earlier in the walls of the American embassy in Moscow. According to the Department, between 1949 and 1964 over 130 listening devices of various sorts were found in U.S. missions in communist countries. Perhaps the most famous case was that of the microphone installed in a wooden replica of the Great Seal of the United States which was presented to the U.S. embassy in Moscow in 1945. It was discovered in 1952, and displayed by the U.S. during a 1960 Security Council debate at the United Nations.

The Czechs attempted to plant one in the bureau of the chief of the Office of Eastern European Affairs in the State Department. A bookcase was chosen as the most suitable place, and a sample of wood from such a bookcase was obtained by a State Department employee the Czechs thought was working for them. A year later a Czech diplomat gave the employee a transmitting microphone that could be placed under the front bottom lip of a bookcase, out of sight. It was roughly the size of a ruler, and capable of being operated by remote control from outside the building. On the designated date, the employee took it into the building but handed it over to waiting FBI men.

In the defence against planted microphones countries have teams of experts touring missions. In Iron Curtain countries, says one expert, 'you always work on the assumption that there is something there'. Some embassies, like the U.S. mission in Sofia, are in a building with government departments on either side – a searcher's nightmare. There are common walls, with Soviet intelligence next door. ('What's a damn sight nicer,' says one, 'is a place in a field with an acre of ground all around you.')

There are a number of routine procedures in searching embassies for electronic devices. The first is a physical search. Secondly, the building is checked with a device that locates metal, rather like a mine detector. Thirdly, a radio frequency probe is used to sweep all the wavebands to see if there are any signals being transmitted. Other equipment is used to check the building's wiring to see if any unauthorised device has been attached to it.

But, despite the care taken and the increasing sophistication of the equipment used, the procedures cannot be totally successful. Bugging equipment can be made that will not register on a metal detector. And sweeping the wavebands for signals will yield nothing unless the bug is transmitting a signal – and today sophisticated transmitters are left dormant most of the time and switched on when wanted by a radio signal beamed in from outside.

The State Department Office of Security came across one case in a communist country where the bug was discovered only because of the howling of a dog. The dog began to whine while an expert was checking the home of a military attaché. The animal was obviously in pain, and appeared to be in heated combat with an invisible enemy in a corner of the room.

Mystified, the engineer stopped work to investigate. After a few minutes' study, he noticed that the parquet floor on which the invisible warrior was waging battle with the dog showed signs of recent tampering – which aroused his curiosity. Pulling up several of the parquet slabs, he uncovered an F.M. device which was transmitting to a distant eavesdropper all the conversations held in the room.

Analysis of this device indicated that it was turned on and off by a high pitched tone inaudible to humans, but disturbing, if not painful, to a dog.

Intelligence experts say that the teams of travelling technicians, however successful or unsuccessful in their searches, do have a deterrent affect on foreign secret services: 'By keeping on checking you discourage them from doing things they'd run rampant with otherwise,' says an American intelligence officer. 'It's like checking people out. You may only find two per cent of them are security risks – but you've got to remember all the people who were afraid to apply because they knew you'd investigate them.'

Although the West concentrates most of its attention on its missions behind the Iron Curtain (and communists on their embassies in the West), all embassies are checked. 'This thing is worldwide,' says a counter-espionage man. 'The only difference behind the Curtain is that you're in their backyard and its easier for them. But intelligence services hostile to us are at work everywhere – not just in their own countries.'

For the actual construction and wiring work in sensitive parts of a mission, countries import their own men. As a result of experiences in Moscow, the United States since 1964 has used the U.S. Navy.

Despite that, embassies cannot be guaranteed safe, and diplomats in 'hostile' countries have to assume that most parts of the buildings are not secure. For this reason, 'vulnerable' embassies will have one specially protected section reserved for sensitive discussions. The system used is that of rooms within rooms, rather like boxes fitting into other boxes. There may be two or more rooms depending on the degree of protection considered necessary. Whatever the number the principle is the same. The outer room will have been checked and searched, and any wiring and construction carried out by safe personnel. The inner room will be sound proof. And it may be even made of glass so that the presence of anything attached to it would show immediately.

Eleven

Diplomats Behind the Iron Curtain

'We are all most polite to our tails; we don't give
them any trouble.'
British diplomat in Moscow

The possibility that his office and his home are bugged is one
of the little facts of life to which a diplomat behind the Iron
Curtain must become accustomed. But it is only one of the factors
that make a communist country a very special kind of posting.
When the surveillance is not electronic, it will be personal. The
few local people who will talk to him are probably spies, as are
the local staff with whom he works. Officials will speak in parrot
phrases. His movements will be strictly controlled. Isolated, he
will be forced to live a vacuum-like existence, collecting hints and
crumbs of information.

His life ought to be impeccable; he will have been warned by
security about approaches, pressures and blackmail attempts.
And at times of bad relations, he may be harassed by the authorities, have his car wrecked by an 'angry crowd' or find himself
condemned in the press. In the West there is a tradition that
diplomats should be immune from personal attacks. Sir Ernest
Satow even maintained that in countries where the communications media is government controlled, there was a *duty* to prevent
such attacks. None of this applies behind the Curtain. The Soviet
press will name 'diplomatic spies' as it did in 1971 when the
newspaper *Isvestia* accused a British naval attaché and three
assistants of gathering information on Soviet shipyards, coastal
patrol boats, docks, anti-aircraft defences and location of air-
fields. The diplomat may even find himself immortalised in book
form as some did in 1949 when the Soviet published *The Truth
about American diplomats*, ostensibly written by a former American citizen, but based on material from secret police files which
was then suitably embellished. A stage upwards, he may be

expelled – perhaps because he has been spying but just as possibly as a reprisal for the treatment of a communist diplomat in his own country.

Many query whether diplomats should be based in communist countries at all. The first argument against is a purely emotional one – that because the communists do not play by the rules, they should be ostracised. After the Canadian Government and China re-established diplomatic relations late in 1970, the British magazine *The Diplomatist* began its report: 'A new Ambassador is soon to join the ranks of those who may have their hair pulled and their faces spat at in Peking. . . . After this cynical Canadian decision supporters of moral stands and fair play on the international scene have good reason indeed to be depressed.' A former diplomat, commenting publicly on suggestions that Britain should elevate its representation in Peking from a *chargé d'affaires*, thundered: 'As it took Russian communism fifty years to destroy somewhere around eighty to a hundred million people, it is clear . . . that the Chinese Reds have certainly not been wasting time, with a score of at least forty million in only a little over twenty years. In the face of these figures anyone who imagines he can get anywhere by appeasing communists is asking for all that is coming to him.' Such arguments – that it is no good co-operating or trying to deal with *them* – are also widely found among military men.

But there are also arguments that missions are not worthwhile on practical grounds. 'What do we gain by it?' argues a right-wing Western politician. 'A bit of trade, a few cultural exchanges, and a minimum of information. Can anyone really say that this is worth the cost and the effort involved?'

And it is true that most information that reaches the West about communist countries is from non-diplomatic sources. Kremlinologists examine every line of the main Russian newspapers, *Pravda* (Truth) and *Isvestia* (News), seizing upon every nuance (despite the fact that it has been well said that the titles of the two papers mean there is no truth in *Isvestia* and no news in *Pravda*). Intelligence analysts sift through the transcripts of monitored communist broadcasts, both those beamed at foreign listeners and those intended for domestic consumption. It was a young woman at an American Government listening post who spotted the Russian decision in 1961 to resume atomic testing, not a diplomat. It was contained in a vague item transmitted by Radio Moscow for publication in a provincial Soviet journal.

The situation is the same with communist China, where at least ninety per cent of the information comes from official sources such as the *People's Daily*, Peking Radio or the New China News Agency. Hong Kong is full of 'China watchers'; even the Russians comb the colony for titbits of gossip, usually small and often false.

Diplomats themselves sometimes feel doubts. Sir William Hayter, after his first year in Moscow, discussed in a despatch to the British Foreign Office whether it was worth maintaining an embassy there at all. He concluded that it was. On balance, most diplomats would agree with him. They claim that, despite the scarcity of information and the lack of diplomatic intercourse, there are still advantages. The first is that the diplomat, though living a restricted life, can get some *feel* of the country. 'It's easy to scoff at this,' says a British diplomat who has served in Peking. 'But it is important. I know of several specific instances where facts were available outside China – but they were interpreted in a different way by those outside and those in Peking. The embassy interpretations turned out to be correct because there the facts had been seen in their Chinese perspective.'

Another, a Scandinavian, argues that a second case for missions in communist states is that they allow diplomats to get some experience of countries whose impact on the international scene 'is no less real for us not liking them'. He says: 'If you've got to live with them – and we have – you can't have a diplomatic service composed of people who have never been anywhere near China or Russia. They may not gain too much there, but the subject is so vital that even a little is better than nothing.'

There is also the claim that Western missions prove to communist countries that *if* they want to be friendly, the West is ready and waiting. 'The last thing you want,' says a diplomat, 'is for communist countries to feel isolated. And that means you have to play your part in keeping a link between them and the rest of the world.' A British diplomat argues that in the case of China this philosophy was proved justified: 'We stuck it out there through some bad times, periods when some of the newspapers were saying we were weak and absurd to stay. But then relations improved to an astonishing degree; the Chinese became keen to improve relations. What we did has paid dividends.'

Even when relations are comparatively friendly, diplomacy in a communist country is still hedged with controls, conditions and frustrations.

The restriction of travel is one factor that makes even the *feel* the diplomat gets of the country debatable. In modern times nations have widely accepted that to fulfil their role diplomats should enjoy freedom of movement. In 1961 this right was written into the Vienna Convention on Diplomatic Relations which said that the host country 'shall ensure to all members of the mission freedom of movement and travel in its territory'.

But the Convention provided a loophole for nations wanting to restrict diplomatic travel, as many already had. It agreed that free movement need not apply to areas and installations closed for security reasons. Both communist and non-communist countries have made wide use of this to control the freedom of each other's diplomats. The first travel ban was imposed by the Russians in 1941. Because bans are followed by retaliations, the practice has spread to many countries of the world. The communists curb the movement of Western diplomats; in the non-communist world, countries that have placed restrictions on communist officials include the United States, Canada, France, Britain, the Netherlands, Italy, Belgium, Greece, West Germany, Japan and the Argentine. Special travel restrictions have also been place by the United States on visiting leaders. Khrushchev, attending the 1960 meeting of the United Nations General Assembly, was subject to the most stringent travel restrictions ever imposed on an official attending the U.N. He was confined to Manhatten Island, and asked to limit his movements to those required for his official mission.

The precise restrictions at any given time vary. It is usually worked on an eye for an eye basis: Britain's diplomats in Moscow cannot travel more than twenty-five miles from the centre of the city without permission; neither can Soviet officials in London.

In China, at the beginning of the 1970s, diplomats were confined to a fourteen miles radius of Peking, an area clearly marked on maps provided by the Chinese Foreign Ministry. There were two exceptions: an artery of about seventeen miles leading to the airport, and a longer one to the Great Wall (though this has been placed out of bounds on occasions when there were military developments concerned with the Sino-Soviet Dispute). Outside of those areas, diplomats are allowed to travel on forty-eight hours notification to five major cities, including Shanghai and Canton, though, normally, seeking permission is only a formality.

Travel restrictions are not only directed between the East and West. Russia and China also impose them on each other's diplomats. In 1970, for example, the Chinese denied the Russians permission to make their annual visit to Manchuria to place flowers on the graves of their soldiers who died fighting the Japanese.

Security is one reason for restricting travel. But for Communist countries there is another vital one. 'They are still terrified of the impact of foreign ideas,' says one American diplomat. 'Allowing us to move about where we liked, talking to people, would be like encouraging a virus.' Soviet suspicion of foreigners is deep-rooted, going back to Tsarist days and to the attempts at foreign intervention just after the Revolution.

It all means that what the Western diplomat sees is little – or is stage managed. Communist countries arrange special visits to 'places of interest' for heads of mission and attachés of various specialities. One Iron Curtain veteran says: 'It's a way of giving diplomats a bit of a breather, and getting over the impression that you are letting them see something. But, all the time, you are closely marshalled together, so that you never even catch a glimpse of something you are not supposed to.'

Although travel restrictions have grown tighter and tighter, there is a limit to how harsh they can be if diplomacy is to continue at all. Diplomats in Peking at the peak of the Cultural Revolution admittedly were almost totally confined and isolated, but that was a very special, and temporary, situation.

But there is another way that the country can show its displeasure of foreign diplomats. All it needs to do is to increase the already considerable surveillance, thus making the diplomat feel even more isolated and harassed than normal. 'They simply make themselves just a bit more obnoxious to us,' says one Western diplomat. 'And they are extremely effective at it.'

At all times in communist countries the personal and electronic surveillance imposes enormous strains. 'Your real trouble about visiting our missions behind the Curtain,' explained one foreign ministry official, 'is that there's nowhere you will be able to ask questions without being overheard. Everyone will be afraid to talk to you.' Perhaps surprisingly, there turns out to be less worry of electronic surveillance in Peking than in Moscow and Eastern European countries. One man who has been in both says: 'You feel very much more relaxed in Peking; it's less of a strain, even though it's such an alien place in all other ways.' A foreign diplomat in China says: 'You get slightly lax about the possibility of bugs – simply because no microphones have ever been discovered in diplomatic walls here. You keep having to remind yourself that there is a possibility you are bugged. But then you feel that it's not the way the Chinese go about things. They conduct their security by keeping personal tabs on all foreigners, and of course foreigners are more conspicuous here than in any other capital city in the world for obvious reasons. And they've their local staff to eavesdrop and look at papers.'

Eastern Europe is different; there every diplomat has to work on the assumption that his conversations can be overheard. Sir William Hayter has recalled lying in bed, wanting to discuss with his wife whether he should resign. But 'Iris and I had always acted on the assumption that our bedroom was microphoned'. Harold Macmillan, the former British Prime Minister, says in his memoirs that he found that the dominating impression of his visit to Moscow to see Khrushchev was that of being surrounded by friends and advisers 'and yet being unable to communicate with them except with very great precaution. This is because you cannot speak in the residence, town or country, put at your disposal. Every room is "wired". You cannot speak in a car, or train, or even outside the house, if it be a small compound or garden. There is (always the) danger of the apparatus picking up what you say. In the British embassy, in spite of constant searches, the modern methods are so good and the modern mechanisms so unobstrusive that (with so many foreign servants etc.) security is almost impossible. This makes everyone rather jumpy and it is a very unpleasant feeling. Those who stay long here either disregard it or get very irritable and nervy.'

Visiting leaders can sometimes ease this strain; German Chancellor Adenauer, visiting Moscow in 1955, travelled in an official German train. The train was equipped with the most modern anti-surveillance devices. On arrival in Russia Adenauer told the Russians he planned to stay on it, and not accept a hotel room.

But for resident diplomats it is constant. 'You do get edgy', admits one diplomat, 'It's not so much not being able to say sensitive things; it's the kind of Big Brother feeling that even your private life is being shared by some faceless Russian.' Communist countries can, however, if they wish, increase even this pressure: they can intensify personal surveillance.

Even during calm periods, diplomats are closely watched and often followed. One Western intelligence officer believes that the reason goes beyond fears of espionage: 'Their counter-intelligence systems are so huge and cumbersome that no one can now cut them down to size. So if you have 500 men and 50 Mercedes earmarked to watch diplomats, you can't suddenly slow down the machine: think of the people who'd be unemployed. The consequence is that the amount of surveillance has to fit the number of people employed, and so you can get the same kind of treatment for a crowd at a cocktail party as you'd get for a suspected spy.'

At periods of bad relations surveillance becomes harassment: a diplomat's car is followed bumper to bumper; on foot, his 'tail' will be only a pace behind. The British Government detailed in 1971 the kind of surveillance directed at a British second secretary, David Miller, before he was expelled from Moscow. He was, it was claimed, subjected to 'extremely close range and intensive surveillance. On two occasions the cars following him had narrowly avoided collision, on one occasion with Mr Miller's own car. Photographers continually filmed him as he was entering and leaving his flat.' American diplomats the same year complained that they were followed by car and on foot wherever they went. In another case, one British diplomat claimed that he was followed around an art gallery by plain clothes men who stood six inches from him while he looked at paintings. In more violent cases diplomatic cars have been vandalised, and diplomats themselves stopped in the street and threatened.

It should, however, be remembered that communist diplomats

in the West complain of similar treatment; the Soviet Government on one occasion described the following of its diplomats in Canada as 'a witch hunt'. And harassment and the rarer violence usually has a retaliatory element; many instances have followed actions by Jewish militants against Soviet offices and diplomats in the west.

To complete the isolation communists post men outside embassies to watch and vet callers – one other way of ensuring that the policy of no contact between foreign diplomats and nationals is enforced.

From the 1940s checks on pedestrians in the vicinity of embassies have become common. In 1956 the State Department protested to the Czechoslovakians that uniformed police had been interfering with visitors to the embassy, forcing them to produce identity documents, then noting down details, and sometimes also questioning them. Earlier, in 1947, the French minister in Sofia clashed physically with police during an argument over whether a French journalist should be allowed to enter the mission. Again, this is not just East versus West. In East Germany a decree of 1963 prohibits private citizens from contacting without permission foreign diplomats – a step directed more against the Albanians and the Chinese than the West who are not represented there. (The decree is reminiscent of a law passed in Britain in 1653 which said effectively that any M.P. who spoke to foreign diplomats, who were frequently agitators, would lose his seat.)

In Moscow two events in one short period of time (1971) at one embassy – the American – illustrate just how effectively missions are isolated by Soviet guards. In the first, in March, a Russian doctor, his wife and two children entered the embassy grounds to ask about emigrating to the United States. About a dozen police ran into the grounds after them, pulling the wife and two daughters onto the sidewalk. The doctor, who grabbed an iron gate and shouted, 'Help me, help me' was 'rescued' by embassy staff, but the rest of the family were taken away. After the United States protested that the Soviet Union had violated international law by entering embassy grounds, a Soviet Foreign Ministry official explained that police were stationed outside the embassy to protect it against 'deranged persons and lunatics'. Two weeks later an elderly Russian tried to slip past the guards into the embassy. He was dragged away by two police-men and taken into a special police office nearby.

Both surveillance and, in some cases, harassment are made easier by the fact that staff in communist countries is locally engaged, and constituted of nationals of the host country. This is at great variance with the Soviet and Chinese practice of not employing anyone in their embassies, no matter how menial the job, unless that person is a citizen of their own country.

From time to time, Western countries have queried whether it is possible to do the same and decided not. The British Rad-cliffe Committee on Security summed up the argument against: 'We came to the conclusion that it would be virtually impossible to find people prepared to undertake these jobs who had sufficient knowledge of the appropriate languages and conditions to do them effectively. From the language point of view alone they would have to be retained in posts for a relatively long period and the longer they stayed the more vulnerable they would be likely to become.'

In the Soviet Union, Western embassies contract their local employees from the Russian Government. In 1970 the number at the American embassy alone was seventy-eight. Yuri Krotkov, a Soviet defector who was involved with the secret police in Russia, has written '. . . every Soviet citizen employed in a foreign embassy – every one, without exception – is certainly a co-opted member of the K.G.B.' Penkovsky made a similarly categoric statement: 'In Moscow . . . the foreign embassies have a great many Soviet people working for them. Each and every one of them is either an agent or has been co-opted by the K.G.B. . . .'

In Peking the Diplomatic Bureau, which is attached to the Foreign Ministry, arranges office or domestic staff for foreign missions. The numbers again are large. The British mission, for example, has translators, accountants and clerks who stamp visas under the supervision of the consul, plus gardeners, mechanics, electricians, plumbers, and an average of two domestic staff for each British diplomat. Diplomats here, as in Eastern Europe, have to assume that every single one of them supplies whatever infor-mation he can obtain. 'Even if they didn't come as informants (which they do) they'd never be allowed to remain with us by the Chinese unless they co-operated,' says a diplomat. Over-friendly staff may vanish: one Chinese translator, who had been in the British army during the war, shared two meals with a British diplomat and then disappeared. The diplomat later heard rumours that the translator was serving with the army in Mongolia.

Not only staff come courtesy of the host government. In Moscow, the department U.P.D.K. is the body that has to be approached for all normal domestic facilities from plumbing to a new cleaner. Sir David Kelly has recalled the problem of wrestling with the bureaucratic machine. 'One of my colleagues had a long correspondence with Burobin (now U.P.D.K.) about the cockroaches in his Embassy. It went to a "high level" and finally was ended by a letter which stated firmly that there were two kinds of cockroaches; one kind could be eliminated, the other could not – and his unfortunately belonged to the latter class.' The Americans in 1972 decided to bypass the system over their cockroach problem. The embassy asked the Orkin Exterminating Company of Atlanta, Georgia, for advice on how to get rid of these insects in the mission building and in diplomatic apartments. The company donated its services and sent a man to Moscow for ten days. *He*, it was explained, used American insecticides which, unlike Russian poison powders, were 'not poisonous to humans and pets'.

Isolated by all these factors, the diplomat is thrown back on his colleagues, and on a few official contacts. The ease and comparative warmth of official contact varies widely. In China, during the Cultural Revolution, officials from the Foreign Ministry only talked to diplomats with Red Guards at their elbows – and then talks were notable mainly for slogans and wrangles. Yet by 1970 China was making overtures: the Foreign Ministry, early in 1971, sent senior officials to a reception to mark the reopening of the British mission that had been burnt by Chinese mobs four years before. A few months later the British acting *chargé d'affaires* could talk at a banquet of Anglo-Chinese relations now being 'in a very happy phase', and later they became even happier.

These are extremes, but hot-cold treatment alternates in all communist countries. Depending on how that country sees its relations with a foreign nation at any given moment, the diplomat may be treated with courtesy and friendship, or be made to realise that he is no more than a barely tolerated intruder. From the point of practical advantages – as distinct from making life pleasanter for the diplomat – it hardly matters though. 'Good relations' may mean the communist country concerned sending more and higher-ranking representatives to an embassy's national day celebrations, or accepting more social invitations. But it hardly means much in terms of practical gains.

In Peking officials talking to diplomats may have stopped answering questions with quotes from Mao. But they still speak in the well-rehearsed official-line, giving nothing away, and instead of quoting Mao, drop in the occasional 'as the *People's Daily* said. . . .'

In Russia, after Stalin, large numbers of minor Russian officials began attending western embassy functions. But diplomats conceded there was never any really close contact, nor any relationship except on the most superficial and formal level.

Invitations to diplomats have the same charade quality. Pietro Quaroni, in *Diplomatic Bags*, has described how diplomats and Soviet officials are allowed to 'mix' at a reception for a visiting head of state:

A gala luncheon is given at the Kremlin for the visitor, followed in the evening by a big reception in the Foreign Ministry – the latter being one of the rare occasions when Russian officialdom is allowed to mix with the corps diplomatique. The word 'mix' is perhaps too strong, because hierarchy is strictly observed. In Room 1, only the heads of diplomatic and military missions are admitted; in Room 2, only the Counsellors and First Secretaries; in Room 3, the rest. The quality, service and presentation of food vary correspondingly. Those in Room 1 can, of course, wander freely in Rooms 2 and 3 if they wish – a process which is irreversible, at least until after the departure of the chief guests and officials. In the centre of Room 1 is a large table piled high with delicacies of all kinds; around it a number of smaller tables for the chosen few, each presided over by a senior Soviet official. The guest of honour sits at the table with Molotov (in my time) and other high Soviet dignitaries. At a certain point in the evening, the British or American ambassadors might be invited to sit with them – although this custom was by no means invariable.

Other events are equally unreal. A Canadian diplomat who had been stationed in Russia, recalls:

Endless hours of an ambassador's time are consumed standing shivering at funerals, or trying to keep awake at children's concerts. In Moscow to celebrate the anniversary of the glorious October revolution they used to summon us to the Bolshoi theatre at 6 p.m. in November. We knew there was going to be a show afterwards with choirs, folk dances and ballets and all the things that Russians are good at. The price for this, however, was about four hours of patriotic tributes to be endured, bolt upright on a Louis XIV chair. Next morning one rose to spend another few hours standing in snow or drizzle watching the jolly tanks roll by in Red Square.

Diplomats need to turn up at receptions though: something may just be said to them, or may be overheard. And, such is the scarcity of information, the diplomat's foreign ministry will want the exact words of what the communist official or leader said – as well as how he said it and what his expression and manner was at the time.

More usually, however, the most a diplomat can hope for to relieve the make-believe at functions is the insults game. In this the offended diplomat can take instant reprisal on behalf of his country – and get home early. The insult may be in the form of words or the presence of an 'unacceptable' fellow guest. At the 1970 May Day parade in Warsaw Americans marched off the diplomatic stand after Gomulka, the Communist Party leader, attacked the 'new, brutal, armed intervention of U.S. imperialism in Cambodia'. In December 1970, West Germany's ambassador left an official celebration in Moscow for the 200th anniversary of Beethoven's birth because an East German official spoke 'on behalf of the German people'.

Given the situation in communist countries, what more can the foreign diplomat do but be thrown back on other diplomats? Even more so than elsewhere he might find it more worthwhile cultivating a colleague from another country than trying to get through to Soviet officials. That other diplomat might be 'in' at that moment – as French diplomats often are in both Eastern Europe and Peking. Diplomats from neutral countries are courted in case they have heard something. The Russians know this, and make use of it in order to spread misinformation. This is done skilfully. Information may be passed to neutral diplomats by Soviet officials in two or three capitals at the same time. That information then reaches Western diplomats, who report it to their head offices. Faced with substantially the same information from widely separate sources, head offices may be tempted to treat it as first-rate intelligence material.

The more beleagured the diplomatic corps and the more difficult information to obtain, the closer the corps and the greater the mutual help. Enemies may, in common interest, start co-operating. During the Cultural Revolution in China the Russians and Eastern Europeans suddenly became friends with Western missions. For a period the Soviets and their partners, though out of favour, were allowed to receive copies of provincial papers denied to the British and French missions. A swap-system evolved: the British and French exchanging intelligence material that reached them from outside (notably, in the British case, from Hong Kong) for looks at the provincial papers.

Adversity brings out the 'best' qualities of *savoir faire* among diplomats. Again in Peking, the British mission was isolated by demonstrating crowds on the day they were celebrating the Queen's birthday in 1967. As usual the rest of the diplomatic corps had been invited. Ambassadors trying to reach the mission were turned back a quarter of a mile away. One athletic Scandinavian diplomat, however, got through. He put on plimsolls, travelled through adjoining gardens, and then climbed over the mission wall. One of the British girls during the attack on the British embassy, which involved physical assaults on many of the women, also showed sterling qualities. A flagstaff, thrown at her, struck her forehead. A diplomat urged her not to cry. 'Cry in front of these bastards,' she said. 'Not likely.'

A wise ambassador in a communist country concentrates a lot of his entertaining and socialising on his own staff, to alleviate the strain. In Peking, foreign diplomats live in international sections, all but the Indians, East Germans, Hungarians, Rumanians and the Russians in two areas. In Moscow, diplomats live in special foreigners' blocks of flats – guarded, like their embassies, by the militia.

But the ghettos do come with luxuries. The living conditions of diplomats in communist countries are even more at variance with those of ordinary citizens than elsewhere. Ambassadors live in huge houses. American diplomats have a country house on seven acres of land outside Moscow as a retreat. Scotch in Russia costs diplomats 70p a bottle and cigarettes £1 per 200. Even in the Cultural Revolution in China the champagne remained available and duty free – and about the only luxury consignment that did not make the British mission was one of frozen birds and other food that rotted at a port because diplomats were not allowed to collect it.

Life, claim foreign ministry men, needs to be made as civilised as possible – to counter the other pressures, not least the attempts that will be made to get them to 'co-operate' with the communist authorities.

Partly because of the pressures, new diplomats will not be sent to Iron Curtain countries, with, perhaps, the exception of Yugo-slavia. Nor, as a rule, will bachelors. Diplomats posted in Iron Curtain countries will spend less time there than their colleagues in capitals like London or Paris; the length of posting for all Western diplomats behind the Iron Curtain is short, often two years.

During that time there may be more opportunities to escape the environment than is usual. British diplomats in China get home leave every year; other Western and African diplomats there may get less but are sent frequently to Hong Kong on the excuse of courier service to give them breaks.

It remains that to be posted to an Iron Curtain mission is a mark of status and of being a coming-man. The first six of Britain's *chargés d'affaires* in Peking since 1950 all became ambassadors elsewhere; Moscow has always been regarded in the West as a top post. But even lower down the ladder it is a posting that counts. 'If we send someone there,' says a high foreign ministry official, 'you can be damned sure we've vetted him out pretty carefully – security and ability wise. It sure as hell isn't a backwater. Though what there is for him to do when he is there. . . .'

Twelve
Communist Diplomats

'Promises like piecrusts are made to be broken.'
Lenin

The communist diplomat is often a spy, usually keeps saying 'no', acts only according to the most detailed instructions from home and, except on very special occasions, keeps himself isolated from the influences of the country in which he is based. This is the stereotyped view, but very largely it is a true one. Western diplomats describe him variously as tough, obstinate, ill-mannered, coldly pragmatic, contemptuous of truth, and of admitting no obligations other than those to be given to his state and the leaders in power.

Some find it hard to accept that he is a diplomat in the recognised sense. He does not negotiate; he repeats instructions like a gramophone record. If the occasion calls for lies, he will lie. The words he uses have their own special meaning; peace, for example, means 'the state of affairs inside a communist country'. His speeches are directed to foreign publics, not foreign governments.

The emergence of the communist diplomat, caring not about niceties nor the means of international relations but only about success or failure, has been a shock to the traditionalists. 'Truth itself has lost its significance,' wrote Sir Harold Nicolson in *Foreign Affairs*. 'Compared to the shining truth of their gospel, all minor forms of veracity are merely bourgeois inhibitions. The old diplomacy was based upon the creation of confidence, the acquisition of credit. The modern diplomatist must realise that he can no longer rely on the old system of trust; he must accept the fact that his antagonists will not hesitate to falsify facts and that they feel no shame if their duplicity is exposed. The old currency has been withdrawn from circulation; we are dealing in a new coinage.' Nevertheless, the communist diplomat exists; communist diplomacy cannot be wished away; and western officials have to accept the reality.

The communist diplomatic apparatus is organised in the same way as that of western nations with foreign ministries, missions and diplomats who report back and pass on messages to the host country. But there are differences. The apparatus is only one part of the international communist machine, and for the Soviet bloc at least it is only meant to be temporary. Immediately after the communists came to power in Russia, world revolution was thought imminent and conventional practices of diplomacy despised and unnecessary. Soviet representatives abroad became Polpreds (formed from the first syllables of the Russian words for plenipotentiary representative) and acted as though they were accredited to the international proletariat and not foreign governments.

It was only when it was realised that the world revolution might take time, that the Soviets decided they must, temporarily, conduct some form of relations with capitalist governments. When international socialism triumphs, however, and the imperialists vanish, the apparatus will become obsolete and disappear.

There are other important differences. Diplomacy is directed towards a missionary creed; it is the end product and not the methods that matter. 'From the point of view of Communist morality,' said Radio Moscow on 20 August 1950, 'only those acts are moral which contribute to the building up of a new communist society.'

It follows that everything that furthers the communist purpose is 'right'; anything which does not is 'wrong'. By this criterion, lying, is understandable and 'moral'. Discussions are but parts of the continuous struggle with non-communists. The State can do no wrong. This often leads to farcical speeches at public meetings. One Soviet diplomat at an international conference on drug abuse spent the first half of his speech stressing how it was a capitalist vice not to be found in socialist countries, and the second part explaining how much money the U.S.S.R. was spending on treatment facilities for addicts. He seemed to find nothing odd in the mix.

Because power is highly centralised in the hands of a small group, or even one man, at home, the communist diplomat exercises virtually no freedom of action. Not only will instructions be detailed, but so too sometimes will even the precise arguments that he must use. He cannot take part in give and take, nor even concede there can be other viewpoints.

All these characteristics give both a strength and a special weakness to communist diplomats. Because ends justify means, the diplomat can smile and offer drinks or fight with gloves off, whichever it is decided is expedient. The instructions may be detailed – but the communist diplomat has no need to worry about opposition parties and anti-government newspapers at home casting doubts on the policies he is told to pursue. Those in power at home can, if they wish, make policies in all fields conform to serve diplomatic needs of the moment. Thus when in 1971 Russia decided to undertake a diplomatic offensive with the West, this could be backed by suddenly increasing the number of Jews allowed to leave for Israel to help provide the right international climate.

There are also weaknesses. A major one is that the distrust and suspicion that communist diplomats must hold for capitalist states both prevents normal contact and makes the objective worth of their reports home highly suspect.

Although Communist diplomats report to their foreign ministry, the power lies not there but within the Party. Foreign ministries in both Moscow and Peking are executive departments. They are organised in the traditional way with geographical, functional and administrative departments. As in the West, the territorial departments are the focal point for contact with missions abroad and foreign diplomats in their capitals.

Unless the foreign minister is high ranking within the Party, he is not powerful and his influence on policy is minimal. In Russia, the minister is not normally a member of the policy-making Soviet body, the Politburo. In both Russia and China it is the Politburo that counts. The Soviet Politburo has its own departments handling foreign affairs, including ones dealing with communist parties abroad. These departments are more powerful than the Ministry. One special feature of the Soviet Foreign Ministry is the Collegium which is said to be unique. Its membership is comprised of senior diplomats, deputy directors, and a 'panel of specialist advisers' who fulfil a policy-advisory role to the Ministry, but although it may have some influence its impact is probably not great.

Dealing with a communist foreign ministry is for foreign diplomats often a thankless, and useless task. In Moscow, Sir William Hayter has compared it with putting money in an old-fashioned slot machine. 'You put in the penny – your question – and in the end, probably, you will get something out: perhaps not what you wanted, an acid drop when you hoped for chocolate, but something; and you can sometimes expedite the process by shaking the machine. It is, however, *useless* to talk to it.'

Communist countries are reticent about their recruitment and training procedures. (Although Russians have been allowed to look at the American Foreign Service Institute, repeated requests for return visits were turned down.) The Soviets, and no doubt other communist countries, place great stress on recruiting men with the right political background and beliefs. V. A. Zorin in *Osnovy diplomaticheskoy sluzhby* (The Fundamentals of the Diplomatic Service) stresses that the party has always worked on the assumption that it is imperative to have 'politically mature people'.

The Soviet diplomatic school, the International Relations Institute, is run by the Foreign Ministry, plus the K.G.B., the Party's Central Committee and the Ministry of High Education. The course lasts six years, of six days a week. Forty per cent of the whole programme is concerned with languages. Apart from that, there are three main areas of study. These involve diplomacy in general (including, for example, the history of international relations), examination of an area of the world, and specialised study of just one country. A Soviet defector, Aleksandr Kaznacheev, in *Inside a Soviet Embassy*, has revealed that there were about 2,000 taught at one time. Admission was by recommendation of a Party district committee, and students fell into three classes: the élite (sons of ministers, generals and high ranking diplomats), K.G.B. officers, and those who have shown outstanding Komosol (Communist Youth) work. About thirty per cent of the graduates went abroad.

What Kaznacheev said then about the secrecy surrounding it is still true: 'The I.R.I. . . . is thoroughly guarded, and its internal affairs and activities are treated as a state secret.' Even more secret, however, is the Higher Diplomatic School. This is probably used for training those already working as diplomats, and party men transferred to the service. According to Kaznacheev, the course there lasts two years. But little else is known of the school.

The Soviet view of the diplomats that emerge from training to be sent out to missions is, perhaps not surprisingly, rather different from the one held by Western diplomats. They are, said L. Fyodorov in *Diplomat i Konsul* (The Diplomat and the Consul) 'politically aware, spiritually pure and morally steadfast'. According to him the basic characteristics of communist diplomats are 'adherence to high principles, party activity, internationalism and humanity. The ethical basis of their personal life is revealed by their devotion to communism, a love of their homeland and other socialist states, dutiful work for the sake of society, human relationships and a mutual respect for all peoples, honour and justice, moral purity, simplicity and humbleness in personal and public life, intolerance of national and rational enmity, and an uncompromising attitude towards the enemies of communism, matters of world peace, and fraternal solidarity with the workers of all countries and all races.'

The Chinese, in formal training programmes for young diplomats do not have a single institute to train all of their foreign affairs specialists. They make use of a number of institutes including the Shanghai Foreign Languages College, the Russian Language School, the No. 1 and No. 2 Institutes of Foreign Languages in Peking, the Institute of Foreign Affairs, and the Academy of Sciences' Institute of International Relations. A number of the larger universities also have diplomacy and language courses. A participant in the 1954 Geneva Conference on Indochina and the 1961-2 Geneva Conference on Laos was impressed by the very large number of youthful Chinese who were not among the 'official' delegates to these meetings. He concluded, reports Professor Donald Klein, that they had been brought along to gain first-hand experience in major diplomatic negotiations.

As with all nations, the number of diplomats from communist states abroad has grown over the years. Russian embassies now have staffs second in size only to American ones. China, which in 1953 had only 154 diplomats serving overseas, had nearly 600 by 1966.

Communist missions are, ostensibly, organised much as other embassies, with an ambassador, counsellors, secretaries, and attachés divided into various sections such as politics, press and culture.

Soviet writers claim that the tasks and the ways of working are the time honoured ones. Fyodorov refers to embassies supplying current information and periodic reports on 'the local political and economic situation, external and internal policies, and on the prospects for developing better relations with the local government'.

And, again according to Soviet sources, the information is gathered in the traditional way. Zorin mentions the need for diplomats to have the widest possible contacts, and claims: 'Conversations even of a semi-protocol nature with such people as Ministers, M.P.s, leaders of opposition parties, Lord Mayors, and also discussions with ambassadors and representatives of countries with whom the Soviet Union has relations have a not insignificant importance from the point of view of improving relationships and in the long run will give a rich fund of information about the internal political position and the external foreign policy of foreign countries, and give a serious basis for further diplomatic activity for the embassy.'

Work at Chinese embassies also appears to fit into recognised diplomatic patterns. Diplomats talk to officials, show films such as the revolutionary ballet film 'Red Women's Platoon' (musical background arranged by Chairman Mao's wife), and give parties and receptions.

But there is a factor special to communist embassies: the power within the mission of the Party and of the intelligence sections. Soviet works lay great stress on ideological work *in* an embassy and on the need for diplomats to keep up to date with Marx and Lenin, and such ideological considerations are no less important in Chinese missions. Party officials try to ensure the 'purity' of the diplomats' beliefs, and also maintain contact with local communist parties.

The intelligence men in both Soviet and Chinese embassies will not only engage in espionage, but will also watch over the rest of the staff. Oleg Penkovsky has claimed that in Soviet missions: 'The K.G.B. men watch absolutely everything that goes on: the purchases people make, how they live and whether it accords with their salary, where they go, which doctors they visit, whom they meet, how much drinking they do, their morals. The K.G.B. listens constantly to what people say. In short, almost every move in an embassy employee's life is known to the K.G.B. Meanwhile, we in the GRU watch the K.G.B. in turn.'

Because of the power of both the intelligence men and the party, the *real* importance of mission members may be unclear to an outsider; a seemingly low-ranking official may be more powerful than his ambassador. Kaznacheev referred to ambassadors being fearful of apparently insignificant attachés, and said that in Rangoon the ambassador was not allowed into the section where the ciphers and most secret documents were housed. Gouzenko, who left the Soviet embassy in Ottawa in 1945, reported similar restrictions on the ambassador there, and instanced one second secretary with direct contact with the Central Committee of the Soviet Communist Party. With Chinese embassies too it is often impossible to see where the real power lies. One experienced Third World official dealing with China – and a frequent visitor to their missions – said: 'You do get situations where the number two strikes you as the more important from his bearing and from what he says. You suspect that he is higher in the party or within some intelligence set-up.'

This does not mean that all ambassadors are lacking in power or importance. A Soviet ambassador may himself be a K.G.B. member. In important countries, he may be a man with sway, even a member of the Central Committee of the Communist Party. Russia's ambassador to the U.S.A. at the time of the Cuban crisis assured Khrushchev that Kennedy would back down. Afterwards, he was recalled. His successor confided to a neutral diplomat that he had been told to report back accurately – not just what would be politically acceptable. In Eastern European satellite states, Soviet ambassadors have been closely involved with decisions within those countries. The Soviet ambassador to Czechoslovakia was believed by many local officials to have played a large part in the decision of Russia to invade the country in 1968.

A similar situation seems to apply with Chinese ambassadors. Those at some posts, for example, Albania or Damascus (which is used as a political base for the Arab world), are probably very powerful figures. Rarely, he, too, may be a member of the Party's Central Committee, as, for example, Huang Chen, the Chinese ambassador in France in 1972.

One question which worries the West is how good and how objective are the reports communist missions send home. There are two unknowns: the accuracy of the information gathered, and how honestly the diplomat reports and interprets it. Communist diplomats in the west lead cloistered lives, isolated both by restrictions placed upon them by the host country and by their own apartness. They work in what are often literally fortresses, sealed from the outside world. Only a small number of them may be allowed to mingle with westerners.

The material they gather appears to come primarily from newspapers, local communists, and officials. At receptions and parties, they are often avid questioners. This applies especially to the Chinese, still less sophisticated than their Soviet colleagues in dealing with outsiders. The atmosphere at Chinese mission receptions is reminiscent of that of European communists of the pre- and immediate post-war periods: lots of lumbering questions, but no conversation. At one, visitors were asked for their views on three obviously predetermined subjects – some by as many as four different Chinese diplomats at different stages of the evening.

The questions are often tortuous. One man, who has left the British diplomatic service but is still involved in the China watching field, was quizzed by Chinese diplomats. They wanted to ask if he was now a spy. 'Had I really left the service; what were my links with the Americans; did I still see my old friends? In other words, all the questions but *the* one.'

Asking questions in return, say Western diplomats, is a waste of time. 'They ask you what you think of the China–Soviet situation,' one says. 'You tell them, and then ask what they think. There is a long pause and you think a deep answer is being formulated. Then you get "The situation was well stated in the *People's Daily* of x date . . ." '

One can hardly help doubting the worth of information collected in such sessions. But given the vast amount of openly available published material in the west, it is probable that Communist diplomats have no shortage of facts. It is doubtful, though, whether they ever absorb enough background knowledge to understand them or the country in which they work really well.

Whatever the worth of the material collected, much however will depend on whether it is reported home honestly. Many western diplomats doubt whether it is; 'To send back reports that do not fit what people at home want to believe would be an act of courage bordering on the suicidal,' one says. 'I doubt if many would risk it. And if they did, how long would they last?'

Others claim that the communist diplomat, knowing that his ministry is not an important one, has little inducement to report honestly. Even if his reports are found 'acceptable' by the foreign ministry, they are highly unlikely to influence events or policies because the power is elsewhere. What his ministry believes is largely incidental.

Considering specifically China, Donald Klein points to conflicting judgements about the value of reports from embassies. 'Some diplomats who have dealt with their Chinese counterparts have been impressed by their knowledge of the country to which they were accredited, and, rightly, or wrongly, assume that much of this information is transmitted back to Peking. Others hold the opposite view, and feel that embassy reporting leaves much to be desired.' Klein believes that reporting is probably cautious and perhaps distorted during periods of high political tension in Peking, and more broadminded and of higher quality when the political atmosphere at home is relatively relaxed.

At least as important is the *way* communist diplomats see things in view of their ideological beliefs. 'You have to remember they are all very heavily indoctrinated before they leave Moscow or Peking,' one western diplomat says. 'I think it highly unlikely that they can report with any degree of what we would call objectivity.' What they see, it is claimed, is what their Marxist training tells them they ought to see.

Trade is an integral part of communist diplomacy. Khrushchev talking to visiting U.S. Congressmen in 1955 said: 'We value trade least for economic reasons and most for political purposes.' Soviet books stress that 'for the Soviet Union and other socialist countries having a monopoly of foreign trade, trade representation abroad has a special characteristic . . . (it) is an integral part of Soviet diplomatic representation.'

The important fact is that Russia's economic structure – with complete monopoly of production and trade – means that the Soviet Union can at any time make available for sale, or buy, whatever will make most political impact. The buying side of this may most importantly be directed at Asian or African countries, but it also provides a diplomatic 'weapon' against the West. East Germany has used its trade to win friends and diplomatic recognition in the Third World. During 1970 its trade with those countries rose by twelve per cent over that of 1969. Many countries gave diplomatic recognition chiefly because of what seemed advantageous trading opportunities. They included Iraq, Cambodia, Syria, the U.A.R., the Yemen, Sudan, Somalia, Algeria and the Congo.

With China, too, diplomatic recognition by other states – such as Italy and Canada – has been closely linked with those countries' desires for trade. Chinese commercial counsellors play a major role in their nation's diplomacy: they normally take part in the top-level negotiations and are sometimes the signatories of the agreements which result.

When it comes to aid, the communist countries have the same advantages they have with trade, and it is also part of Communism's 'total diplomacy'. Again it can be directed where it will have most political impact (though, it should be noted, the West has also much adopted this approach too). For receiving nations, communist aid has the advantage at least that rapid decisions can be made by the Soviets or Chinese without them having to be pored over by legislators. Many diplomats in the West claim that communist aid is often directed at propaganda projects such as steel mills and dams that have an immediate public relations impact.

China in the 1970s has increased its aid, both in total value and the number of recipient countries, simultaneously with its active attempts to negotiate trade and diplomatic ties with many nations. Much economic and military aid has been directed at the developing countries and here there has been a marked struggle for influence between China and Russia. China has publicly warned governments to beware of Russian aid because, claims Peking, the Soviets tie it to trade or then try to interfere in a nation's internal affairs. Russia has the greater resources, but China the advantages that its brand of Communism appeals to the peasantry and that it gives the developing world a high priority. In 1970 China became the Communist world's main supplier of aid to developing nations, outstripping Russia, albeit temporarily. In that year, for example, China had about 6,000 civilian experts working in Africa compared with Russia's 2,400. In addition to these, however, there was China's main prestige aid project, the £169 million Tanzam railway in Tanzania and Zambia. During construction this will involve the help of Chinese estimated to range in number from 5,000 to 12,000. This Chinese commitment was made after the West refused to help, and foreign diplomats were forced to concede that the terms on which the aid was given were 'extremely generous'. It is free of interest and repayable over thiry years. In Zanzibar the Russians and East Germans have also been almost totally ousted by Peking. The Chinese also supply training camps for South African liberation organisations in Zambia and Tanzania.

The biggest recipients of Russian aid have consistently been Egypt, India, Afghanistan and Iran. The priorities have been establishing political influence in key areas (Egypt and India) and the preservation of friendly neighbours (Iran and Afghanistan).

Receiving countries have grown to be wary of both East and West in the aid game, however. In India disillusionment has come from Parliamentary committees over the quality of some of the aid. They have expressed alarm over huge financial losses sustained by a number of Soviet-sponsored development projects. Among the complaints – steel mills that the Russians estimated would produce steel at a capital cost of £150 a ton, but which looked likely to be £222 a ton. Because of Soviet failures, the plant would open nearly two and a half years late – and the Indian Government would lose almost £18 million. The Russian's overbearing attitudes, and disregard for local advice, have also been criticised – something familiar to U.S. aid workers.

What neutralist countries have increasingly pursued is 'balanced' aid from both East and West. They would like to feel there is total truth in the viewpoint expressed in the African magazine *Drum*. The magazine likened taking aid to milking a cow. African countries were prepared to milk the communist cow as long as it made no demands on them. 'A cow's job is to yield food quickly. If it does not, it can be done away with.'

There is another aspect of communist diplomacy which is vital: there is no separation between policy and propaganda. Communist officials seem to find it difficult to believe that other countries can take any other attitude. At an inter-governmental conference on Cultural Policies in Europe in summer 1972, the Soviet Minister of Culture told his fellow delegates: 'Governments should try to make a new kind of man by integrating culture to the total system of politics which governs their countries.' Communist countries reflect this conviction internationally as well as internally.

It has been estimated, in *The Techniques of Soviet Propaganda* a study prepared for an American Senate Committee, that the total of all types of communist propaganda – worldwide – involves 500,000 personnel and an annual expenditure of about $2 billion. 'This effort is aimed at the some one billion people outside the communist bloc; thus it may be said that Moscow with some participation from Peking, spends $2 a year for every free man it intends to subjugate . . . the equivalent amount allotted annually by the United States to worldwide propaganda is one and a quarter cents per person. With the addition of budgetary provisions for this purpose by all other free nations, the total amounts to almost two cents. The Soviet propaganda effort is thus roughly 100 times as great as the entire free world. . . .'

The range of the communist propaganda apparatus is wide. Some of the machinery, such as propaganda broadcasts, are also common to the West. But the difference lies in size – and in the advantage gained by such helpmates as Friendship societies, local communist parties, and International 'Front' organisations such as the World Federation of Trade Unions and the World Peace Council. The vastness impresses, even though it should be remembered that some of the propaganda tasks of communist countries are carried out in the west not by governments but by other bodies including religious organisations and private foundations. TASS, the Soviet news agency, and the New China News Agency (N.C.N.A.), are part of the propaganda machine, adjusting news to fit objectives. Books play a great part in the propaganda offensive. In one year Russia published and circulated about thirty million books in foreign languages, according to its Ministry of Culture. Cultural exchanges are geared to stressing aid and technology with developing countries, and the arts and sciences to win prestige in the west.

China's propaganda machine appears to differ only slightly from that of Russia, being modelled upon it though adapted where necessary to fit special Chinese considerations. In the Chinese service, there have been cultural counsellors since the mid-1950s. These probably keep in close contact with N.C.N.A. correspondents serving abroad, and also act as a link with the 'friendship' associations. Much of the Soviet and Chinese propaganda is directed at each other: as part of the war of words, broadcast transmissions are beamed between the two countries. Russia has accused China of endangering the safety of aircraft by jamming transport radio bands with propaganda broadcasts.

The communists export only what fits the image. A particularly bizarre example of this happened in Britain in 1971 with an exhibition of Soviet art and design at London's Hayward Gallery. Four years of negotiations preceded the exhibition. An agreement was made in Moscow on items that would be included, and the control of the exhibition was given over to the Russian authorities. The items that were later sent from Moscow did not include some that had been agreed upon; these, needless to say, were ideologically unsound ones. But what happened afterwards was even more extraordinary. Russian officials arrived in London, toured the galley, and ordered out about fifteen unacceptable exhibits, obtained outside Russia. One was a reconstruction of a room designed by Lissitsky. Because it was impossible to remove it, the Russians ordered it to be sealed and papered over – so that even its very existence was hidden.

Thirteen
Vatican and New Nation Diplomats

VATICAN DIPLOMACY

'How many divisions has the Pope.'
Stalin

In 1971 the Pope's 'Foreign Minister' was in Moscow opening a diplomatic dialogue with the communists. It was thirty-six years after Stalin's famous remark and the first visit by a Papal envoy since the Revolution. But, as a Vatican official has said, 'One thing the Church can afford to do is not to rush.'

The Vatican diplomatic machine is active and impressive. It sends out ambassadors (which it calls Nuncios) and in return receives resident missions from about half the world's nations. To many, it seems strange that in the latter half of the twentieth century, a Pope should be sending and receiving diplomats, but the power of the Vatican in international affairs is probably at least as great as that of a middle-ranking nation such as Britain.

Like all diplomatic machines, the Vatican foreign service seeks to advance its own interests. Its particular concern is to ensure conditions in which Catholics can freely practise their religion and in which the faith can be spread.

To obtain what it wants the Vatican, like other diplomatic services, will bargain, offering concessions or help in return. Poland, for example, with a Catholic population of thirty million, needed the Church's co-operation in keeping the country calm after the riots by students and workers in 1970 over rises in basic food prices. President Tito has enlisted its aid to try to prevent separatism in Yugoslavia. The Americans enlisted the Pope's help in trying to persuade North Vietnam to free prisoners of war.

The Vatican has long experience in international diplomacy. The first emissary of the Pope was sent to Constantinople to the Eastern Roman imperial court in the fifth century. The present machine owes its origins to the early days of modern diplomacy when the princes, as a sign of their independence, sent representatives to all the courts of Europe, including the Papal court. The Popes, in return, sent out their own envoys, and a special office had to be set up in Rome.

Vatican City (or more accurately the Holy See) is today the world's smallest independent state with an area of a little over 108 acres and a resident population of about 900. It is all that exists of the old Papal states of Italy and southern France. By 1870 only Rome remained of those states, and this was annexed by Italy when the protection of the French was withdrawn. In 1929, under the Lateran Treaty, Italy recognised the sovereignty of Vatican City.

At the Vatican, the Cardinal Secretary of State, the most powerful man after the Pope, is charged with relations with civil governments. Below him, an under secretary of state controls the diplomatic machine. The sixty or so countries that keep diplomatic representation there are by no means all Catholic, a sign that nations regard relations with the Pope as important in a practical sense. The countries include Cuba and Egypt, and it has been stressed that no major power conducting a far-reaching foreign policy has been able to remain absent from the Holy See for long. In 1972, the only major powers unrepresented were Russia and the United States. And even the United States had two years earlier created an official link with the Vatican, though short of diplomatic relations. President Nixon appointed Henry Cabot Lodge official American emissary to visit the Vatican two to three times a year. Among the tasks envisaged was seeking support for U.S. foreign policy.

Modern states have relations with the Vatican for purely pragmatic reasons. Because the Pope, as leader of millions of Catholics throughout the world, is a force they seek to ensure that the Vatican's influence is favourable or, at least, not hostile. The French, for example, strive continuously to explain their Middle East policies in the hope of avoiding open criticism from the Pope.

President Roosevelt asked Pope Pius XII to refrain, at least for a period, from any public statement against the bill to extend lend-lease to Russia – a measure to which many Catholics in America were opposed.

Hitler made skilful use of the Vatican in 1933 when, with an eye to votes from the Catholic Centre Party, he pledged himself to friendly relations with the Holy See. In July that year the Nazis concluded a concordat (treaty) with the Vatican which gave the Church the right to regulate its own affairs in Germany. It was soon broken by the Germans but the value of the agreement for Hitler was that it came at a moment when the Nazis were in desperate need of prestige. And what better than an agreement with the Pope?

As the plans of the Church touch affairs in many, if not most, nations, the Vatican is also a good listening post.

Napoleon recognised the strength of the Pope in world affairs. An envoy about to be sent to Rome asked him how he should treat the Vatican. Napoleon replied: 'Deal with the Pope as if he had 200,000 men at his command.'

On its side, the Vatican will deal with any nation – if it thinks this is in its interest. Religious differences are no bar to diplomatic relations. Like nation states, the Vatican does not consider that the views of a foreign government or how it came to power is the important factor. What matters is that it does hold power. Even in the case of the Kremlin, it is not the ideology of the communists that debarred relations – only Russia's non-toleration of its Catholics. 'International life,' says Father Robert Graham in *Vatican Diplomacy*, 'would be seriously handicapped if the states could have official intercourse only with those regimes which they approved. The papacy does not therefore draw the line, diplomatically at heretics, schismatics, infidels and pagans.'

It is not, however, so pragmatic when it comes to women. In 1970 the West Germans wanted to send to the Vatican Mrs Elizabeth Mueller, a diplomat with counsellor status. The Vatican refused to accept her. 'It is a tradition that diplomatic representatives accredited to the Holy See be of the male sex,' said a Vatican official. Women diplomats have been allowed in the Vatican – but they have been of low rank, and not, like Mrs Mueller, high enough in the hierarchy to take over from an ambassador in his absence.

Ambassadors to the Vatican present their letters of credence. Speeches are made in the normal way, and are devoid of any controversial points. A new British diplomat, in 1970, for example, used his to outline his government's policy, and the Pope, in reply, spoke of friendly co-operation between Britain and the Church, of a united Europe being a source of strength and stability for the world, and sent his greetings to the Queen.

There is ceremonial. The Swiss guards, in their costumes designed by Michelangelo, present arms with their halberds, bands play national anthems. The missions are usually small and the diplomats professional members of their country's foreign service. There are, of course, no consuls, nor commercial or military attachés.

As with diplomacy generally, there are sometimes diplomatic clashes. After Pope Paul gave audience to leaders of African resistance movements, the Portuguese delivered a protest note and then recalled their ambassador for 'consultations'.

Ecclesiastics destined for the Vatican diplomatic service receive special training at the institution *Pontificia Accademia Ecclesiastica*. Abroad, missions, headed by the Nuncios, are composed of counsellors, auditors, secretaries and attachés. The Nuncios, who are usually titular bishops or archbishops, have a double function – representing the Pope before the civil government and also before the Church in the country. They differ from apostolic delegates with whom they are often confused; the latter deal only with the Church within the country to which they are sent, and they are not accredited to the government and do not have a political role.

Britain, although it has a mission at the Vatican, has no Papal ambassador in London – a situation stemming from a distrust of papists developed in the days of attempted invasions by continental powers from the reign of Elizabeth I. The Apostolic delegate in Britain, though not on the Diplomatic List, is accorded diplomatic courtesies by Catholic missions in London. There is a social side to Vatican diplomatic life abroad. Receptions are held, for example, to mark the anniversary of the coronation of the Pope.

Vatican diplomats report, represent and negotiate just as their nation state colleagues. There are strong attempts to extend the Church's influence in the underdeveloped world (here its reputed wealth is an embarrassment, and the Pope has been forced to give speeches saying the Vatican's riches are not as great as people believe). Much of the diplomatic activity of recent years has been directed towards Eastern Europe where there is a Catholic population of sixty million. New policies of co-existence were launched by Pope John XXIII, a man whose attitudes were sharply different from those of his anti-communist predecessor Pius XII. A number of leading communists have called at the Vatican to pay respects since the early 1960s; and by 1972 two communist heads of state, President Podgorny and President Tito, had paid official visits. In seeking a détente with communism, Vatican thinking has been parallel with that of most Western nations. A Vatican diplomat, Mgr Agostino Casaroli, widely known as the Pope's foreign minister, has moved to and fro between the Vatican and Eastern Europe. The diplomatic activity has been intense. In 1971 Vatican and Polish officials had their first official contact since Poland became a communist state after World War II. The three days of talks included discussions on the normalisation of the religious situation and specifically raised the questions of priests having to do military service and being forced to swear allegiance to the Polish state. The same year Tito paid his visit to the Pope telling him their points of view on international questions were 'near or identical'. Yugoslavia and the Vatican have had a protocol of agreement since 1966, and full diplomatic relations since 1970. In Hungary the voluntary seclusion of Cardinal Mindszenty for fifteen years until 1971 in the U.S. embassy in Budapest made negotiations difficult (Hungary for some years was willing to let him leave but the Cardinal's conditions for going were unacceptable). Despite that, a concordat was signed in 1964. In it the communists agreed that the Pope might in future name new Bishops.

In 1971 Mgr Casaroli paid his first official visit to Moscow to deposit on behalf of the Vatican the document of its accession to the Treaty of Nuclear Non-Proliferation. The Pope, though unlikely ever to have a nuclear weapon at his control, wanted to give his official support as an example. A more practical reason was talks with officials of the Foreign Ministry. Afterwards, Mgr Casaroli said he believed 'the Vatican and the Soviet Union can develop parallel and converging actions for the achievement of peace. I want to stress that for the first time in 50 years we have put an end to monologue to open a dialogue.'

While the Vatican was urging concessions from the Russians,

the Soviets were seeking support for their proposal of an all-European security conference.

Bargaining goes on in other countries. Some of the fiercest battles have been conducted on the Vatican's own doorstep with Italy. When divorce was legalised in Italy, on 1 December 1970, it was done so despite the fierce disapproval of the Pope. The following day the Vatican was backing an appeal for the repeal of the new law.

For Vatican diplomats, the Catholic countries generally have provided some of the more difficult diplomatic struggles. The Vatican has concordats with a number of nations. Talks on revising one signed with Spain in 1953 began between the Spanish ambassador at the Vatican and Mgr Casaroli at the end of the 1960s. Nearly two years later a working report which they initialled, was sent to the Spanish episcopal conference to be countersigned. At a plenary meeting the Spanish bishops threw it out. The old concordat gave the Church special privileges in Spain – including a state subsidy estimated some years ago to be £9 million a year – in return for General Franco's right to nominate candidates for vacant bishoprics. The compromise – found unacceptable by the bishops as still going too far in the direction of the state – would have ended this situation, but would have given the Spanish head of state the right to be consulted by the Vatican on all important clerical appointments. This compromise was finally agreed however. Later that year it was called into practice when Pope Paul carried out a shuffle of the hierarchy in Spain – but was forced to strike a balance between Vatican liberal tendencies and the regime's conservatism.

Vatican diplomats have been constantly active in other fields. Nuncios have acted as intermediaries in bringing opposition parties together, as in Bolivia in 1970 when the President and the Army Commander in Chief, who had led a rebellion against the government the day before, were brought together for talks at the Vatican embassy. (In 1940 the Vatican was used as one of the contact points for talks between the British and Germans who were anti-Hitler. The Pope himself agreed to act as an intermediary between any new anti-Nazi German regime and the British.) On more general policies, the Vatican lent its voice to Communist China's admission to the United Nations some time before Peking's membership was agreed, and has been wooing that country assiduously.

In the struggle to fight birth control, huge diplomatic offensives have been launched. Late in 1970 the Secretary of State instructed all Nuncios to use their influence on governments. At the United Nations, the Vatican's three man mission of observers lobbied delegates.

In recent years there have even been signs that the Church is anxious to bring the huge Roman Catholic aid network closer to diplomatic aims. The network, responsible for about $1,000 million a year, is larger than that of any country other than the United States.

And Vatican diplomacy also has a large propaganda element. There is radio and television broadcasting. The Vatican's daily newspaper *L'Osservatore Romano* is as official as *Pravda* or the *People's Daily*. And not least of the propaganda attributes is the Pope himself, who skilfully makes sure his views on world issues are widely known.

NEW NATIONS

'The first actions of a new nation are to start an
airline and to join the diplomatic rat-race.'
Western diplomat

For the new and developing nations diplomacy presents special problems. Once they become independent – as more than sixty have since World War II – they need some kind of diplomatic machinery to conduct relations with other states. Yet they are lacking in money and manpower, in expertise, and in training facilities. There are the problems of trying to assess what they should attempt to achieve diplomatically and how, and they are not helped by the fact that the returns of diplomacy are difficult or even impossible, to evaluate.

The diplomatic services of new nations have ranged from a handful of staff to many hundreds. It may be so small as to represent no more than a token presence on the world stage; Tonga has only one overseas mission – in London – staffed by just two men, a high commissioner and a first secretary. On the other hand, it may be so large as to portray the grandiose delusions of its head of state as did Ghana's under Nkrumah (even in 1970 Ghana had 579 diplomats – more than India and nearly twice as many as Australia).

Western observers are often cynical: to many, new nation diplomatic services are useless status symbols costing money the small countries can ill-afford and producing diplomats with little to do but flaunt their privileges.

New nation diplomats, not surprisingly, see that view as totally unfair: 'Given that a diplomatic service is essential for any nation,' says one African diplomat, 'countries like mine have at least as great a need as any of the big, rich countries.'

A number of new nations begin by deluding themselves that they will play an important role in world politics. They are quickly disillusioned. The ambassador at one embassy, of a country that became independent in the late 1940s says: 'At the start it was political work, and it was not felt proper for a head of mission to concern himself in such things as economics or trade. Now we realise that this is what we must be doing; we want hard cash and better prices for our commodities.'

The big powers have to be lobbied, especially says one, 'now that developed countries show ever-increasing tendencies to concentrate on their own internal problems'. How major countries act does concern developing nations. Countries with a large dependence on a single agricultural crop are particularly vulnerable to how their bigger brothers behave. Thailand needs to export rice for example, so how much the United States decides to grow itself is crucial to Thailand's well-being. The decisions that American rubber companies make with regard to building synthetic rubber plants are vitally important to Malaya's economy.

As persuaders, the developing countries have some advantages: as members of the Third World and of regional and other blocs they have influence beyond their national power; there are opportunities for playing off the wealthy nations against each other; like other nations, they can reach out to public opinion at least in democratic states.

A major aim for all new nation diplomacy must be to lobby for financial and technical aid. Aid means cash, either in grants or loans (with or without interest) and technical assistance in the form of the provision of experts. In theory it is the developed world's altruistic way of trying to bridge the increasing gap between it and the other two-thirds of the world. In practice it is much used as a means of pursuing self-interest – to achieve political results or to gain strategic advantages or to promote exports by insisting the aid is used to buy goods from the donor country, often at inflated prices.

It is a post-war newcomer to diplomacy, but its image, at first high, has fallen sharply over the years. There has been growing disillusion by both donors and receivers. Some donor countries expected to see instant effects; criticisms of waste have produced political disquiet; and rich nations have become increasingly concerned with their own balance of payments problems. Receiving countries resent the terms and conditions on which it is given. Shortly before retiring as prime minister of Malaysia, Tunku Abdul Rahman, said of Japanese aid: 'Although Japan furnishes loans, it takes back with the other hand, as if by magic, almost twice the amount it provides.'

In the late 1960s, ninety per cent of the non-Communist world's aid was dealt with on a nation to nation basis and not multilaterally, a situation many concerned with international aid are trying to change. New nation diplomats have to struggle to persuade richer countries to grant aid and without too many strings attached (not an easy task: by the late 1960s only two per cent of the United State's aid was not tied to the condition that it must be spent on American goods).

But there are strict limits to what the new nation diplomat can achieve. Countries given aid are often decided upon not by their need or the eloquence of their leaders or diplomats, but by international politics.

Henry S. Rowen and Albert P. Williams in a Rand Corporation paper, 'Policy Analysis in International Affairs' stress that with America: 'Funds are not allocated so as to maximise third world economic growth, but rather to support the economies of countries in which the United States has substantial political interests. Aid may support economic growth policies in order to impart a progressive image to the recipient government. Or aid may be aimed at preventing economic collapse in a country where such collapse would seem to be disruptive of international order.' Japan uses aid as part of its trade diplomacy although by 1972 there were indications that it was beginning to realise this could not continue so blatently. Most of Britain's aid goes to Commonwealth countries. In the late 1960s the major part of France's aid was to overseas territories and departments still officially part of France and to French-speaking African countries. German aid is spread more widely.

Starting a new diplomatic machine from scratch is a formidable undertaking. Apart from creating a foreign ministry, a civil service hierarchy and a series of missions, there is much nitty-gritty: regulations for the service, welfare support (ranging from education allowances to helping with the hire purchase debts if a diplomat has to move suddenly).

New Commonwealth countries have been given ten 'guiding principles' for starting a diplomatic service, among them: 'Be conservative about opening overseas posts, don't do it unless there is an essential requirement. In the work of the ministry, concentrate on your main national interests. Be flexible in your planning; what seemed to be a vital national interest a couple of years ago doesn't necessarily look the same today and what seems vital today may not seem so in two years' time.'

They are all sensible. Yet the principles may have taken second place to the immediate problems of money and manpower.

Because diplomatic services are expensive even the large, wealthy powers have been cutting their foreign service machines. The problem is especially acute for new nations with strictly limited amounts of foreign exchange. Whatever money is allocated will have to be equated with needs at home. Ideally, the choice would be made rationally. Often because a foreign service is a symbol of status, it gets too high a priority. Contrariwise, because money spent at home can be *seen* to have been spent, the new diplomatic machine may be expected to do too much on too little.

Whatever the financial situation, skilled manpower will almost certainly be short. There will be competition for resources between the foreign service and home departments. It is not simply a question of filling low ranking jobs, but of staffing missions at all levels. Initially outsiders – from lawyers to military men – are often brought in. A further complication sometimes is the need, politically, to reflect different internal elements of the country overseas.

The new nation often has to take the best available, hoping to improve the quality later. There is also a frequent tendency to hand out ambassadorships to political nominees. This arises not only from a shortage of manpower, but because the head of state or foreign minister wants people he can trust personally. In 1972, for example, most of Sri Lanka's ambassadors were political appointees, although they were generally men with knowledge of government like the delegate to the U.N. who was a former secretary to the Treasury. 'In that,' says one, 'it is not straight political patronage. But naturally the people chosen are ones sympathetic to the views of the government.' The ambassadors have the right of direct approach to the prime minister. One explained he would not use this for routine matters, but he would on anything of importance.

This, in turn, produces longer term problems for a foreign ministry at home. Direct reports by the political appointees to the foreign minister or head of state mean that the civil servants are by-passed and their role demoted.

Even after the initial recruitment, problems do not stop. An influx of young men at the start means rapid rises to higher diplomatic positions. Because they reach these at a comparatively early age, those who join afterwards can be caught in a bottleneck – facing untold years of non-promotion.

Training, like recruitment, will probably have to consist of making the best of what is available. International organisations and other countries give some help. Guyana, for example, received advice from the United Nations and its future diplomats were attached to various missions such as the American in Chile and the New Zealand in New York to gain some experience. Countries that accept trainees from foreign countries to be attached to their staff for a period of time include America, India, Australia, Britain, New Zealand and Canada. The Carnegie Endowment has arranged training in America and Geneva, and the Commonwealth Secretariat in London accepts diplomats on two to three week attachments. The British government has arranged courses at Oxford university covering subjects such as history and international law.

With training, developed countries have all the advantages: accumulated experience, a higher level of education to work on, and training facilities. Many developed countries concentrate on 'in service' training – young diplomats learning as they work. A new service cannot do this. Nor if it is small, and staff is in short supply, can it – at a later stage – easily release staff for specialist or mid-career training.

All diplomatic services like to rate language training high – but it is costly. This is particularly so in the case of 'hard' languages; to teach an Australian third secretary Chinese or Japanese, for example, costs about A.$20,000.

The first diplomats, arriving at their new posts, feel like pioneers. Most know little of the country or capital, and hardly anything of its background. Ideally some priorities will have been fixed for the mission but instructions will probably be minimal. And, because at home things are probably equally as confusing, requests for advice may either not be answered or the reply may be so negative as to be useless.

For many new diplomats it is not long before the first visiting delegations descend. New nations have a tendency to send experts abroad even for jobs that diplomats could well handle themselves. The experts exert pressure to preserve that state of affairs; they, too, like to get overseas, and they want to build up direct contact with their foreign opposite numbers.

If the delegation is at all high-powered, the diplomats almost certainly find they are expected to be combination guides-party-throwers-travel agents and bankers. Diplomats report cases in which delegations have appeared to regard the embassy or high commission as being at their personal disposal. Some visitors have threatened penalties against a head of mission or his staff when all their wishes have not been fully met.

To mitigate the financial and manning problems, many countries resort to multi-accreditation. Under this system the embassy is based in one country, but the ambassador is also responsible for one or more others as well which he and his staff will visit periodically. Botswana, for example, with a diplomatic service of only thirteen at March 1970, had ten diplomats abroad at four missions, including the United Nations. The high commissioner in London was also accredited to France, West Germany,

Norway, Sweden and Denmark. His colleague in Lusaka
also 'covered' Kenya, Uganda, Tanzania, Malawi and Ethiopia.
The Swaziland ambassador in Washington (one of three overseas
missions staffed by the country's eight diplomats operating
abroad) also represented his country at the U.N. and in Ottawa.
In 1968 Guyana and Yugslavia agreed that their permanent
representatives at the U.N. should also be accredited to each
other's capitals – while staying in New York. Guinean ambassadors to London seem to make a point of varying their bases,
although it is not clear whether this is for purely personal prefer-
ence or whether there is some deep political reason. The one who
was accredited in 1971 chose to live in Rome. His predecessor preferred Washington, and the man before that settled in Paris.

There are inherent difficulties with multi-accreditation. Those
countries in which the ambassador is not resident may feel they
are being treated as inferiors. More practically, if two countries
covered by the same ambassador ever clash, can he report objectively on the situation – and, even if he can, will anyone believe
it is objective? Another system has emerged in more recent years,
without notable support to date. This is that of plural representation whereby an ambassador represents more than one country.
There can be several variations on this: the same man may handle
the affairs of two or more countries; separate men can represent
their own countries but share a common mission; or separate
missions can be headed by the same man. Experiments so far have
been led by Commonwealth Caribbean countries. But, again,
there are problems – not least the fact that the interests of two
countries, even if on the friendliest terms and with close links, do
not always exactly coincide. In one experiment Guyana and
Barbados shared a representative in London. The ambassador
concerned reported that he found no problems of conflict of interest, but there were minor worries: 'such as which flag I should
fly on my car'. This was solved by having a V-prong made for the
radiator cap on his car so both could be flown together.

The problems faced by new nations have to be borne in mind
in looking at what their diplomats are like once they start operating. Highly developed countries may find the majority of them
lacking – emotional, often pompous, unsophisticated, verbose, and
given to over-emphasising the protocol and ceremonial.

They can be notoriously touchy if they feel they are being slighted in any way. It is not just the diplomats who feel this way; it is the establishment as a whole, including their ministers. An incident in Australia, in winter 1970, illustrated this. A Zambian delegation arrived in Canberra for the Commonwealth parliamentary conference – to find no Zambian flag flying outside Parliament House. The delegation's leader, the minister of development and finance, was convinced the flag had been cut down. A special investigation, ordered immediately, decided that the rope had frayed and broken in the wind. But the delegation refused to stay, and flew home.

In many capitals, heads of protocol confirm that their toughest resident diplomats are the newest ones. Many young entrants of new nations, said the report of a Commonwealth seminar, look at their chosen career as constituting 'either a series of lively parties or stimulating conversation or of James Bond-type activities', an impression derived from novels and films and from observing the conditions in which diplomats from some wealthy countries work in their own capitals. Certainly, from talking to young new nation diplomats, the reasons for joining their country's foreign service emerge as fairly basic. The two most common reasons given by far were 'It's exciting', and 'It gives an opportunity for travelling'.

The misconceptions may die as some claim (glamour giving way to hard grind), but this seems not to be born out by observing the diplomats of many new nations. The living standards are high, the social life grand. A western diplomat says sadly: 'The old countries have begun giving up the big flag-waving parties. Now the new ones have caught the disease.'

There is another problem: the sociological and psychological strain of a developing country diplomat launched into an unfamiliar society with a different living standard.

For new diplomats, whose countries were under colonial rule not long before, the combination is heady. Either they act without confidence and with undue respect or they are openly aggressive.

Africans, in particular, seem to see constant discrimination against them. In London they have protested to the foreign secretary that police victimise them. One claimed that he and his colleagues were frequently followed by police, stopped and asked about the ownership of the cars in which they were travelling. The feeling they are being persecuted is strengthened by the letters they receive from non-diplomat nationals visiting, or resident in, the country. One ambassador pushed over his notes about a case currently concerning him: a man arrested for loitering in a large store. He claimed that he was simply browsing through letters and books, and that action had been taken because of his colour.

To ask a new nation diplomat whether he is not over-reacting or taking his new status too seriously, is to invite angry replies; simply to raise such questions is to query his nation's sovereignty or to label him and his colleagues as somehow inferior. He also justifies the grand parties as practical necessities: 'We must build up a circle of influential contacts and friends and this is the best way of doing it,' claims one Asian. The fine houses may be essential 'because when I invite someone here what he sees reflects my country'. The insistence on the finer points of protocol is 'especially necessary' in the case of a small or developing country: 'The American ambassador doesn't have to *show* he is someone; I do. I don't mean someone as a person; I mean someone who represents his country,' an African ambassador argues.

Some observers compare it with the days of Western diplomacy when ambassadors jostled and fought each other to establish their precedence: 'Like that, it will pass'. But, even if there is need for small nation diplomatic services, they have in the way they stress the trappings and the privileges given new strength to just those frills that should have been long dead and forgotten.

Fourteen
Diplomats at the United Nations

'I never tire of repeating that there is nothing wrong
with the U.N. except the members.'
Lord Caradon, former British permanent
representative at the U.N.

The United Nations has an air of unreality. Diplomats of over
130 nations talk, scurry and lobby in a glass palace that seems a
million miles divorced from the city of New York outside. 'You'll
find,' says one resident diplomat, 'that we all behave a little unnaturally. That's because this is an unnatural place.'

The purposes to which the diplomats' states have pledged
themselves are grand: peace, human rights, justice, and social
freedom. But the diplomat at the United Nations finds himself
working at an organisation whose worth in achieving them has
been increasingly questioned. A number of the ultra-traditionalists
of diplomacy doubt the need for its existence; to some what happens there should not even be called diplomacy.

One American diplomat-critic complains: 'The main work
seeks to be getting enough votes together to carry some resolution
which even if it is passed will never be acted upon.' The public
seems to share the disquiet. Twenty-five years after the foundation
of the U.N., an American presidential commission reported that
it was 'becoming increasingly incapable of dealing with the
grave issues troubling the world'. And it noted that whereas in
1965 an opinion poll showed that eighty-four per cent of the
public believed the U.N. was the last best hope for peace, by 1970
only fifty-one per cent believed that to be so.

And, as many U.N. diplomats will concede, much of the public
debate does make the organisation seem farcical. Long speeches of
platitudes or denunciation are followed by seemingly even longer
ones. 'But that doesn't mean that the United Nations is not
needed,' says one Indian. 'In a world with so many individual

states and so much interdependence, it just has to exist. But you have to remember that the U.N. is composed of individual members all with their own ideas.'

It is true that in the modern world, foreign relations can no longer involve just one nation talking to one other as they did in the past. Multilateral diplomacy, where negotiations take place between many nations, has been an essential development. The U.N. is far from being the only multilateral forum. Today there are more than 150 inter-governmental organisations, some like NATO and the E.E.C. important in a foreign relations sense.

These organisations are a vitally important part of modern diplomacy. Research by Professor Chadwick F. Alger shows that only one-eighth of the world's nations have diplomatic representatives in more than half the world's capitals. But seven-eighths have organisational affiliations with more than half of all the other countries. 'Organisational ties thus provide communication links between many nations that have no bilateral exchanges of diplomats,' he points out. Even among such organisations, the United Nations is rather special. It is not only multilateral in the sense that meetings take place in which many participate, but it is also parliamentary in that there are public debates and votes on resolutions with diplomats forced to lobby for support. It goes even further than this however. Much bilateral negotiation takes place between its walls; and a great deal of the diplomatic activity is as private and secret as in the most traditional diplomacy. It has, additionally, the factor that at the U.N. a diplomat is not representing his nation to just one other country; he is representing himself and his nations to all the other states that are members and also to countries which are not but which keep active delegations in New York. These 'permanent observers' include West Germany, the Vatican, South Korea, South Vietnam, Switzerland and Monaco. The Germans and the Koreans each have an office of about a dozen diplomats.

Among the basic principles on which the U.N. is organised are those of open debate, one member one vote, and a non-political civil service. There are six principal U.N. organs: The General Assembly, comprised of all members; the Security Council, with five permanent members (China, Russia, America, Britain and France) and ten non-permanent elected for two year terms; an

Economic and Social Council; Trusteeship Council (supervising the administration of certain non-selfgoverning territories); the International Court of Justice; and the Secretariat. Voting in the General Assembly on important matters, such as peace and security, is by a two-thirds majority, and on other questions by a straight majority. The Assembly can only make recommendations. The Security Council, on the other hand, can make decisions binding on all U.N. members. But the permanent representatives can veto any decision and thus make the Council powerless. In addition to the six principal organs, the U.N. family has more than twenty major international organisations, programmes or agencies, including the U.N. Children's Fund, the U.N. high commissioner for Refugees, the World Health Organisation and the World Bank.

The headquarters of the United Nations, on an eighteen-acre site backed by the East River, are a permanent reminder that this is a new type of diplomacy. The thirty-nine-storey slab-like Secretariat block with its east-west façades surfaced in blue-green glass and aluminium, is flanked by the low, sweeping General Assembly building. Inside there are carpeted corridors, lounges and dining rooms, countless offices, and debating chambers. The meeting and conference halls are a contrast with the palatial, sometimes crumbling, embassies identified with traditional diplomacy. In the General Assembly meeting hall, a single shaft of sunlight enters through a four foot diameter circular skylight. But it is the battery of microphones and the presence of the television cameras that most registers. The quiet whisperings of traditional diplomacy have no place in this part of the U.N.

The building is a mini city with its own security force, printing plant and fire fighting unit. Visitors are induced to attend meetings, take guided tours, lunch in the delegates dining-room, shop at the bookshop, use the post office and take something home from the gift and souvenir centre. They are urged, though, to 'refrain from applause' at meetings. It all looks deceptively open and democratic. What the visitors see is indeed real – though only a part of what the U.N. really is.

Delegates soon learn to navigate the corridors and to absorb its ritual (a high official or diplomat obviously striding on a mission of importance, for example, is left alone and the usual bows, nods and handshakes temporarily abandoned). But they have to learn to live with New York as well, and its impact on diplomats is powerful. The violence of New York has made the U.N. an increasingly less popular posting: several newcomers show more preoccupation with the prospect of surviving than of winning diplomatic battles. They arrive already warned (in booklets sent to them) that they should fit a triple lock on their doors; colleagues will have stressed the need to find a home in a neighbourhood where they and their visitors can come and go after dark in some safety.

The Chinese, needing an apartment and office building after their admission to the U.N., bought a ten-story motel on the West side of Manhattan. But they were worried about crime, and only took the building after being assured there was less crime there than in the more fashionable East side. In 1971 a special U.N. committee on Relations with the Host Country was set up to deal with security and the safety of the worried diplomats. Ironically, the following year the committee's chairman, Zenon Rossides, the delegate from Cyprus, was mugged and robbed. Three men attacked him and his wife early in the evening in Central Park, put ropes around their necks and took watches and Mrs Rossides' engagement ring.

New York, exciting though many people find it, is hardly a temple to the quality of life in other respects, with its noise, rush and traffic jams. In the winter of 1971, after a week of debate in which diplomats had complained about crime, overcrowding, and harassment by extremist groups, the United States felt obliged to defend the city. An American delegate reminded diplomats that their governments had chosen freely to site the U.N. in New York rather than in a pastoral setting, a mountain retreat or an idyllic island. 'New York as a seat of diplomatic activity may be worse than some places,' he said. 'I dare say it may be better than some others.'

It remains that the city and the organisation are not natural good neighbours. In the mid-1960s a special body, the New York City Commission to the U.N., was set up because of the antagonism between the two. This body, which operates with a staff of about a dozen plus forty volunteers, starts worrying about the diplomat the moment it hears he is being posted to the U.N.

He is sent an information kit. It tells him to make sure his marriage is valid according to American law, contains details of some costs like baby-sitting charges, advises on tipping, gives guidance on dealing with landlords, and has practical tips like 'Don't leave crumbs out in the kitchen for cockroaches'.

New nation diplomats have special problems in New York. Those from black nations are often hit by discrimination. The trauma of moving from a developing country to a highly sophisticated one is particularly acute in the case of New York. Wives often find they cannot cope; even everyday gadgets may be totally unfamiliar. Often there is a language difficulty. One diplomat's wife I came across could speak only an African dialect, ruling out any communication with all but her husband.

And New York just does not like its diplomat population. Special events, like the U.N.'s twenty-fifth anniversary, worsen traffic jams. A New York cab driver summed up popular feeling: 'Maybe we should let the bums take over the island and all move out for good.' There is especial resentment at the diplomatic affluence and privileges, most notably the diplomat's immunity from the motoring laws.

Just how seriously the diplomat takes the United Nations and what happens there depends on his country. In the main, developing countries are passionate believers in the organisation, and send their best men there because it is the focal point of their diplomacy.

It gives them near global diplomatic coverage in one place. And the cost to them is comparatively small: the less developed countries, though constituting two-thirds of the U.N. membership, contribute less than five per cent of the budget.

In voting terms, the developing countries are powerful. The growth of membership has completely changed the General Assembly. The fifty-one original members were predominantly Western orientated nations of Europe and the Americas. Today, provided they agree among themselves, developing countries have a large built-in majority. The nations, which form into blocs, are not a cohesive group. But one bond binds them: anti-colonialism and issues involved in that question, including South Africa and Rhodesia. (On this there have been mixed successes. New nations have been helped in their transition from colonial status.

But Rhodesia and South Africa have remained unshaken by all the resolutions. . . .)

Western diplomats often believe that the new nations, practising their heady independence, are making the U.N. look foolish, bringing it into disrepute and illuminating its weaknesses. 'They can push through a resolution on anti-colonialism,' one Italian says. 'Everyone knows it can never be enforced. So the thing just looks as foolish as it is.' Others, particularly the Americans, point to the discrepancy between this voting power and real power in the world.

But with the General Assembly only able to make recommendations and the major powers having the veto in the Security Council, it is sometimes hard to see what the smaller powers can achieve. Some diplomats believe they are able to exercise some power. Lord Caradon has said that middle and smaller nations 'can often propose what the super-powers can accept but which the super powers could not themselves initiate'. New nation diplomats believe too that, even if they cannot force action, they can make the big powers show publicly where they stand. One diplomat from a small Asian country says: 'You are aware from very early on that unless the big powers agree, there is nothing that can be done. But what you can do is to exert moral pressure. On, say, Rhodesia, you can put down a resolution that you know just will not be implemented. We are then accused of carrying out acts of futility, because everyone knows no action will follow. But what these critics forget is that by doing it you can expose the immorality of the big powers.'

But many will confess to growing disillusionment. A major cause of the U.N.'s weakness, says one African, is that the large powers insist that their own crises are dealt with outside the organisation. These have included the Berlin blockade, the Cuban missile crisis, the invasion of Czechoslovakia, Vietnam, and Northern Ireland. Arms control, of vital import for all states, depends not on the U.N. but on Washington and Moscow.

Another African admits: 'There are times when I feel so very frustrated. One sees so little being achieved. I try to console myself by the reminder that in diplomacy nothing good is achieved dramatically; the dramatic events are usually bad like the declaration of war.' Another's private consolation is: 'Until we can find something better, we have to live with this.'

Larger nations including American and Russia attach much less importance to the United Nations. Heads of mission are carefully chosen because they are on display to the world, but mostly the organisation is not seen as a central point of the world struggle. One diplomat from a major power summed up the U.N.'s worth as 'good training for younger diplomats'. Large-nation diplomats are more cynical about the endless meetings. 'Mostly U.N. diplomacy is very tedious,' says one. 'Just talk, talk, talk.' A colleague complains of 'the hours of boredom, with people going on for ninety minutes and no one ever getting down to the subject; you just want to scream.' Another, an English diplomat, described his major job at the U.N. as 'sitting on committees that are discussing anti-colonialism as the whipping boy'. A former President of the Security Council, and a great believer in the need for the U.N., confided sadly that he believed it would be many, many years before U.N. diplomacy had any real impact. 'It is a good place to gauge the tensions of the world,' he said. 'But the decisions are rather meaningless. Perhaps to get so many people working together is asking for Utopia.'

This does not mean that the major nations like being outvoted on issues. Western diplomats work hard to lobby support: ambassador Henry Cabot Lodge, when head of the United States delegation to the U.N., pleaded with a Senate appropriation hearing, for a table to seat forty – to feed delegates during attempts to line up their votes. And diplomats as individuals like trying to gather votes. 'When you are lobbying, it's quite exciting,' says one Briton. 'There's a lovely Machiavellian quality to it, and if you get a vote promised it's something tangible.'

Larger powers have used the organisation – often for saving face or for buying time. In 1968 the United States took to the U.N. the case of the spy ship *Pueblo* captured by North Korea. America never expected results; the intention was to buy time to stave off extremist right-wingers at home who wanted action against North Korea.

Veteran U.N. based diplomats seem to share a world-weary look. This contrasts with the excitement of newcomers from new nations – keen, anxious to be involved in everything when first they arrive. This soon fades. Most diplomats though, appear to like the atmosphere. 'It hasn't got the class of being at a post in a capital,' says one French diplomat. 'But what you get instead is the sheer spread of it all: many subjects and talking on them to Americans, Europeans, Asians and Africans.'

Disregarding the impact of their work – or the lack of it – U.N. diplomats are busy with endless meetings: 'When I'm back at home, I see so many unnecessary people around me with nothing to do. Here I feel I'm doing three people's work, and I'm being fully exploited. I like that.'

Relations between diplomats of all nations appear good – even when their countries are on bad terms. And diplomats say there is no race or colour prejudice inside the U.N. – a statement that seems to be supported by observation. A few do get 'over-involved': like diplomats based too long in one country, they go 'native'. Here it is not becoming too Americanised, but too un-objective about the organisation in which they operate.

U.N. diplomats seem especially characterised by their professionalism in pleading their country's views – ones often in conflict with their personal feelings. One British diplomat who has often argued points he doesn't believe, says: 'Perhaps it's because of my training but it doesn't keep me awake at night because I voted one way that was against what I personally think is right. You accept that there is another side to every case, and you get quite good at arguing something you don't believe without losing your moral sense. After all, you'd have to be very bigoted to believe that every case had only one side – your own.'

A woman diplomat recalls being called upon to oppose a resolution which she personally thought was a good one. Her principal opponent was an Indian delegate who pleaded his case passionately. Afterwards, moved by his obvious sincerity, she told him that she actually agreed with his proposal. He told her: 'Well I didn't. It was a damned silly suggestion.'

Missions at the U.N. range from the very small to those that number over a hundred people, such as the U.S. or Soviet delegations. They are normally headed by an ambassador, whose appointment, unlike that of an ambassador to a national capital does not have to be cleared with the hosts first. Nor can the secretary general of the U.N. declare an ambassador *persona non grata* – though the United States could expel him for, say, spying.

Diplomats at the U.N. mostly look like clean-cut businessmen.

Sombre dark suits predominate. There are some national characteristics. The Americans have a reputation for naivete; the British are said to be good at committees – useful in an organisation that, in 1970, held 6,570 meetings. The French are often described as being 'impossible – even where their friends are concerned'. This stems, it is said, from the fact that they often tell other delegates they will do X – and then do Y: 'Sometimes you never know what they'll do right up till the moment of voting.'

The Russians are regarded, as always, as rigid, slow-moving and terrified of deviating from detailed instructions. Publicly, a Soviet delegate would never concede there is anything wrong with or in Russia. One admitted privately at the end of a party that 'every country, including mine, has weaknesses'. Why didn't he say that in public then? 'How could I?' The Russians, though, do have a high reputation for background intelligence. Western delegates have been deeply impressed by information quoted during discussions on many major topics. It is perhaps too soon to characterise the Chinese representatives. The first impressions have been of their charm. But the Chinese diplomatic service has a history of switching its smiles on and off on order.

The U.N. is a mixture of open, public diplomacy and secret talks and negotiations. It is this mix, say its defenders, that gives the U.N. its unique and important position in diplomacy.

The public side is, obviously, the most familiar. Defenders of the U.N. system claim advantages in open conference diplomacy, among them that publicity can sometimes prompt a surge of international opinion affecting how countries will act. But it is this side that is often most open to criticism.

It is not only that conference delegates, particularly from small countries, do get carried away by the heady excitement of their own oratory. Often, and increasingly, open conference diplomacy has been used for its propaganda impact on people outside the U.N. Much of what happens at the organisation – inside and outside meetings – is designed to appeal to home audiences. After Communist China's maiden speech, for example, the American ambassador to the U.N. issued a statement referring to it as a 'disappointment' which contained 'empty cannons of rhetoric'. His statement was designed to appease conservative U.S. opinion.

At the United Nations, obtaining publicity is easy because of the large resident press contingent.

This should not, rationally, be an argument against conference diplomacy, but against its abuse by governments. Some diplomats, however, see any publicly conducted diplomacy, as inherently useless. They agree with Alfred Duff Cooper who, in his memoirs, said 'All negotiations whether concerning the sale of a horse or a proposal of marriage must be carried on confidentially.' The central claim is that open negotiations are limited in what should be their aim – reaching agreement – because diplomats arguing in public have to state their opinions and then find it hard to adjust and compromise.

But when diplomats at the U.N. want agreement, the real work is never done in public. Firstly, certain committees of both the U.N. and the specialised agencies are held in private. Secondly, and most importantly, when there are open meetings the crucial negotiations take place privately and secretly before they begin. The decisions are fought out between individuals and groups in the corridors, over meals and drinks, and during coffee breaks. A resolution may be altered forty times as it goes around outside, before reaching the point where its wording has enough supporters. All Security Council decisions, say diplomats, are sorted out outside, one of the reasons the Council always starts its meetings late.

What emerges often, of course, is a resolution so full of compromise that it means nothing. It may be so vaguely worded that it can be held to mean two completely different things. A European diplomat talking of his involvement in one U.N. committee, with over thirty members, says: 'You can't freely discuss awkward issues like birth control on which no one could agree. So you work behind the scenes and fudge up some language that will mean one thing to them and another to us. You do reduce it to mumbo-jumbo words. But I think it does contribute to international relations – you learn to get on with people.'

Different blocs of countries may work out their own compromises – and then make further compromises in discussions with other blocs. For a country or group of countries involved in lobbying, all the diplomatic manoeuvres of threats and promises and warnings can be, and often are, used. Ideally, though, threats should be used more sparingly than in bilateral diplomacy; because of the nature of the U.N. they rapidly become known to many countries and can be self-defeating.

The lobbying by the United States and its supporters, notably Japan, over the Communist China issue in 1971 provided an example of full attempts at persuasion. The Americans were fighting to keep Taiwan in the U.N., and lost. During the lobbying, President Nixon concentrated on heads of state; the secretary of state worked on foreign ministers; the State Department played on diplomats in Washington; and U.S. ambassadors abroad lobbied governments. At the U.N., the U.S. delegation operated a system of threats and promises on other delegates; many were reminded of old favours. Some were warned of help that might not continue in future. The Japanese backed the American offensive, and hinted to delegates that they might be planning to expand investment in certain countries of the world if. . . .

A delegate may 'sell' his vital vote in return for a change in a resolution. The occasion on which the United States used her veto for the first time, in 1970, was brought about by Spain doing such a deal. The Africans needed one vote to ensure the passage of their resolution which tried to force the U.K. to take further action in Rhodesia. Spain agreed to support it in return for the abandonment of two clauses demanding sanctions against South Africa and Spain's neighbour, Portugal.

Secret diplomacy also takes place within the U.N. on a bilateral basis. The building is particularly well-fitted for such diplomacy. Because there are so many diplomats, constantly meeting, eating and drinking together, passing in corridors, it is easy for two of them to engage in private negotiations without anyone knowing what is happening. The end of the Berlin blockade in 1949 was announced in a men's lavatory at the U.N. The Russians, wanting to call off the blockade because it had been made largely ineffectual by airlifts, had the problem of just how to do it. Between sittings of the Security Council Yakov Malik spoke to Dr Philip Jessup, of the U.S. delegation, in the men's room. He told him that Russia would end the blockade if acceptable arrangements could be made with the United States.

Governments may also use their representatives at the U.N. to try to find out information concerning one other country. An amambassador can just 'accidentally' bump into another and, in the course of a general conversation, ask him a specific question.

Some countries instruct their U.N. delegates to make contacts with 'unfriendly' countries at the U.N. while having little or no relationships outside. Spain, for example, conducted many of its negotiations with the communists inside the U.N. building. And in cases where countries break off diplomatic relations with each other, they normally keep a link open through their U.N. representatives.

It follows from the dual nature of the work at the U.N. – public and private diplomacy – that the ideal representative there should combine the traditional diplomatic skills with those of a good politician. Not all have this combination, and some diplomats concentrate on say lobbying, leaving colleagues to make the speeches. Diplomats also claim that there are specific qualities that are essential, among them the ability to keep one's temper, patience, and mental agility because of the constant switch of subject matter. Oddly, however, precision – often listed as one of the main qualities for diplomats – is one often *not* needed at the U.N. where the objective may be to formulate something so imprecise that everyone can read into it what he likes.

The power of a U.N. diplomat generally is not large. Even more so than diplomats in national capitals he is executing clearly defined policies. There have been exceptions (India's Krishna Menon, for example, negotiated a resolution over prisoners of war in Korea that made possible a ceasefire without specific instructions on detail). Delegates whose communications with their home governments are poor may freewheel a lot during discussions – though, usually, taking a cautious attitude in voting. And the degree of independence does alter. At one time when the United States could count on a balance of power in the U.N. its mission was regarded as important and was called 'The State Department on the East River'. The British, under the Wilson Labour Government, was represented by a minister of the Government rather than a career civil servant.

But today control is close. Western diplomats joke about Communist colleagues being afraid to take any decision, no matter how minor, on their own initiative. But they too have to constantly refer back. The American delegation is in telephone contact with the assistant secretary of state in charge of the Bureau of International Organisations in Washington between ten and fifteen times a day. The assistant secretary pays personal visits, sometimes as many as ten in a month, and when there are important debates in the U.N. the procedings are relayed live to his desk.

Apart from highly limited power over important issues, U.N. diplomats suffer from a shortage of the diplomatic refinements compared with their colleagues in capitals. Ambassadors to the U.N. present their credentials. But, instead of carriages, uniforms and bands, there is a five to ten minute chat with the secretary general. There is no doyen because arrivals and departures are so frequent. But there is a system of precedence. At the beginning of the General Assembly each year, names of countries are taken from a box by the secretary general. The order of precedence is taken from the name first drawn in alphabetical order in the English alphabet. In 1970, for example, Bulgaria was first and Brazil last.

There are however a few niceties. At the Security Council delegates serve as president for a period of a month in turn and there is a tradition that each time there is a new president, a delegate speaking for the first time that month praises the old one and welcomes the new. And there is a heavy social side. But, compared with that in national capitals, it is a bit heavy and worthy, characterised by rather deep conversations. Clothing is less formal – 'no long dresses and white gloves like in Bongo Bongo,' says one woman diplomat. One piece of ceremonial holds sway: parties for countries' national days. But the great social period is between September and December when foreign ministers are visiting, and three receptions a night are not unusual. Diplomats attend – but 'everyone understands that it's just showing the flag and they don't mind if you just call in and shake hands'. The chief of protocol greets foreign ministers arriving at the airport – sometimes six or eight in a day, the first at eight in the morning and the last at midnight. On one occasion, the chief of protocol had just greeted one dignitary when he heard the Irish foreign minister was arriving ahead of time at a far distant point of the airport. He saw a police car, rushed over to the driver: 'Are you Irish?' he asked. The driver replied 'You bet I am.' The protocol chief reports – 'With sirens sounding, he got me there.'

In an organisation like the U.N. the staff of international civil servants are important. Their role, many diplomats agree, is increasing, partly because of the complexity of the issues being discussed. Because they remain as delegates come and go, they represent the permanent force and this gives them a strength. The documentation they provide can influence diplomats by what it contains and the points it stresses.

The U.N. in New York has a staff of over 4,000; globally, the U.N. staff is 35,000 with the largest concentration in Geneva where there are so many international agencies. In New York, the secretary general and the under secretaries and their families enjoy broadly the privileges and immunities granted to diplomats. Others get immunities ranging from national tax exemptions, immunity from acts performed by them in their official capacity, and the right to import free of customs duty their effects when arriving to take up service in New York. They take an international oath of allegiance to the organisation, promising to discharge their functions and regulate their conduct in the interests of the U.N. 'and not to seek or accept instructions in regard to the performance of my duties from any government or other authority external to the Organisation'. Many diplomats note that after a time, international civil servants often become ingrained with that loyalty – 'they no longer really consider themselves Dutch or American, but U.N. men'.

Recruitment has to be carried out not only on grounds of competence for the job, but also on nationality. The ideal behind that decision was that the result would be a mixture of cultures and ideas. In practice it has led to nations fighting for more positions for their own nationals. There have also been examples of jobs remaining unfilled for months while applicants were sought from countries with small representation. The biggest national contingent is the American (filling nearly nineteen per cent of the jobs at the end of 1968). Russians at the same date occupied just under six per cent. At the other extreme were countries like Burundi with one national on the U.N. New York staff – .05 per cent of the total.

U.N. staff at New York often have what one diplomat describes as 'that devitalised look'. They are part of what is an incredible, and frequently inefficient, bureaucracy. And often diplomats blame them – sometimes unfairly. 'They do,' as one claims, 'have their own language gone mad – a form of gobble gook.' Instructions given by the U.N. office in Geneva for filling out a form in early 1971 said: 'If the form with the information printed on it is not submitted, the information should be transcribed on the form which is submitted.'

It is not only the language – but the flow of the papers on which it is printed. In 1970 the U.N. spent over $29 million to fill over 773 million pages with words reporting its own activities. Press releases run up to 8,000 pages a year – many copies, it is conceded, wasted because ones not sent to newspapermen go to delegations who already get official records of the same meetings.

The U.N. has been facing seemingly endless financial crises (and it seems ironic that such is its position that philatelists, who buy U.N. stamps, collectively form the ninth largest contributor to the organisation's budget). The cry from outside has been for more efficiency. Dr Kurt Waldheim soon after becoming secretary general, said his most urgent task was to cut administrative expenditure and drastically reduce overstaffing. Insiders believe though that inefficiency and bureaucracy are going to be as easy to cure as ending crime in New York City.

Although U.N. staff usually get the blame, often it should rest with diplomats and their governments. Some diplomats love helping set up new committees on which they can sit. Conference chairmen will condemn the paper flow – and a few days later call for a huge report to be prepared. And, to say the least, diplomatic priorities sometimes seem odd. Late in 1970 UNESCO, one of the U.N. family, adopted a proposal to introduce Arabic as a fifth official language. It was estimated that the total cost for hiring interpreters, and translators and producing the documents in the first two years alone would be an extra £360,000.

Conclusion

The public view of the United Nations reflects the major criticism made of diplomats generally: that they are men of no real power engaged in activities which, in reality, have no effect on world events.

During the 27th Session of the General Assembly, which ended in December 1972, the delegates met for 1,500 hours and passed 153 resolutions. They dealt with such well-worn subjects as colonialism, disarmament, the Middle East and nuclear testing, all important issues but ones where the UN's impact over the years has been notoriously small.

At least U.N. diplomats can point to something – the number of resolutions. It is even more difficult to try to provide any kind of balance sheet for their colleagues working in national capitals. What did they do that mattered? Was their existence worthwhile?

Diplomats themselves sometimes confess to feeling doubts about their value. Several elderly ones admitted that as they neared retirement they looked back and wondered whether they had achieved anything. One European ambassador, running a large and imposing mission, felt that, rationally, the embassy could well be replaced by a public-relations/information office, lobbying journalists and sending diplomats around the country to give lectures and film-shows.

Yet, with this rare exception, diplomats seem happy with the diplomatic machine. Admittedly there are things that might be improved – increased recruitment of new diplomats more widely representative of their countries; more men with economics backgrounds; perhaps more interchange with industry and other government departments; and better training. The machine, in other words, might need some tiny adjustments – but, basically, it is still as essential and meaningful as ever.

A few of the reviews had made some recommendations that did not quite fit that cosy viewpoint. There was the Duncan Committee's view, for example, that British missions in all areas but the important ones should become 'selective' posts specialising in one function such as trade. And there was the recommendation of the German Commission for the Reform of the Foreign Service that small embassies in Africa and Central America be closed and replaced by missions covering regions rather than single countries.

But these could be fought off: the reviewers did not understand the actuality of inter-state relations. Embassies had to remain or small states would feel snubbed; all the countries concerned had a vote at the United Nations; and diplomacy was a two-way trade. Even the thought of 'demoting' embassies in small countries, replacing them with less elaborate set-ups, was unthinkable. Diplomats agreed with Sir Douglas Busk who, in *The Craft of Diplomacy*, wrote: 'Imagine the likelihood of any foreign head of government granting a private interview to a junior officer; yet there have been British politicians so ignorant that they have advocated such courses.'

At the same time diplomats were being forced to concede that they, and their foreign ministries, were becoming even less powerful. In Washington it was useless asking State Department officials about developments in major foreign policy matters. They just did not know. At this level, their usefulness appeared to stop short at loaning Dr Kissinger the occasional expert.

Even more so than before the diplomat could hardly claim he was playing a major role in negotiation, or exercising important influence on international affairs.

There seems little doubt the trend will continue. In Britain, with the country a member of the European Community, the Cabinet Office became the 'command centre' for decision-making on Europe. The Foreign Office was just one of the departments involved.

In looking at the future of diplomats it is easy either to be beguiled into believing that the diplomat is simply a victim of misinformed opinion, or to think all of them could be sent home and international events left to a roving band of trouble-shooters and jet-travelling experts.

Diplomats need to exist in foreign capitals because nations have to carry on a continuous dialogue on a countless number of subjects – not just the big questions of war and peace or major trade agreements or disarmament, where increasingly the work of advice and negotiation will be taken from their hands.

Take that away and diplomats will emerge as what they really are: civil servants who happen to be working abroad. If one accepts that, there is need for radical changes in the machine. The problem of the world's diplomacy at the moment is that it is still constructed as though diplomats were dealing with great events, as though ambassadors did in full power represent their nations, and as if the people of one state would look at the representatives of another in their midst and be influenced by their presence.

It is worth looking back on the diplomat's range of work – representation; communicating their government's views to another country; reporting; trade and economic tasks; influencing overseas public opinion through press and information work; cultural activities; and the whole range of consular functions.

It can be seen that with the single exception of representation they are straightforward civil service jobs. And in doing them the diplomat needs no more than any other civil servant: an office in which to work during the day; a home to go to at night.

But the reality, as we know, is far from that. The home is (at ambassador level) a mansion; lower down the scale it is still splendid. The office is not just a working plant – but (with rare exceptions) a stone or concrete embodiment of his country's 'greatness'. And because he is a 'diplomat' he has to be surrounded with all the protocol and trappings of office.

What one criticises is not that the diplomat exists – but the scale on which he does so. For the diplomat to report, to pass on messages, to give out information, none of these trappings are necessary. 'Diplomats today,' Geoffrey McDermott, a former British Foreign Office minister with ambassadorial status has written, 'are glorified journalists; and since a good many journalists are spryer and quicker on to both the news and its significance than they, it is permissible to wonder why they are so glorified.' Even if one accepts that they remain more than journalists, the point about glorification remains valid.

It is representation that is responsible for the over-elaborate nature of the plant and the living conditions. The claim is that houses must be large because the diplomats must entertain; the embassy and the ambassador's residence must be splendid because they represent a nation. Yet who does it really impress? Can anyone really claim that the views of foreign states are changed or even influenced by such things? The whole representational side, one feels, has become largely superfluous – except as part of some international play-acting. Forced to try to justify it, diplomats claim that it remains essential because everyone else does it. One hardly needs to be cynical to suggest that half a dozen major countries getting together should be able to solve that problem.

With the fiction that diplomats deal with great events discarded and the outdated representational side removed, it would be possible to look objectively at the tasks that remain. Some of them at least are questionable. The trade role, one feels strongly, has been given to diplomats because it provides an acceptable way of making use of manpower that already exists. Whether that manpower or the machine is the best one for the purpose seems to have been a secondary consideration. Even diplomats, as we know, have grave doubts about the work they are asked to do in this field. With the best will, it is hard to see what precisely they achieve. Action has been mistaken for achievement. It is at least worth asking whether industry could not – and should not – do the job itself (as it does with notable success in some countries).

The same might be said of information work. Newsletters and background material are poured out to politicians and journalists. I know no politician who, as a result, believes he is better briefed (understandably the material is regarded as suspect) or has felt he should change his mind on a subject. Few journalists would approach a foreign embassy to obtain information about what was happening in that mission's country. They know from experience that the information will have been gathered simply from guidance sheets or newspapers; the journalist is better telephoning a colleague on the spot.

Cultural and aid work in their execution even if not in the policy decisions that lie behind them are so divorced from diplomatic knowledge that only as a time-filler at a small post could they be justified.

So what might one do? Andrew Shonfield, director of the Royal Institute of International Affairs, has made one interesting suggestion: That member states of the European Community replace their separate embassies in most of the underdeveloped countries with joint embassies. Such work as export promotion and cultural relations could remain national but be handed over to a separate organisation. Conventional embassies would remain in perhaps a couple of dozen capitals including Moscow and Tokyo.

This would be a start, because what diplomacy needs is a complete re-think followed by a massive pruning operation – fewer embassies and much smaller staffs at those which remain. It would have to be accepted, however, that there would be cuts in personnel not primarily for the sake of saving funds but because much of the work should disappear.

If it is felt that there must be a presence in small states abroad, it could be just that. All that is needed is either a regional embassy, per the German Commission recommendation, as a token. Alternatively, if it were felt justified, the embassy could become a simple two-man office. If the host country were going to feel snubbed, by all means call the civil servant in charge ambassador – it is only a title. Ideally the small office would concentrate on a specific function. If it were aid, the 'diplomat' would be an aid expert.

Diplomats would, of course, argue that a country cannot make its mission in a foreign state specialise in only one subject because the host nation may want to discuss other matters also. But that is not really an argument. The mission could still act as a postbox, passing on that country's views and, later, giving its own government's reply. In actuality that is all that happens in many cases now.

Larger embassies would remain in major or important capitals. One does not have to query their existence to wonder whether they too have not got out of hand. Is it really essential, for example, for the British embassy in Washington to have over ninety diplomats, nearly 200 experts from other home departments, and 110 military men? Day to day dialogues on many subjects may be necessary, but to that extent?

None of this is to claim that diplomats are not impressive as individuals. Mostly they are. Like all professions, diplomacy may have its fools – but I found fewer than I have among politicians, lawyers, businessmen or in my own journalism. Nor is it to believe that abroad they do not fill their time. But with what? is the question.

Much time and effort goes into the mechanics of diplomacy rather than an end result. The Americans and the Russians, for example, recently concluded ten years of discussions that will result in new embassies being built in each other's countries.

Sometimes it is on matters that one feels could have been dealt with without the presence of a high-powered diplomat. As American ambassador to Paris, Arthur K. Watson's main priority was the flow of illicit drugs via France into the United States. When he left at the end of 1972 he regarded the reduction in the supply as his main achievement. It was a real and tangible one of course. But did it need an ambassador to achieve it? One suspects that this was precisely one of those problems where president to president notes could have had the same effect.

Frequently it is work for the sake of work because someone at home wants it. A very senior Latin diplomat, for example, spent a considerable amount of time attempting to get one of his own nationals returned home to face trial. It was meaningless from the beginning because the 'offence' was not recognised in the host country and that was made clear at the start. But the discussions went on and on.

The diplomat, to a large extent, is the victim: he does what he is asked. It should change, but it is doubtful whether it will. Those diplomats – and they are many – who say they would not discourage their sons from entering the profession are right. In the year 2,500 politicians may still be attacking the increasing number of diplomats; priorities may have been changed yet again; there may have been more tinkering with the machine. But it is a fairly safe prophecy that the Corps Diplomatique will still be there – even bigger than ever.

Bibliography

BARGHOORN, F. C., *The Soviet Cultural Offensive: the Role of Cultural Diplomacy in Soviet Foreign Policy*, Princeton University Press, 1960.
BARNETT, VINCENT M. JR (ed), *The Representation of the United States Abroad*, Praeger, 1965.
BLANCKÉ, W. WENDELL, *The Foreign Service of the United States*, Praeger, 1969.
BUSK, DOUGLAS, *The Craft of Diplomacy*, Pall Mall, 1967.
CARDOZO, MICHAEL H., *Diplomats in International Co-operation: Stepchildren of the Foreign Service*, Cornell University Press, 1962.
DULLES, ALLEN, *The Craft of Intelligence*, Weidenfeld and Nicolson, 1964.
GALBRAITH, J. K., *Ambassador's Journal*, Hamish Hamilton, 1969.
GRAHAM, ROBERT SJ., *Vatican Diplomacy*, Princeton University Press, 1959.
HAYTER, SIR WILLIAM, *Russia and the World*, Secker and Warburg, 1970.
HAYTER, SIR WILLIAM, *The Diplomacy of the Great Powers*, Hamish Hamilton, 1960.
HAYTER, SIR WILLIAM, *The Kremlin and the Embassy*, Hodder and Stoughton, 1966.
KAUFMANN, JOHAN, *Conference Diplomacy*, A. W. Sijthoff-Leyden/Oceana Publications, New York, 1968.
KAHN, DAVID, *The Code Breakers*, Weidenfeld and Nicolson, 1966.
KAZNACHEEV, ALEKSANDR, *Inside a Soviet Embassy*, Robert Hale, 1963.
LONDON, KURT, *The Making of Foreign Policy: East and West*, J. B. Lippincott, Philadelphia, 1965.
NICOLSON, SIR HAROLD, *Diplomacy*, Oxford University Press, 3rd edition, 1963.
NICOLSON, SIR HAROLD, *The Evolution of Diplomatic Method*, Constable and Co., 1954.
PEARSON, LESTER B., *Diplomacy in the Nuclear Age*, Harvard University Press, 1959.
PENKOVSKY, OLEG, *The Penkovsky Papers*, Ed. Frank Gibney, Collins, 1965.
PHILBY, KIM, *My Silent War*, MacGibbon and Kee, 1968.
QUARONI, PIETRO, *Diplomatic Bags*, Weidenfeld and Nicolson, 1966.
REGALA, ROBERTO, *The Trends in Modern Diplomatic Practice*, Dott. A. Giuffré, Milan, 1959.
SATOW, SIR ERNEST, *Satow's Guide to Diplomatic Practice*, 4th edition, ed. Sir Neville Bland, Longman, 1968.
SORENSON, THOMAS, *The Word War*, Harper and Row, New York, 1968.
STRONG, MAJOR-GENERAL SIR KENNETH, *Intelligence at the Top*, Cassell/Giniger, 1968.

TETLOW, EDWIN, *The United Nations – the First 25 Years*, Peter Owen, 1970.

THAYER, CHARLES W., *Diplomat*, Harper and Brothers, New York, 1959.

VAGTS, ALFRED, *The Military Attaché*, Princeton University Press, 1967.

WILLIS, DAVID K., *The State Department*, Christian Science Publishing Society, 1968.

WILSON, CLIFTON E., *Cold War Diplomacy*, The University of Arizona Press, 1966.

WISE, DAVID, AND ROSS, THOMAS B., *The Invisible Government*, Random House, 1964.

WOOD, JOHN R. AND SERRES, JEAN, *Diplomatic Ceremonial and Protocol*, Macmillan, 1970.

Among published reviews and reports, particularly valuable ones are:
The Changing Patterns in the Organisation and Conduct of Foreign Policy. Report on a Commonwealth Seminar held in Singapore 9–14 March 1970, Commonwealth Secretariat, London.

Toward a Modern Diplomacy. A Report to the American Foreign Service Association, *Foreign Service Journal*, November 1968.

Report of the Review Committee on Overseas Representation. (The Duncan Committee Report), H.M.S.O., 1969.

Index